JULIE ANDREWS

JULIE

STEPHEN PALEY

ANDREWS

A Biography by
ROBERT WINDELER

G. P. Putnam's Sons, New York

To My Grandparents
AND
FOR ENGLISHWOMEN EVERYWHERE

Illustration will be found
following pages 66 and 194.

Preface

LIKE many other Americans, I first became fascinated with the phenomenon of Julie Andrews during *My Fair Lady*. I had worn out one copy of the cast album and was well into my second when the Wednesday afternoon came that I skipped school to spend three rapturous hours in the balcony of the Mark Hellinger Theater, watching the beguiling blond, blue-eyed Briton being brilliant in what, even then, I suspected was probably going to be the greatest musical comedy of my lifetime.

For the next ten years I followed her successsive triumphs from a distance, and I first saw her up close at the Academy Awards in April, 1966. That was the time she lost to Julie Christie. My blind date (for I had just come to California and didn't know anyone to take to one of the most glamorous evenings a man could ever offer a woman) sat on my right—she thought she looked like Elizabeth Taylor and kept arranging her borrowed sable stole. Dorothy Manners, the longtime associate of and successor to Louella Parsons, was on my left, constantly complaining in my ear because *Ship of Fools*, her favorite movie of that year, wasn't winning anything. I paid scant attention to either of them, because three seats away, on the aisle (was a nominee, presenter, and acceptor), on the threshold of one of the most insane and inexplicable stardoms in the history of Hollywood and at the same time as excited as a schoolgirl at her second prom, sat

Julie Andrews. I was riveted by that dichotomy and have stayed more or less that way since.

We didn't meet until early October, 1966, at the Los Angeles airport. We had flown from New York to Los Angeles on the same plane, the day after the *Hawaii* premiere, but she had slept the entire way. And so coming off the airplane we met formally, and that was the start of the *Time* cover story, a project that was to absorb me off and on for almost the next three months (the story appeared on December 23, 1966). Those sessions of intensive interviewing took place at her home in Beverly Hills in the afternoons (she was in one of those very rare between-pictures periods) and always—like the rehearsals for *My Fair Lady*—included tea.

I have observed Julie Andrews at work, at home, and with her new husband, Blake Edwards, for almost as long as Edwards himself, if not in quite the same way, during the years he was making *Thoroughly Modern Millie, Star!* and *Darling Lili* and I was working as a Hollywood correspondent, first for *Time*, then for the New York *Times*. I have found her to be thoroughly accessible, approachable, and cooperative, even when this book was first a possibility and then a reality.

We first discussed the idea of my doing a book with her, at lunch in her dressing room toward the end of *Star!*, clearly not the calmest, most uncluttered time for her, but certainly propitious in that it was the peak point of her stardom. She at first thought the whole idea of a biography at that stage in her life to be "presumptuous and premature." Her father, Ted Wells, had prepared a volume of his reminiscences as the father of a superstar, which at that time she was trying to stop the publication of, as tactfully as possible, finding that "a bit of bad taste." (They compromised, and some of his material appeared in an English women's magazine, after she approved every word of the manuscript; the rest she retained the rights to, through her own company.) But as the months wore on and we discussed it again, once in her trailer outside Paris during *Darling Lili,* again not a quiet time, she thought perhaps it would be a good idea to do a series of "conversations," something which she could do very well indeed and which was an easy format in which to pick and choose only the subjects that she wanted to discuss.

For many reasons I decided to go ahead on my own, with a biography as I had originally planned, while agreeing that many things involved with show business and stardom are premature, presumptuous, and even tasteless. Therefore, I wrote this book about Julie Andrews, the most interesting movie star—both as a person and as a phenomenon—of my particular tenure in Hollywood. The book is premature only in that it is the story of a half-life, one not yet half over chronologically or in terms of human and professional potential.

This then, is not an "authorized" biography, and I am glad of it. That way lies the Jackie Kennedy-William Manchester syndrome, and I want no part of it. Miss Andrews did not approve this manuscript and may not approve of it. But it is not, one hopes, an uninformed biography, and in it I have tried to be something Julie much admires, totally truthful. I liked Julie Andrews, as a person and as a performer, or I could not have spent a year of my life researching and writing this volume. I have found, in three years of knowing her, that she has, as Blake Edwards once told me, "some interesting negative qualities, too—her need to be liked, for example. We all have it to some degree; she has it more than most." I like her in spite of those too, or is it because of them?

Writing about such a completely contemporary subject, I found it essential to draw on the journalistic writings of others about Julie Andrews (this is the first book) ; I am particularly indebted to the editors of *Time* magazine, under whose auspices much of the basic material in this volume was collected; to Joan Barthel, whose piece on *The Sound of Music* in the Sunday New York *Times Magazine* provided much of the basic material for the chapter on that movie; to Anne Leslie, writing in the London *Express,* and Mary Blume of the *International Herald Tribune* for their perceptive interviews with Tony Walton and Julie, respectively; to Roy Newquist of the Chicago *American* and to my predecessor as Hollywood correspondent of the New York *Times*, Peter Bart (and for one or two things that have nothing to do with Julie Andrews). And I am grateful to Judith Crist for trying to teach me, at Columbia University, what to do with my love of movies.

ROBERT WINDELER

Introduction

IN late December, 1955, just before the start of rehearsals
for *My Fair Lady*, Julie Andrews was at home in Walton-
on-Thames, with her mother, stepfather, and two younger
half brothers, Donald and Christopher. The season before
she had captivated Broadway as Polly in *The Boy Friend*,
but at the moment the thing that pleased her most was that
she would be with her family this Christmas. Alan Jay
Lerner, the librettist and lyricist who, with composer Frederick Loewe, had transformed George Bernard Shaw's *Pygmalion* into a musical, was spending his holiday in New York,
preoccupied with the problems of the production and less
than pleased.

"I had given Julie a copy of the play to think about over
the summer before we went into rehearsals," he recalled.
"Her first tryouts had not been very good. I told her I would
see her when the rehearsals began. Julie had no sense of being
a star, none of that sense of obligation that a star has toward
a play. The others, Rex Harrison and Stan Holloway, turned
up several weeks ahead to talk over their parts. Not Julie.
She sent us a letter from London saying she would arrive on
the day rehearsals began, not before, because she had promised to take her two little brothers to a pantomime. It was so
different, so unbelievably unprofessional, that we were
amused rather than annoyed."

Twelve years later, almost to the day, Julie, an international superstar, finished *Star!*, the musical screen biography

of Gertrude Lawrence. It had been her most ambitious project by far, and she was exhausted from months of not only playing but being another English musical sensation. At the cast closing party that Friday night before Christmas, 1967, Julie appeared only briefly, as usual drank nothing alcoholic, and stayed just long enough to have some supper of beef Stroganoff with director Robert Wise and his wife. She disappeared to her dressing room to do some last-minute packing, she said, for her trip to Switzerland with Blake Edwards and her daughter, Emma, the next morning (Emma and her governess would stop for a few days in New York to see her father, Tony Walton, and join Julie and her director-beau in time for Christmas Day). Half an hour later I drove across the dark, empty lot at Twentieth Century Fox to Julie's dressing room. I found the star slumped over a dressing table, at that point almost speechless with laryngitis, hand addressing the last of hundreds of Christmas cards to old friends in England and new ones in America. She stayed there for another two hours, worrying about things like what kind of shaving lotion to send the teen-age boys at Hathaway House, her chief charity ("Nothing too fragrant, do you think Old Spice would be all right?" she asked me).

Those small acts, for which she would have been forgiven had she forgotten them, were (like postponing the start of her major Broadway success to attend a "Panto," the entertainment form that had occupied most of her teen-age years) pure, if somewhat compulsive, kindness. The years and circumstances had changed her in so many other ways ("Although I can recognize the girl who came here in 1954, it's hard to identify with her," she said), but no matter how ambitiously or successfully she pursued her career, she would never pursue it at the expense of her family or what passed for her family at any given time. Really for the first time I knew the public had been instinctively right about Julie Andrews. To contradict Mae West, goodness had everything to do with it.

The niceness may have been more nurtured than natural —and indeed there was nothing in Julie's background to suggest that it was inbred. Yet it was rare enough in the context of the entertainment world and long-standing enough to be real. And most important of all, it shone through, and at a time when there was a surfeit of women of the world.

Julie Andrews was not conventionally pretty, and at the start of her career her major asset seemed to be her singing voice—still her strongest asset twenty-two years later. She is tall, five feet seven, her legs are too thin (when Tony Walton first met her they were "chocolate-covered"), her feet too big (size eight A), and her swooping nose is covered with freckles. She was not the sort of lady who was inundated with marriage proposals. Her former secretary, who earlier had worked for Joan Fontaine and Zsa Zsa Gabor and intercepted many, said Julie never got one—except from Blake Edwards, but that was verbal and not in the morning mail.

Yet at the start of the 1970's, Julie sat at the top of the movie profession that had scorned her as recently as seven years before.

In the late 1960's it was fashionable, and generally accurate, to declaim the death of the old Hollywood star system. In those years of *Romeo and Juliet, Bonnie and Clyde, The Graduate,* and *Oliver,* all huge hits without huge names, a major motion-picture studio could not take a young girl from the chorus or the country or the corner drugstore and make of her a Rita Hayworth, a Lana Turner, a Kim Novak, or a Shirley MacLaine. The major male stars, Paul Newman, Cary Grant, and Steve McQueen, could get high prices per picture but couldn't guarantee the sale of many extra seats if the picture was bad. Even Richard Burton and Elizabeth Taylor, the best-paid team in cinema history ($1,000,000 apiece per film, against 10 percent of the gross for each, often plus a producing fee), could no longer assure the box-office success of anything.

Julie Andrews was the one astonishing exception to the

"new" Hollywood (where big pictures were still made, bigger than ever, and money was freely spent), and yet she was hardly a relic of the old. A child of World War II, the product of British music halls, a broken home, and three unforgettable Broadway successes in a row (and a woman who still contained too many of the phobias and self-doubts that resulted from that background), Julie was the one star who always made money. While other superstars meant merely big prices, Julie meant big business. *My Fair Lady* made $7,000,000 during her two years in it on Broadway, another $4,000,000 during her eighteen months as Eliza in London. *Mary Poppins* took in $44,420,000, a Walt Disney record. She took a modest, black-and-white antiwar film, *The Americanization of Emily* (only her second film attempt and her own particular favorite), and made it triumphant at the box office. She was almost solely responsible for making *Thoroughly Modern Millie,* an even more modest and frequently uneven spoof of the 1920's, into one of the most seen movies of all time and a record moneymaker for its studio, Universal. And *The Sound of Music,* in which she starred, was simply the most successful motion picture ever made; by the start of 1970 it had taken in more than $120,000,000 and kept its studio, Twentieth Century-Fox solvent for three fiscal years.

The motion-picture career of Miss Andrews was just eight movies old in 1970 (and only her first two films, *Mary Poppins* and *Emily,* were of any enduring artistic merit), and yet she commanded the highest fee of anyone in the business, $1,100,000 against 10 percent of the gross, for that eighth picture, *Darling Lili,* written, produced, and directed by Blake Edwards, who was also only the second great love of her life. She conquered virtually every medium of entertainment she attempted, and besides the best-selling movie of all time, she made the most successful Broadway show, *My Fair Lady,* and two of the top-selling recordings in history, the scores of *The Sound of Music* and *My Fair Lady.* Not since Mary

Pickford in the first years of silent films had anyone burst onto the screen with such seemingly lasting and total impact.

Then suddenly, in late 1968, there was a series of setbacks, and Julie appeared to plummet from public favor quicker than any star since Ingrid Bergman, with whom she felt an affinity. *Star!* opened to disastrous reviews and an even more disastrous box office. Julie's affair with Blake Edwards had deepened to the point where she was depending on him for most major decisions. ("She's like locked up in a room," observed one producer at Paramount, where *Darling Lili* was being filmed. "She doesn't make a move without his permission.") And worst of all, the British and American press that had been so kind to her throughout her career turned as one man against her.

But having survived as a child star and as a gawky adolescent, Julie Andrews was well equipped to survive as an adult. Only thirty-four on October 1, 1969, she had been an entertainer for twenty-two solid years. "It means a sense of identity to me," she said. But thrust on stage from the age of four, by her mother and stepfather, taken from school at age twelve to sing full time, forced to exploit a "freak" voice with a range of four octaves, and sent to America to support the family before she was nineteen, Julie eschewed not only a childhood, but a girlhood and part of a young womanhood as well.

To anyone watching Julie Andrews on the screen or stage, she is the essence of sunshine, the soul of contentment. And much of the time off-screen she has the same warm disposition, and it is as real and luminous as the California sunshine that streams into the very open, very white eight-room house in canyon country in Beverly Hills, where Julie lives with Blake and her seven-year-old daughter, Emma Kate Walton. She actually whistled walking around that house, as one imagined Mary Poppins, Maria Von Trapp, or Millie Dilmount would and as Gertrude Lawrence even did.

Like any other woman, of course, Julie had several other

sides. She was at times lonely, angry, frustrated, anxious, exhausted, and even bitchy. She could be ribald, totally withdrawn, patronizing, distant, chilly and boring. She demanded and got eleven dressing rooms at Paramount for *Darling Lili* —for no visible reason. With her large frame (125 pounds), boyish hairdo, and a prominent jaw, she was surprisingly sexy, dainty, and feminine. Not so surprisingly, she was a good mother. And although her fans might have been shocked to discover it, she was only beginning to emerge as a woman. Julie Andrews was a star before she became a person.

A close woman friend in Hollywood, Dr. Elsie Giorgi, said of Julie: "She needs a period of belonging to herself. Anybody who's gone through what she has deserves it. She is thirty-four, going on eighteen. But now she is learning to be with herself, and her future happiness depends on how well she learns it. She is strong, though, because she exists through herself and not through the limelight. She writes her own dialogue."

Blake Edwards, for three years her friend, whom she finally married in November, 1969, observed: "All that bad background was bound to have made her insecure and to give her a deep need to find out who or what she is. Having to search has been good for her. Boy, when you explode on the horizon the way she did, you are bound to be insecure and searching. Not that she's neurotic; she isn't at all. She's got quite a cross to bear. I'd hate to be Mary Poppins."

Actress Tammy Grimes, a longtime acquaintance, said: "The more superstar she becomes, the more real she has to become or she won't know who the hell she is."

More than anyone else, Julie herself was aware of her need to spend a great deal of time in self-examination. She arranged her life to assure the maximum amount of time with her daughter, probably the only person with whom she was completely safe, herself, warm, and in love. But she also arranged time alone to think. She had been in psychoanalysis for five years. And Svetlana Beriosova, her good friend from the Royal Ballet, said: "Julie works just as hard at her life as she does in her profession."

Julie had always played Galatea to a Pygmalion. At first it was her resented stepfather, Ted Andrews; then there came other Svengalis: Charles Tucker, Cy Feuer, Moss Hart, Tony Walton, Robert Wise. "She has no real conception of her capabilities," Tony said as far back as *My Fair Lady*. "It's all there—just needs a bit of dragging out." But Blake had been the most influential, and he was embarked on a search of his own. "The biggest problem with me is that there really is no Blake Edwards," he said. "I've gone in too many directions so far. Success makes you too aware of the details and apparatus of our business." Yet the attempt to find themselves caused some people in Hollywood, like scriptwriter (*The Graduate, Catch-22*) Buck Henry, to wonder: "I wonder who the hell they were before they were Julie Andrews and Blake Edwards."

Julie was ambivalent about most things, even about being an American: "My British roots are strong, I don't know why. I live in America, and my work is here." At times she seemed ambivalent about her work. "There was a time when I couldn't conceive of not working, of not keeping terribly busy," she said after *Darling Lili*. "But I've grown relaxed and less driven. I have no plans to work to a certain age and retire. But there's less urgency, suddenly." She was annoyed that she seemed to be making only one picture a year, and yet she wanted six months off in between them.

"You have this panic, this weight," she said. "You cope with it day by day, and sometimes everything is chaotic on the surface. I need order, desperately, but I can't have it. And there's never any time. And then there is this very great loneliness. It is hard, the pressure; often I get headaches. But one hopes it is not for nothing."

No one becomes as insanely big a star as Julie Andrews became without great force of character, whether she recognized it or chose not to. She was fond of her friend T. H.

White's explanation of why Lancelot was the greatest knight: He had the potential to be the toughest and cruelest. She had far too much self-restraint ever to show real toughness or cruelty, but she might have been capable of both. That she made it without either was the wonder.

White wrote a poem to Julie in 1962, during the Broadway run of *Camelot*, which was based on his book *The Once and Future King*. The poem, called simply "Julie Andrews," appeared in a red-bound privately printed volume of White's verse. Julie had number 22 of 100 copies. A companion poem to Richard Burton was on the page facing hers. White had also started to write a parody of Cavalier poet Robert Herrick's "Upon Julia's Clothes," the first line of which reads: "As in silks my Julia goes," with the second line to be an unflattering comment on Julie's nose. (He thought, being a woman, she would be offended; she would have been delighted, but he never finished it.)

The poem he did write read:

> Helen, whose face was fatal, must have wept
> Many long nights alone
> And every night men died, she cried
> And happy Paris kept sweet Helen.
>
> Julie, the thousand prows aimed at her heart,
> The tragic queen, comedian and clown,
> Keeps Troy together, not apart
> Nor lets one tower fall down.

Occasionally the towers did crumble, of course.

JULIE ANDREWS

JULIE ANDREWS

he had determined from the early children's theatricals that Julie belonged on stage.)

At any rate, the separation, divorce, and subsequent custody arrangements were accomplished amicably on the surface at least ("there were no fights, no loud scenes, thank God," recalled Julie), and "the next thing I knew a personality as colorful and noisy as show business itself—another Ted—came into my life." Julie was five or six when she went to live with her mother and new stepfather whom she disliked on first meeting. "He thundered across my childhood," she said. "My Mum wanted me to call him 'Uncle Ted,' which I was opposed to instantly. To avoid muddling I did end up calling him 'Pop' and my real father 'Dad' or 'Daddy.' "

The Andrews' (Julie's name was legally changed) at first were "very poor and we lived in a bad slum area of London. That was a very black period in my life. I hated my new house and the huge man who seemed to fill it." But Ted and Barbara Andrews as a permanent vaudeville act began to catch on, and the family moved to Beckenham, Kent, and finally, when Julie was eleven, back to Walton-on-Thames, where they bought a house called The Old Meuse. Mrs. Andrews later discovered that her own mother had worked there as a maid, and she continued to live in it long after her only daughter became famous and even after her second husband, Ted Andrews, died of a stroke in 1966.

Sometimes Julie attended the Cone-Ripman School in London, which taught acting and ballet in the morning and more conventional subjects in the afternoon (and where Aunt Joan Morris reappeared to teach between sessions of her own dancing school, which were erratic because of the war). Ted and Barbara Andrews achieved greater and greater fame as a second act in vaudeville. "We were never top of the bill," Mrs. Andrews recalled. "After all, we were musical and not comedy, and the comedians got the best billing. But we were the second feature, a good supporting act with a drawing room set and ballads—nice family-type entertainment." Sometimes, as they had to move around the country with the act, Julie would go to other schools. Sometimes, because of the war, there was no school to go to.

"In all fairness I truthfully do not know to this day whether I started in show business because of my parents or circumstances or what," she said. "But I was under everyone's feet. My stepfather, not knowing what to do with me (and I think in an attempt to get closer to me), sent me off to a singing teacher. They discovered that I could sing." That was when she was seven. But her mother recalled that the voice really was discovered in an underground air raid shelter in Beckenham when Julie was eight. Ted Andrews led *a cappella* community singing in the shelters during air raids to take the neighbors' minds off the "doodlebugs" (pilotless aircraft) falling around them. During one of these air raids, Julie, who had been outfitted with a whistle and opera glasses to watch for doodlebugs (Beckenhamites tended to ignore official air-raid warnings and go into the shelters only when German planes and doodlebugs were virtually overhead), joined the singing, soaring powerfully an octave and sometimes two above the general pitch. Mrs. Andrews took her to a specialist, who confirmed that the "bandy-legged, buck-toothed child" had "an enormous belting freak voice with a range of four octaves and some fierce high notes. I sounded like an immature Yma Sumac."

Ted Andrews was delighted with his stepdaughter's newly discovered talent, and he forced her to develop it. He sent her to a new voice teacher, Madame Lilian Stiles-Allen, a renowned concert singer and "wonderful woman," who stayed with Julie until she was a superstar. "It's thanks to her that I didn't do more damage to my voice with all that singing when I was young, and later in *My Fair Lady*. I used to go watch her give lessons to all her other pupils. Then I would take lessons twice a day. She had an enormous influence on me. She was my third mother—I've got more mothers and fa-thers than anyone in the world."

One of those fathers, Ted Andrews, pushed hard. To avoid overstraining her young voice, "I was made to practice singing only a half an hour a day, but it seemed like much longer than that. I loathed singing and resented my step-father. He acutely embarrassed and upset me by asking me to perform. But he was a very good disciplinarian, and I later was grateful that he had made me take singing lessons. It gave me an identity which later became very necessary. With-out it I would have been ten times more mixed up than I was." Toward the end of the war, during school holidays—when there was school—Julie was taken to the theater in whatever city they were to watch her mother and stepfather at work. "I enjoyed school, and like any other small girl, I wanted to be just exactly the same as everyone else. No matter how hard Mummy tried to make this come true for me, I *was* different. The girls I envied most were good at games; I was awful. And nobody had to go home and prac-tice singing as I did."

But Julie kept practicing and developed a perfect pitch that musicians twenty years later would marvel at. "I'm firmly convinced one can develop perfect pitch; you don't have to be born with it," she said. "I was one of those child-brat prodigies, and for my age I had an immensely powerful voice. It was to everyone's great surprise that it was there; there were no vocal musicians in my family." (People who did not know that Ted Andrews was not her real father as-sumed she inherited it from him.)

Julie sang for friends, depending on her mood. When she was ten, the war ended. "Then came the day when I was told I must go to bed in the afternoon because I was going to be allowed to sing with Mummy and Pop in the evening." Julie recalled having to stand on a beer crate to reach the micro-phone and singing a solo (but she didn't remember the song) . "It was such immense fun that I did it several times more, during school vacations, on an odd Tuesday night when it was not desperately important. My mother played the piano, and my stepfather sang. Once in a while I joined him in a duet. It must have been ghastly, but it seemed to go down all right."

For Julie to appear in these unbilled, spontaneous "surprise bits," the Andrews' would have to get permission from the theater managers. "Some of them wouldn't take a chance on a rather ugly nine- or ten-year-old child—they thought my parents were quite out of their minds—but the ones that did take a chance were very nice." After two years of these occasional beer-box appearances, Ted Andrews decided that Julie was ready for a career of her own.

There had been a suggestion that Julie go to RADA, the Royal Academy of Dramatic Art, but as Barbara Andrews explained it, "We decided that a little toughening up as far as the theater world was concerned would be good. So we took her into our act. Let's face it—it didn't hurt the act either."

Besides being a talented tenor, Ted Andrews was "a whiz at selling anything," his stepdaughter recalled. One day in October, 1947, when Julie had just turned twelve, Andrews and Val Parnell, managing director of Moss Empires, the largest booking firm in England and owners of the London Palladium and Hippodrome and theaters all over the provinces, were playing golf. Andrews persuaded Parnell to come home with him to hear Julie sing. Andrews went "out to the garden and yanked this scruffy kid wearing a smudged smock into the house to sing an aria"—"I am Titania," from *Mignon*. Parnell was impressed enough to sign Julie for a review, *Starlight Roof*, that was about to open at the Hippodrome. And it was through Parnell that Julie met and signed with Charles "Uncle Charlie" Tucker, who was her manager until 1965.

Parnell assigned Julie to do the much tamer "Skater's Waltz," but the night before the opening, October 22, he de-

cided that the naïve girl singing the simple song wouldn't go
with the rest of his sophisticated review (which starred Pat
Kirkwood and comedians Fred Emney and Vic Oliver), and
he fired her. "My mother and my agent descended on him
and said, 'You've got to give this girl her big break,' and all
that sort of awful nonsense." Parnell relented the afternoon
of the opening but asked her to go back to Titania's aria
from *Mignon*, "a song ten times more difficult than the one
I'd started out with."

On opening night, her aria, which fortunately she knew by
heart, was a success, and she reached F above high C with
ease. Her routine involved sitting in the audience with her
mother until it was time for her song. She went onstage, ex-
changed a few lines of dialogue with Vic Oliver, sang, walked
back down into the audience and on out the theater without
waiting to take a second curtain call at the end of the show.
Performers under the age of fifteen were prohibited by London County Council regulations from being in a theater
after 10 P.M. The "Polonaise" and Julie got all the notices
the next day. "I only had that one song, but fortunately it
stopped the show," she said.

For this, her professional debut, Julie got the grand sum of
$200 a week, or rather her parents and Charles Tucker got it.
All the girl got was a raise in her allowance from 40 cents to
$1 a week. The rest was supposed to go into a trust fund for
her. Barbara and Ted Andrews turned down the first offer of
a pantomime at $400 a week, saying they were determined
that she be neither spoiled nor overworked. But Charles
Tucker took her under his wing, "and the buck teeth were
seen to immediately." The two of them settled down for a
year's run at the Hippodrome. "I haven't really stopped
working since," she said at the height of her movie career,
"except for the odd holiday once in a while."

Julie remembered herself as a physically "hideous" child,
with pigtails, crooked teeth, "very bad legs" and two eyes
that at times moved quite independently of each other.

There was little she could do about the legs, but she corrected the eye condition by using the eye exercises developed by Dr. William H. Bates. She felt she got by on her "freak" singing talent, especially during the Hippodrome run. "I knew no other profession, no other life," she said. "I didn't know that it was not good for a twelve-year-old girl to be singing in a sophisticated review. I just thought I was the luckiest girl alive."

Starlight Roof led to Julie's being tapped for a royal command variety performance at the London Palladium on November 1, 1948, a month to the day after her thirteenth birthday. Danny Kaye, a court favorite, was invited from America to headline the vaudeville show, and the Nicholas Brothers and George and Bert Bernard were also on the bill. Julie, who was described in the official announcement October 14 as "A 13-year-old coloratura soprano with the voice of an adult," was the youngest solo performer ever chosen to perform before royalty at the Palladium. Queen Elizabeth, the wife of King George VI and later queen mother, and Princess Margaret were there, and although Julie said she didn't remember it exactly, the queen said, according to newspaper accounts at the time: "You sang beautifully, Julie, and we enjoyed it very much." The selection was again the "I am Titania" from *Mignon,* on which she had nearly "bust a gut taking a top F twice nightly" for a year. She never missed that F above high C, although she confessed twenty years later that she had missed other notes and that same one since.

When her year at the Hippodrome was up, Julie began to tour music halls all over Britain. Ted and Barbara Andrews were an established act, and sometimes she would perform with them as a family act, and more often as a single act, for which she earned £75 a week. Either way, "this was the daughter of Ted and Barbara Andrews that everyone had come to see. My mother and stepfather had become big stars, and I was in effect part of the act." She followed them into radio and later into television. Her schooling, which had been sporadic at best, was abandoned entirely in favor of a governess and chaperone, who taught her for four hours a day for the next three years, until Julie stopped altogether. "I bitterly regret not having had more education," she said.

She played provincial theaters from one end of the country to the other—"endlessly, it seems"—and starred in panto-mimes—holiday "fairy-tales-in-song." "I was always the prin-cipal girl who was rather wet and makes goo-goo eyes at Our Hero and gets him in the end." Julie played in *Humpty Dumpty, Jack and the Beanstalk,* and *Little Red Riding Hood.* She was Princess Balroulbadour in *Aladdin,* and she played the title role in *Cinderella. Aladdin* and *Humpty Dumpty* each ran a full year at the London Casino, and it was during the latter show, when Julie was thirteen and he was fourteen, that she met Tony Walton. His father was an orthopedic surgeon in London, and he also lived in, but was not related to, Walton-on-Thames. "We met on a train going back to Walton from London," she said twenty years later. "I was playing the egg in *Humpty Dumpty*—rather Freudian. He had seen the show, and we started talking. We've been friends ever since."

As Julie's career expanded, Ted's and Barbara's began to slip. She was playing the best of the remaining vaudeville houses, and they were playing the second-best. One summer at the seaside resort of Blackpool, Barbara Andrews remem-bered, "We were on the pier, and she was in the big theater in town—really a step above us." Ted and Barbara played less and less frequently. Finally, they retired altogether, al-though Ted took a nine-to-five job briefly, and Julie, who was making between $400 and $500 weekly, began to support the family (the Andrews' had two sons, Donald and Chris-topher), Tony remembered, and even put one brother through school. "It's something we've never spoken of, but I can see now that it hurt terribly," she said. Work followed work, and "I couldn't think of anything else I could do or wanted to do." Tony said that up until *Camelot* she had a "guilt feeling about taking it easy." "If I hadn't been around, I suppose they'd have found a way to support themselves," she said of her dependents.

Things were so bad ("weird and plenty seedy" was the way Tony put it) that Julie from her earliest years wrote phony diaries that were "filled with fanciful images of what a beautiful, happy family life she had and what a glamorous existence she led," Tony remembered. Ted Wells saved a story she wrote when she was about five that read: "Wuns the wos a mother and father. The motheer wanted a litl girl and boy. It was Crisms, the night Santer Claus hee cam to bring the two babis. Wen the muther woke up she was so pleesed she loot arfothem and they live hapleevrovter." When she was eighteen, in New York for the first time, to open in *The Boy Friend* she idealized her stepfather and his retirement in this gush: "He has *such* a lovely voice. He used to sing ballads like 'Love, Could I Only Tell Thee How Dear Thou Art to Me.' I'd rather listen to it than anything. Mummy always wanted to be just Mummy so Pop gave up show business." The truth was, Tony said, that for those years from age thirteen on Julie was "head of the family and it was a grade-B movie existence."

"To be truthful, at the time I think I thought I was happy," she said. "Children bounce back rather quickly from all their troubles. At any rate, I would go around saying how happy—how desperately happy I was. I fancy I was protesting too much."

"She was an unhappy girl" recalled the boy next door in Walton-on-Thames (her boyfriend briefly when she was seventeen) Tancred Aegius, now an advertising salesman with Lord Thompson's newspapers. "Her mother and stepfather were always drunk—on liquor that she had paid for. It was sad." (Need anyone wonder why, as an adult, she regarded all alcohol—except the occasional weak Scotch, bullshot, or mulled wine—as poison?)

Julie couldn't always decide whether she wanted to live with her mother or her father (and sometimes she wasn't able to live with either; when Barbara Andrews was pregnant with Christopher, Julie stayed with Mme. Stiles-Allen four or five days a week). She knew she was "precocious, a loner, I enjoyed the company of older people." She spent a good deal of time with Ted Wells both because she wanted to and because he had liberal visiting rights written into the agreement when he relinquished custody of her. "I guess I mostly wanted to be with Mother because she seemed to lead a rather colorful existence; she supplied the rougher, bawdier side of my life. My real father filled in the love of the countryside, outdoor sports, reading. When I was with him, we led a quiet, more relaxed life. My stepmother was a wonderful woman, but I must admit I found it hard to live with my stepfather."

Still, she and Ted Andrews shared a profession, one that in a very real sense he had given her. "At least all the time growing up, I knew I could sing. I thought that was rather good. Of course, I didn't ever dream I would be singing after my childhood. I used to think: 'What am I going to do when I grow up?'" And they went to see other theaters together, even if only for professional reasons. One night Julie and Ted Andrews went to see *South Pacific* in the West End. "That was the first big musical I'd ever seen. Pop said, 'Just for one night we'll make it special.' He put on a dinner jacket. Afterward I talked about how wonderful the music was. My manager, Charles Tucker, said, 'Someday, Julie, Rodgers and Hammerstein will be writing songs for you.' (*The Sound of Music* was for Mary Martin, but the second *Cinderella* in her life, the TV special, was for her.)

Julie played in pantomimes ("Most of the time I was kept in short, short dresses, patent leather shoes and ankle socks, trying desperately to look ten years younger than I really was, growing a bosom and feeling wretched about that"), touring companies and vaudeville until she was eighteen and had gone as far as she could go in that medium. "I came on the scene when vaudeville was on its last legs. I mostly sang bastardized versions of operatic arias." She had kept up with her singing lessons but had no concentrated drama training or, in spite of her Aunt Joan, any serious adult-type dancing lessons. "I still really don't dance," she said after finishing *Thoroughly Modern Millie,* and before I learn to, I'd really like to learn to play the piano."

Cy Feuer, half the producing team of Feuer and Martin, which was mounting the New York production of *The Boy Friend,* the London hit starring Anne Rogers, was casting his company in England. "We wanted as many English actors as possible because we wanted to reproduce it on Broadway as close as possible to the original [which was being left intact in the West End]," he recalled. "Someone suggested to Vida Hope, the director, that there was a girl working in a play in Leeds in Yorkshire who might be what we wanted for the female lead." Feuer and Miss Hope took a train to Leeds to see Julie. "It was some crazy play with music about Ku Klux Klansmen in the Ozarks or something like that. Julie was only eighteen at the time." It was, in point of fact, *Mountain Fire,* in which Julie played her first American part, a backwoods girl with what she thought was a Southern accent. "When I went to the United States and heard a real Southern accent, I nearly died of shame," she said. Feuer was first struck by the atrociousness of the dialect and secondly by her breaking off her dialogue and beginning a song, *after* which the leading man and the orchestra came in. "She started to sing, and her pitch was perfect and her voice was delightful. Later, we went to dinner, and she was thrilled and excited at the prospect of starring in a play on Broadway. We, of course, thought she was perfect for us."

Julie herself described *Mountain Fire* as a "bomb, an incredible disaster. I accepted a very limited engagement, thank God, and played a Southern belle from Tennessee. The story was all about Sodom and Gomorrah and bootleg whiskey and Lot's wife turning into a pillar of salt. I can't tell you what went on. You've never heard a worse accent than mine. I got pregnant by a traveling salesman—in the play, of course—and thank God the miserable thing closed before we got to London."

Vida Hope had actually spotted her and virtually signed her on as Polly Browne the previous Christmas performing in her first *Cinderella* at the Palladium. "My first thought was: 'Oh, good Christ, the idea of leaving my home and family'—I couldn't do it. I had toured on my own all through England, but suddenly the idea of two years in America was too much." The Andrews' were all for it, and so was Charles Tucker, so at length Julie did "what I always did when I had a tough decision to make. I asked my Dad, my real Dad, the wisest and darest man I know. He advised me to see America while I had the chance and pointed out that the show might not be a hit and might last only a very short time. I decided to go if I could get them to agree to a one-year contract instead of two [the usual for the star of any show, especially an established musical hit]. Charles Tucker did get them to agree to a one-year contract and an increase in salary as well. It was the first time I really put my foot down on something. I wouldn't have earned enough to bring my family over and they certainly couldn't afford it, so one year was it."

Her parents had to "sign her over to us because of her age," Feuer said. But he was struck by her maturity. "Most performers at that age are very amatueurish, but even then she had great equanimity and poise. She didn't rattle. She had a very good dramatic ability even then; she was an instinctive actress."

And so Julie Andrews first came to America in August, 1954. Her first home was the seedy Piccadilly Hotel at Forty-Fifth Street and Broadway. Only its name was English. "It was during an immense heat wave, and I had one room with one tiny window." That was too much for the lead in a

Broadway musical, even one who had known early poverty and tacky English music halls. She wasn't earning enough for an apartment of her own, but she and Dilys Lay, a redheaded young comedienne who played Dulcie in *The Boy Friend,* shared what Julie termed "a modest suite in the modest Park Chambers Hotel on Sixth Avenue (which, down at our end near Central Park you might call New York's Bloomsbury)." It had a bedroom, a living room, and a stand-up kitchenette. The rent was not exactly modest, even in New York in the mid-1950's, $275 a month, payable in advance. "It made a horrible hole in our budget," said Julie, and the girls had to get an advance on their $100-a-week rehearsal salaries to pay the first month. Almost two-thirds of Julie's $400 a week salary during the actual run of the show went for taxes, Charles Tucker, and parental and sibling support. "I had no sense of money or of taking care of myself," she recalled years later. At the rooms in "Bloomsbury" Dilys cooked dinner, while Julie did the shopping, made tea, and washed the dishes. They later acquired a maid, but Julie spent her nineteenth birthday (the day after *The Boy Friend* opened) surrounded by floral tributes by ordering bacon and eggs ("Champagne and caviar?" "Not a drop, not a grain") from room service and writing her mother a ten-page letter, "though I'm afraid it did get rather eggy," and, of course, reading "those precious reviews." She pronounced it "a marvelous birthday; except for the fact I wasn't home I think it was the best birthday I've ever had or am likely to have."

To make the suite more livable, the girls hung red paper bells from the ceiling. They bought an electric broiler to learn to cook American-style, and a dachsund named Melanie, which they gave to each other for Christmas, both having missed their dogs at home (Julie's was a Welsh corgi, Hump short for "Humpty"), "the sort the queen has—no tails and sweet little faces and tiny little bodies—such lovely dogs!") and finding stuffed poodles no proper substitute. Julie's half-brother Donald would kick Hump to make him

bark into the phone at Julie during the transatlantic calls
that took the rest of her salary. One of their many male admirers gave them a TV set, and watching Charlie Chan films
and old English movies on the Late Show quickly replaced
going out to midnight showings of features. "We have a
sworn pact in blood not to wait up for the Late *Late* Show; it
makes the management quite queasy if we don't sleep
enough," Julie told an interviewer. They went out often, at
first with young Englishmen from the Old Vic company,
which was also in New York, later with "some American
chaps." Julie found the main difference between them to be
that "a British friend asks you where you would like to go,
but an American says you're going *here,* or *there.*" "And usually both; with Americans one does get around a bit," said
Dilys.

Around a bit included nightclubs, of which there was no
exact equivalent in England: El Morocco; the Latin Quarter
when Mae West was holding forth; the Stork Club; and 21.
"Johnny Ray and Frank Sinatra, dreamy," Julie said of two
singers she had seen. "Our dates were annoyed. They forgot
we watch other performers with a professional air." The girls
also went to movies, although Julie, who was homesick much
of the time—as she had feared she would be, made the mistake of seeing *Beau Brummel,* "full of wonderful shots of
Windsor Castle, which is close by our house. I came directly
home and called Mummy, although I'd been steeling myself
not to." And there was shopping for things like nylon "marvelous full" petticoats that weren't yet readily available at
home.

Julie at first didn't like New York: "too large, too humid,
too noisy, too crowded, too expensive. I was frightened of it."
Then there was "the soggy tea bags and ghastly water," but
there were also "poppets": New York cab drivers; the second
teller from the left at Manufacturers Trust Company; and
other "people you love in spite of everything." She loved
American drugstores, so much more comprehensive than

English chemists, "cream cheese and jelly sandwiches and your wonderful milk shakes—ruinous but marvelous—your beer is fine for me, light, as the commercials [which she didn't like] say, but I'm afraid an Englishman wouldn't like it." Other American likes included Dixieland and Benny Goodman and New York's East Side, "so neat and uncluttered and clean, and every girl is as attractive as Margaret Rose."

Professionally it was much rougher. Because a whole new *Boy Friend* company had been started for the Broadway run, leaving the hit London company whole, there were weeks of rehearsal before previews started," Julie recalled, "from 10 A.M. right through till 4 o'clock the next morning." There were no out-of-town tryouts, but more weeks of previews in New York. "How they work on Broadway," Julie wrote home long before she realized what movie hours could be. "If the first call is for 10 A.M., you've got to be there on the dot, and not a minute is wasted—it's detail, detail all the way. Every gesture, every line, is gone over again and again. But it's fun and terrific experience. If I miss anything at all it's not backstage but at the front of the house. Theatres here haven't got the regal atmosphere and character they have in London. You get the impression the people who designed them had only one idea: to pack in as many customers as possible."

Despite all the work, things did not go well; the American and British production teams fought. Cy Feuer took over the director's job from Vida Hope. "I had to learn a wholly new way of acting for this show—my own style was rather quiet— I was awful," Julie recalled more than twelve years later. During previews one day Feuer took Julie outside to the theater's fire escape. "He sat me down and he said: 'You were simply lousy last night. You're trying to be clever and it's dead. You're way, way out and sending it up rotten'—he really let me have it," she remembered vividly. "He said, 'Believe everything you say—be Polly. If you do that, you'll be a success. If you don't, you'll be a disaster.' Thanks to Cy and his words of advice, I *was* Polly. I did it because I was told to do it."

Feuer years later refused to talk about what he did to help Julie and the others in the cast who were equally foundering. "It would be very unbecoming of me and I couldn't teach Julie very much. Dramatically she had it all along. She performed far beyond the ability of anyone that age." And offstage she was, in Feuer's view "a marvelous person to work with, a very sweet person. She did everything you asked without complaint and was a lot of fun. There's some kind of bubble inside her. She was just everything you could ask for in a performer, and always on time for rehearsals and performances."

"I realize now," said Julie in Hollywood in 1965, "that the high point in my life was coming to America. I was very aware, even at the time, of having some door open somewhere and passing through it. I was on my own, and standing on my own two feet for the first time. I was having to function as an independent person, where before I'd been a guarded child."

The opening night of *The Boy Friend*, September 30, 1954, at the Royale Theater realized no one's worst fears. Sandy Wilson's light parody of a 1920's musical, about a little rich girl at a private school on the Riviera who falls in love with a messenger boy who turns out to be as rich as she, was pronounced by Brooks Atkinson, then the dean of the then "Seven Butchers of Broadway," to be "a delightful burlesque . . . of the standard musical play of the Twenties . . . extremely well done in manuscript as well as on stage. [Wilson] has written book, songs and lyrics with satirical inventiveness; and someone has directed it with great ironic skill [Vida Hope was still listed as director on the program, but gossip had gone around]. It is hard to say which is funnier: the material or the performance." Atkinson called Dilys Lay "a miniature Beatrice Lillie," but said, "It is probably Julie Andrews, as the heroine, who gives 'The Boy Friend' its special quality. She burlesques the insipidity of the part. She keeps the romance very sad. Her hesitating gestures and her wistful shy mannerisms are very comic."

Feuer attempted to explain the impression she had made in his show, one not solely or even mostly attributable to her voice: "This girl is tall, she has large features—which are great for the stage; you can see her a mile away. People like that take light. They don't disappear into the scenery. Taken singly, those features may not be so much, but the way they're put together, they turn out to be attractive. She is a kind of built-in leading lady, has a kind of built-in dignity and a kind of built-in musical know-how."

In November, 1954, Julie was awarded feature billing by Feuer and Martin, the only member of either the New York or London cast so honored. "We're having a terribly good time, *The Boy Friend* company," she said when it happened. "We're all so young and happy. I didn't need to be especially thrilled when they told me they were going to give me featured billing. I think it would be being a bit of a big shot to actually look at my name up there." The first evening it was up, Julie arrived at the theater in a taxi, just having practiced her scales for a full hour ("my voice really needed it; I was so stale"), trying hard to keep her face turned from the marquee that said:

THE

BOY FRIEND

SMASH HIT MUSICAL COMEDY

WITH JULIE ANDREWS

Finally she looked, said softly, "Ah, there it is," and the man who was in the cab with her said, "Sure enough, her eyes were shining."

The following April, Julie returned from Ebbets Field in Brooklyn and her first American baseball game to find that she had been promoted even further, to co-star (with John

Hewer, who played the messenger boy, the romantic lead), "in recognition of their contribution," said Feuer and Martin. The marquee then read:

JULIE ANDREWS   JOHN HEWER
IN
THE BOY FRIEND
SMASH HIT MUSICAL COMEDY

Julie pronounced herself "thrilled" but remained somewhat unimpressed. "Here you make a star out of practically nothing too quickly," she said, somewhat ungratefully and self-deprecatingly. "In England you have to prove yourself over a long period in a variety of roles. In England I wouldn't be considered to have arrived yet—we adopt more of a wait-and-see attitude there. Here one has one hit and, whoosh! Well, I'm English, and I'm waiting and seeing."

"She took the triumph right in stride; it didn't go to her head," Feuer remembered. "She was the same sweet girl as always. We never had any problems with her." And Dilys Lay said: "Julie would never pull that big star stuff. If she did, I'd say, 'Oh shut up, friend.' " Other honors came, like one of the twelve Theatre World Awards for promising new personalities (other winners that year included Anthony Perkins, for *Tea and Sympathy,* Barbara Cook for *Plain and Fancy,* and Captain Von Trapp himself, Christopher Plummer, for *The Dark Is Light Enough*). "But the mink-and-diamond stage of stardom is still, I can assure you, a million miles away," she cabled an English evening paper. Actually it was a little more than a year away.

Years later, Julie's memories of *The Boy Friend* included her friend Millicent Martin, then in the tiny part of Nancy but "now *the* Millicent Martin" (the cast had also included Moyna MacGill, Angela Lansbury's mother, as Lady Brockhurst), and Anne Rogers, another friend, who had stayed in London as Polly. One day in Hollywood after *Thoroughly*

Modern Millie Julie mused on the possibility that if Miss Rogers had come to New York to do *The Boy Friend* instead of she, she might have got *My Fair Lady* and "be sitting here now in place of me," rather than touring the United States in *Half a Sixpence* and doing the London company of *I Do, I Do*. Julie also remembered her mother's flying over to New York to stay after the opening, leaving in Walton-on-Thames the man most responsible for it all, the stepfather who had insisted on singing lessons "to break the barrier between us. But of course that didn't work out very well. It was rather like a husband teaching his wife to drive. It only increases the tension."

II

ONE OF THE more famous telephone calls in theatrical history came to Julie Andrews in April, 1955, slightly past the midpoint of her year in *The Boy Friend.* A representative of Alan Jay Lerner and Frederick Loewe, the adaptor-lyricist and composer of a musical version of George Bernard Shaw's *Pygmalion,* was calling routinely to see when Miss Andrews would be available, as she had been suggested for the part of Eliza Doolittle. "When I told him I would be free in August [although *The Boy Friend* would run for 485 performances, into January] he almost fell off the other end of the phone. They had assumed I had a two-year contract like everyone else in the company," she said. "I thought 'What are these Americans going to do to poor George Bernard Shaw?' I really had grave doubts, but because I thought I'd get too homesick, I was free at just the right time."

She auditioned for Lerner and Loewe, as she also did for Richard Rodgers, who was casting *Pipe Dream.* Rodgers wanted her, but Charles Tucker allowed that she had been offered the lead in the musical version of *Pygmalion* (the title *My Fair Lady* had not been decided on yet). "Dick was absolutely wonderful about it and said *My Fair Lady* would be the wiser move," said Julie. "I got the part and things went on from there. Until *My Fair Lady* I wasn't doing anything for the sake of anything except that I was told to; it was my job. The year I had spent in *Boy Friend* was one of the best of my life. I learned a lot about timing and comedy from American audiences. I am a slow learner, or I used to be, and it was a marvelous experience to learn on the job and get away with it."

Learning on the job was also to be an important part of her experience with *My Fair Lady*—"a monstrous task. Shaw simply terrified me. The singing part was the only thing I thought I might somehow do. When it came to acting, I was simply awful at first and terrified of Rex Harrison. It was obvious I needed a lot of attention."

Shaw had described Eliza Doolittle, in his stage directions for *Pygmalion,* as "perhaps 18, perhaps 20, hardly older." Lerner (whose book Julie described as "wonderful—you can't tell where Shaw leaves off and he begins") had kept that conception. But Julie, who was twenty at the time, was the only one who came close to the correct chronological age. Mrs. Patrick Campbell, for whom Shaw had written the play, was forty-nine when she appeared in it in London in 1914. Lynn Fontanne was thirty-nine when she played Eliza for the Theatre Guild in 1926, and Gertrude Lawrence was forty-four when she played the flower girl at the Ethel Barrymore in 1945. Even Wendy Hiller, the definitive Eliza as far as *My Fair Lady* was concerned, was twenty-six when the picture *Pygmalion* was released in 1938, and Julie Harris was well in her thirties when she played Eliza on television.

But at the start of rehearsals, January 3, 1956, Julie's ingenue age and her singing voice were all that were right. Rex Harrison hated the whole idea of working with this silly little girl who would walk into the theater and start practicing her scales loudly. This irritated Harrison considerably, probably because he was incapable of doing scales. Alan Lerner admitted "she aged ten years on the road—onstage, of course." "I wouldn't be at all surprised if there weren't times when they all thought of sending me back to London," Julie said ten years later.

She worked hard at the role that Harrison recalled she had

been the only choice for (once Lerner, Loewe, and Moss
Hart had signed him as a male "star," they could take Julie
without worrying that she was an unknown). She ran the
Wendy Hiller-Leslie Howard *Pygmalion* "countless times
and bawled every time" to learn the part (as had Alan Lerner in order to write the libretto, appropriating the film's,
rather than Shaw's original, ending). "Although she had
never done any acting really, she tackled it marvelously and
the results were there for all to see," said Rex.

"Dear Moss Hart was like a Svengali," Julie remembered.
Hart had "met her for the first time at the first rehearsal," he
said later. "She was charming, but it seemed to me that she
didn't have a clue about playing Eliza. About the fifth day I
got really terrified that she was not going to make it." Julie
told friends during rehearsals that she thought she knew
what Hart wanted, but that every time she tried to do it,
"something comes up in front of me," and she described herself as clawing like a crab at a glass wall with Hart on the
other side. The director canceled general rehearsals for a
weekend and spent two days alone with Julie to see what
could be done to develop her performance.

He looked back on the time as "the days of terror," and
she as "the now famous, dreaded weekend." He said, "It was
the sort of thing you couldn't do in front of a company without destroying a human being. We met in this silent, lonely,
dark theater [the New Amsterdam] and I told her, 'Julie,
this is stolen time, time I can't really afford. So there can be
no time for politeness and you mustn't take offense, because
there aren't any second chances in the theater. There isn't
time to sit down and do the whole Actors Studio bit. We
have to start from the first line and go over the play line by
line.' With someone not gifted, this would have meant nothing, this rehearsal in depth."

Both days, from 2 to 6 P.M. and 8 to 11 P.M. (the mornings had to be devoted to costumes for Julie), "we sweated it
out," she recalled. "He bullied and pleaded, coaxed and ca-

joled. He made me be Eliza." Hart would say things like "You're playing this like a Girl Guide," "You haven't any idea of how to play that," "You're not thinking, you're just oozing out the scene," "You're gabbling." "Those two days made the difference," Hart said. "She was neither affronted nor hurt. She was delighted. We were both absolutely done in, exhausted. But she made it. She has that terrible English strength that makes you wonder why they lost India."

"Come Monday—though I probably dropped halfway back again through sheer nerves at facing the company—he had really given me an insight as to how the part should be played," Julie recalled. "I really did need a strong guiding hand. It was such a big musical and I had so little courage. I didn't know what Eliza should be, a whiny girl or a gutsy girl, a weak character or a strong one. Moss supplied the route, the direction, and as the nights went by, I absorbed Eliza more and more," aided by frequent fifteen-minute refresher sessions with Hart in the powder room at the Mark Hellinger Theater, where the play would open, while the rest of the cast continued rehearsals onstage.

"Moss Hart was a dear man," Julie said almost a decade and a half later. "I wish he were still alive. I feel today that he would be extraordinarily close, and there certainly have been no other men who have helped me more. But at the time he made me infuriated, and scared and mad and frightened and in awe and full of an inferiority complex, while knowing I could do it, he worked and worked and worked on me."

Even during her three-and-a-half-year run in *My Fair Lady* (two years on Broadway, eighteen months in London), Julie "was never really sure, on any given night, that I had enough strength to do the whole thing flat out. It was an extremely difficult role and I wasn't really up to it. I found it an enormous weight every night and I can't remember a single performance when I didn't wonder to myself: 'Am I going to get through it tonight?' and 'I'll have to save myself a little in this song so that I have enough voice left for my next number.' It was such an enormous show—the screaming, the singing purely, the singing on the chest, the great dramatic requirements and everything—that I honestly don't think I could do it today."

Harrison remembered that it was at first difficult for Julie to do the long Shaw dialogue scenes, "but she certainly overcame that quickly. The other thing she found difficult, and Audrey [Hepburn] did too, was to get the gutter quality in Liza—that's a very exacting thing." He also recalled that during rehearsals whenever he played a deadly serious scene, Julie would burst out laughing. "It was a form of nerves, I think. She was really only a kid at the time, and it must have been a frightening experience for her. I always asked her why she laughed, and she never did tell me." (She didn't remember laughing, particularly.)

Julie took great delight in the fact that she learned her Cockney from an American, Alfred Dixon, a former actor who had been teaching pronunciation for twenty-five years. Some Britons took great exception to an American's teaching a British dialect, but Dixon, who had catalogued, he said, all the world's inflections, was as close a vocational cousin to Henry Higgins as could be found. "One of our problems at the beginning was our too-faithful use of the Cockney dialect," said Julie. "We received so many letters saying they did not understand us that we had to tone it down. The trouble with the dialect is that it varies slightly between men and women and between that in use today and in the period of the play, which is Edwardian. In those days the men were different. Their voices were deep and low, and the women's were shriller and sort of high."

In Shaw's original script, the only part he wrote phonetically was at the very beginning, when Freddy, looking for a taxi for his mother and sister outside Covent Garden, knocks Eliza's flowers into a puddle. Liza says to Mrs. Eynsford-Hill: "Ow eez ye-ooa san, is 'e? Wal, fewd dan y'de-ooty bawmz a mather should eed now bettern to spawl a pore gel's flahrzn than ran away athaht pyin. Will ye-oo py me f'them?" ("Oh, he's your son, is he? Well, if you had done your duty by him as a mother should he'd know better then to spoil a poor girl's flowers and then run away without paying. Will you pay me for them?") "That's certainly a mouthful," said Julie, who was forced to pick up her pronunciation of the rest of Shaw's other Cockney lines from Dixon. Her own favorite was, "Oi woodn't 'ave et it, only oi'm too lidy-loike to take it aout of me maght." ("I wouldn't have eaten it, only I'm too ladylike to take it out of my mouth.")

Unlike most musical-comedy hits that gestate over a long period of trying out, rewriting, and reworking, *My Fair Lady* had the look and feel of a winner almost from the first. For one thing, the creators and cast had total confidence in the property and were not tempted to make major changes. There was an overall ultraprofessionalism among the participants (although the English principals in the cast, which also included Stanley Holloway as Alfred Doolittle and Cathleen Nesbitt as Mrs. Higgins, insisted on a daily tea break at four, during rehearsals, and producer Herman Levin said that English biscuits were always served with tea that was actually brewed in the dressing rooms practically abutting Lindy's). The Columbia Broadcasting System, which had moved into other forms of entertainment than radio and television with its financial investment in the show, for purposes of authenticity made a recording of the bells of St. Paul's Cathedral in London as a sound effect. The church bells would strike the "second quarter" during the Covent Garden scene, when Higgins studies Eliza's Cockney speech. By the time of the New Haven tryout in February Julie was confident enough to be a solid part of a successful show, and by the Philadelphia tryout, in early March, the word was out that *My Fair Lady* was the next big hit and Julie Andrews was the next big Broadway star. Out-of-town viewers and reviewers were moved to superlatives. During the last two weeks in Philly,

Julie, Harrison, Lerner, Loewe, and Levin were besieged by
New York friends for opening-night tickets—at the rate of
ten bids for each ticket. Julie and Harrison cut off their
phones and left word that no long-distance calls were to be
put through. She was reminded of her "waiting and seeing"
remark after the triumph in *The Boy Friend* and was asked
if she had changed her mind. "No, because we still haven't
opened in New York," she answered.

When they did open in New York on March 15, 1956, at
the Hellinger on Fifty-First Street, with Mrs. Barbara Andrews among the glittering audience, all doubts about the
progress of her musical-comedy career were ended. Julie and
the others heard tumultuous ovations after every song (she
sang eight) , but she went to Sardi's to await the reviews still
uncertain. "When I saw the big sheaf of newspapers coming
in, my heart dropped. But the reviews, they were wonderful.
I came right home and put through a call to London to my
father. It was eight thirty in the morning over there, but I
don't think he had slept much during the night."

"Bulletins from the road have not been misleading," wrote
Brooks Atkinson in the next day's New York *Times*. " 'My
Fair Lady' is a wonderful show. . . . To Shaw's agile intelli-
gence it adds the warmth, loveliness and excitement of a
memorable theatre frolic." Atkinson praised Shaw's "crack-
ling mind" and said it was "still the genius of 'My Fair
Lady,' but he also extolled Lerner's lyrics, Loewe's "en-
trancing love music and a waltz" ("I Could Have Danced All
Night"), Harrison's Higgins, Miss Nesbitt's Mrs. Higgins,
and Holloway's Doolittle. "Miss Andrews does a magnificent
job," he said. "The transformation from streetcorner drab to
lady is both touching and beautiful. . . . Miss Andrews acts
her part triumphantly." And Walter Kerr said in the New
York *Herald Tribune:* "Miss Andrews descended a staircase
looking like all the glamor of the theater summed up in an
instant."

The day after the opening a line formed at the Mark Hellinger box office that was to continue for the next eight years, shattering all Broadway attendance and revenue records. The show was completely sold out every night for more than two years, and eighteen months after the opening it was impossible to get reservations for six months hence. And in the first year of its release the original cast record album outgrossed the show (not counting the premium that went to scalpers who often got $100 a pair of tickets) and sold 1,000,000 albums for $5,000,000. (In London these records were legally unobtainable and went for $50 an album.) It was to become the best-selling original-cast album of all time.

A national touring company did as well as the Broadway one, the movie sale to Warner Brothers was for $5,000,000, and the London and other foreign versions, the records, and the films would bring the total gross receipts to in excess of $85,000,000 over the next fourteen years. The Broadway production became the longest-running musical in history— 2,717 performances over eight years. Julie, a major reason for the success of the venture, became the hottest property on Broadway, inundated by dozens of offers to better her already respectable $2,000-a-week salary, the first international leading lady since Gertrude Lawrence had arrived in New York in 1924, singing "Limehouse Blues" in *Charlot's Revue.*

"Toast of the town," she said at the time, with more than a trace of sarcasm. "I haven't time to be toasted very much. It is true that I receive a great many invitations but I can accept only a few. I dare not go out before a matinee and the next day I am recuperating." She was at first back in the modest suite at the Park Chambers, by herself this time, since Dilys Lay was in London ("my first time alone ever, but not so terrifying as I had imagined"), but then she moved to "a minute flat in the East Sixties with a sweet little patio in back and a proper cooking range." She spent much of her free time with Tony Walton, who by then was her more or less publicly acknowledged boyfriend of twenty-two, who had come to study scenic design in New York in April, 1956. He called for her after every performance, and they spent as many days as possible in the country. She took a short winter vacation the year after the opening, and she and Tony and her business manager turned down invitations to Nassau, Bermuda, and Jamaica in favor of Bear Mountain, New York, out of season. She took along a new camera she had bought at a discount house after calling the business manager to see if she dared spend the money.

She was still incurably homesick (especially in spring: "I love American autumn, but British spring is wonderful") and sent recorded Dictaphone letters several times a week to the family at Walton-on-Thames, where a similar recording machine was used for return airmail. And the best thing about her new affluence, as far as Julie was concerned, was that she could afford to fly members of her family over to New York for visits ("It makes the year go so much faster") and to ship them presents. She decided that her future career should allow her to live in England most of the time and spend three or four months of the year in the United States working. She preferred her homeland, she said, because "it's small, I like the smallness of England. It's all so big and vast over here, it really knocks you off your feet." She looked forward to the spring of 1958, when she would take the show to London, just a half an hour by train from Walton, and picnics on the Thames and "the daffodils yellowing in great clumps outside my window." She bought bunches of daffodils from the man outside her subway stop (no taxis to work for this fair lady) but found they were not somehow the same.

She slept late, until 11 A.M. or 12 noon, a schedule that was almost clock opposite to what her moviemaking schedule would be years later. She hired a studio to practice her singing for an hour once a day, eschewed the cheeseburgers she had learned to love (to keep her flower-girl figure), and tried to sleep nine and a half hours a night. The telephone backstage and at home rang constantly. "People expect so much more from you," she observed of stardom. "More letters, more effort, more entrances. Then if you don't produce, they think you've gone bigheaded." Julie tried with effort and letters but put her foot down on entrances and avoided big parties and nightclubs altogether. She and Tony would more often than not after the show go to the Windsor Pharmacy at Fifty-Eighth Street and Sixth Avenue for a Windsor Special, "a banana thing with wads of coconut cream." One of the things people most expected from Julie was tickets to *My Fair Lady,* but she couldn't get them, even for her "discoverer," Vida Hope. "I know she didn't believe me. Nobody does. I don't know where everybody comes from," she said.

Stardom meant a reversion to her innate shyness, a longing for simplicity ("I really wouldn't mind retiring, I really haven't much desire to go on to bigger and better things—what could be bigger and better than this?") and intermittent insecurity: "I still feel terribly unsure sometimes, as though I've tackled something miles above me."

But it also meant settling in for the two-year run she had dreaded in *The Boy Friend,* getting reconciled to steamy central heating, which she blamed for a series of colds she got when she had reported for rehearsals and for infrequent throat dryness during the run, and getting excited about "being involved with a show so good that Ingrid Bergman spent three of her thirty-six hours in New York at it—she came backstage later and she even used my WC." And then if she didn't like her beige dressing room with pale-blue chintz curtains and a navy armchair, the theater manager told her: "You can have it done in solid gold." The one immediate tangible result was that she and Tony got into the reserved-seat hit movie, *Around the World in 80 Days,* on the strength of her name when they couldn't get in by standing in line.

Julie spent some of her time denying to reporters that she and Tony were engaged, as her mother and stepfather were having to do in London. For her twenty-first birthday, he gave her a brooch in the shape of a laurel wreath ("what kings used to crown their queens with," she explained) that she wore on everything, and it seemed that the future course of the romance had been decided, although they were putting off the engagement because Julie had to do Eliza in London and Tony had to take his exams for the scenic design union in New York. For the same birthday, Charles Tucker gave Julie her first fur coat, a black seal, but she seemed to have lost some of her former acquisitiveness. "Every time I'm tempted by something elaborate I hear Mummy saying: 'Simplicity, simplicity,' " she said.

After the opening, Julie was the problem child no longer, but the darling of most of the cast and management of *My Fair Lady*. Moss Hart said she reminded him of Gertrude Lawrence, whom he had directed in *Lady in the Dark,* and he added: "She has this curious kind of glacial calm, as though she came down from Everest each day to play the show, instead of from a hotel room." Stanley Holloway, who played her father, said, "This child isn't spoiled one bit by success—it's hardly believable in an age where teen-agers are so worldly. I'm lucky to have her for a stage daughter. She *might* have been a scene-stealer." And even Rex Harrison, with whom she had had a few minor run-ins, and Julie came to an understanding, a mutual respect, and an arm's-length liking.

Among the rest of the cast Julie was known as the Rock, simply because she would stand solidly by, waiting for Harrison to amuse himself and try to rattle her by switching bits of stage business around. She also had trouble dancing with him ("He's left-handed and hence left-footed and starts the waltz from the left side—it can be confusing") and throwing slippers at him. She kept missing him and finally got so mad in rehearsals she heaved with all her might and hit him square in the forehead. "He stood there dazed, like a hurt child," she remembered. "Then he immediately begged for a lighter pair of slippers." On subsequent nights her aim improved (she was supposed to hit around the shoulders), but the impact was not so great. Julie remembered that she had been "shaking at the thought of working with him—one heard awful things about Rex, how rude he is and all that—but I think his years had mellowed him. He was charming, sweet, and wonderful to work with and wonderful to know. One would imagine that he'd been doing musical comedy for years, and yet it was his first one."

Harrison, who ended up playing Higgins as long as Julie did Eliza—two years in New York, eighteen months in London—longer counting the movie, for his part said ten years later: "She is very nice to work with, absolutely the same offstage as on. She is marvelously even, her performance doesn't vary; it is highly professional from the word 'go.' Julie was always—a very boring old word—a good trouper. She plowed on through thick and thin. One thousand performances over three years in three thousand hours; four months and five days of twenty-four hours a day—I had my secretary figure it out one day—that is quite a hell of a long time to have been vis-à-vis with somebody, through summers hot, winters cold, that sort of thing. She has an honesty and integrity, an openness. I think she has a quality of the English equivalent of the girl next door. She reminds me of some of the English ladies at Metro [Goldwyn-Mayer], Greer [Garson] and Deborah [Kerr]. She is not quite the same as they, but she has that very same quality that has appealed to movie audiences over the years."

(Despite all that vis-à-vis-ness, Julie and Rex saw each other only very occasionally in later years, and never on purpose, at "things like the Academy Awards," said Julie, grinning. They never discussed Audrey Hepburn's getting the movie part. At one Hollywood dinner party in late 1966 that they both attended, they were at opposite ends of the table and didn't speak at all during the evening, just waved and blew kisses, which could probably only happen between two show-business people.)

The fifty-four-minute-and-twenty-second Columbia recording that was to become the best-selling original cast album ever was done in fourteen hours at a converted Gothic church at 207 East Thirtieth Street in Manhattan on a Sunday ten days after the Broadway opening. Lerner rewrote and rearranged lyrics. ("For God's sake, get me to the church on time" became "Be sure and get me to the church on time" to ensure that the record could be played on radio and television. This prompted Stanley Holloway, whose number it was, to mock: "Be Shaw, be George Bernard Shaw to get me to the church on time.") Loewe and Franz Allers, the conductor—who at one point was conducting with one hand and holding up his pants with the other—changed tempos and orchestrations, and some instrumentalists were given their very own microphones. Goddard Lieberson, executive vice-president of Columbia Records, supervised both studio and control room, where Loewe was pounding a wooden shelf and shouting things like "Hit the D! Hit the D!" and "Cymbals, Cymbals! Cymbals!"

The session started at 10 A.M. with Holloway and chorus singing "With a Little Bit of Luck," which he accompanied with gestures and soft-shoe routines. Julie arrived just after lunch, and by the time she had sung two of her eight songs, "Show Me" and "Wouldn't It Be Loverly?" she remarked that her nerves were raw. Harrison, in a green waistcoat, arrived at three forty-five and talked "You Did It," with Robert Coote as Colonel Pickering. "I Could Have Danced All Night" came next and then dinner. Julie, Harrison, and Coote did their dance steps for "The Rain in Spain" to keep in the mood, although sound effects rendered them unnecessary.

A barefoot Harrison played the violin with the orchestra during other people's songs, but he reluctantly gave up his chair when the time came to do "I've Grown Accustomed to Her Face." Julie and Harrison did their duet, "Without You," and Mr. Allers asked the orchestra for "two minutes of silent prayer please." Harrison's "Why Can't the English?" and "I'm an Ordinary Man" and Julie's "Just You Wait" finished the recording session just after midnight. The drums were so strong during "Just You Wait" that Julie began imitating a drum majorette at her microphone. Within thirty-six hours of the end of the session, the first pressings were being produced to fill advance orders for 100,000 records.

The London *My Fair Lady* was almost a reprise of the New York one, although Julie had to "brush up on my Cockney and put back the heavy accent that I had had to tone down." Sally Ann Howes, a British stage and screen star, like Julie a former child star (*Thursday's Child*) and the daughter of a show-business father, actor Bobby Howes, made her Broadway debut in February, 1958, as Julie's replacement. Edward Mulhare came in opposite her in Harrison's role. And Julie, Harrison, and Holloway left to repeat their roles in the London production, opening on April 30.

Julie arrived home on April 6, after a holiday with Tony in Paris, Venice, and Klosters in Switzerland. She had stayed away because her Broadway success had made her "comparatively rich," and if she had arrived any sooner, she would have been eligible for British income tax on her American earnings. This situation was to keep her from coming home many times in the next decade of stardom. She flew into London airport with 260 pounds of excess baggage and a canary given to her by the *My Fair Lady* cast, which she had named Mr. Pocket, after the Alec Guinness character in the movie *Great Expectations*. Seven more trunks were on their way from America. Ted Wells, her brother John and half sister Celia, and a score of friends met her at the plane from Zurich. The girl who had flown to New York for *The Boy Friend* four years before with just two battered suitcases, arrived in the Alaska sealskin coat Charles Tucker had given her, a pearl-and-gold ring from Tony on her right hand, a clinging American-designed white wool dress and a seed-pearl-and-gold locket, another gift from the *My Fair Lady* cast. She went home to Walton-on-Thames for a night, then moved to a suite at the Savoy for the start of rehearsals.

Tony had stayed behind in Switzerland but returned to England in time for opening night at Theatre Royal in Drury Lane. Tickets proved to be as hard to get as they had been in New York, and there was an air of excitement unusual for a London opening, based on the ecstatic reports emanating from America over the past two years. Theatre Royal, hard by Covent Garden, where two of *My Fair Lady*'s scenes are set, had a larger stage than the Mark Hellinger (although a smaller seating capacity), and eight singers were added to the chorus. Zena Dare, a distinguished British actress, made the final appearance of her long career in the role of Mrs. Higgins. Leonard Wier was recruited six days before the opening as a replacement in the part of Freddy Eynsford-Hill.

For the whole cast, but especially for Julie, who had played in *Starlight Roof* in pigtails a short ten years before, and Holloway, long a favorite in London, opening night of *My Fair Lady* in its spiritual home was triumphant. Most Londoners came away agreeing that the musical was indeed as good as the Yanks had said it was. The audience, in white ties and dinner jackets and long formals, gave the show a four-minute standing ovation at the final curtain. There were eight curtain calls and would have been more, but the conductor broke into "God Save the Queen." The critics generally were fulsome. Those critics and playgoers who had seen the show in New York as well felt the musical had had a beneficial sea change, and they found Julie's Eliza, in the words of one, "More mature, commanding and subtle."

The opening had another effect, in that one minute after midnight the previously banned New York recordings of *My*

Fair Lady began to be played on commercial television and radio. A new version, the single best *My Fair Lady* album of the approximately sixty that were issued, was recorded in suburban London's Walthamstow Town Hall, on a rainy Sunday in October, 1958. This was the stereo version (although a monaural pressing was made at the same time) of the original cast, and Julie told me ten years later that recording it provided the one really angry scene she had caused in her professional career: "I was recording [Just You Wait,] 'Henry Higgins' and I was yelling and screaming my lungs out, as the song required. But in the playbacks I didn't hear what I knew was there. By that time I had done the show for something like two and a half years, and I knew what I was talking about. I got really mad, and the sound engineers very sweetly agreed to turn whichever knobs had to be turned, and we redid it. And that was that."

On August 8, 1959, Julie played Eliza for the last time. She confessed to being "tired tired" but not "bored tired" of being "part of a legend. You don't want to go on, but suddenly you don't want to go, either," she said. "The old firm, the old job, becomes very dear." For the thousandth time she took her applause on closing night, but that time tears rolled in rivers through her stage makeup. The audience joined hands and sang "Auld Lang Syne." The cast gave her an ovation, and Julie rushed offstage to her dressing room, where she stayed for more than an hour, crying. She later was hostess for a party at the theater. The next night her role was taken over by Anne Rogers, the original Polly in *The Boy Friend*.

After both versions of *My Fair Lady*, "my voice was in a ragged state from night after night of belting," Julie said. "Then I had my tonsils out—at age twenty-three. I thought I would never sing again. I very tentatively and timidly took on *Camelot*. It was an enormous period of anxiety about my voice. The next eighteen months were a miracle to me—I got my voice back. Svetlana Beriosova also remembered that "she was very worried about her voice before going on in *Camelot*; she wanted to be in top form for that."

"*Camelot* was just about my size and weight, a good level for me, and I enjoyed it so much more than *My Fair Lady*," Julie said after *The Sound of Music*. "Queen Guenevere was my favorite role so far." As Guenevere, a lesser part in a lesser Lerner and Loewe musical, Julie established herself as a full-time Broadway star. Three hits in a row was no fluke, and she picked up another substantial credit during her eighteen-month run in the part (she did not do the London company). She found "working with Richard Burton was exciting," and he termed her one of his "three favorite co-stars, the others being P. O'Toole and E. Taylor." Modestly, she said that after *Camelot* "it was a question of degree. I wasn't a star, but I wasn't unknown either."

Camelot had begun to come about in early March, 1956, in Philadelphia, when it was apparent that *My Fair Lady* would be a hit. Lerner, Loewe, and Hart took an informal pledge to work together again, and shook hands all around. After the *My Fair Lady* opening, they began to look for an idea. They considered and rejected musicals based on *Huckleberry Finn, Children of Paradise,* and *Father of the Bride,* the Spencer Tracy-Elizabeth Taylor movie. A Sunday newspaper review of the late T. H. White's *The Once and Future King* intrigued them enough to read it and then agree on the witty retelling of the King Arthur legend for their adaptation. They bought the stage rights from the author, who was then living on the Channel island of Alderney. The writing was completed in July, and rehearsals began in September, 1961, under the title of *Jenny Kissed Me*.

Because the star, composer, lyricist-librettist, and director were the *My Fair Lady* team, great things were expected of *Jenny Kissed Me*. The advance ticket sales produced a new Broadway record. Julie recalled: "We all believed in the book immensely and thought it would be a very beautiful musical." But there was trouble on the road in Boston. Then Moss Hart had a heart attack, and Alan Jay Lerner filled in as director. Julie by this time was an accomplished professional and the least of anyone's worries, but Richard Burton, while an experienced actor, was a newcomer to Broadway musicals (and he, like Harrison, would only talk-sing), and the third lead, Lancelot, was being played by a nervous novice from Canada who *could* sing but wasn't so sure of his acting, Robert Goulet. The problems one by one were resolved, and the retitled show opened at the Majestic Theater on December 3, 1960. Most critics, like the New York *Times'* Howard Taubman, found *Camelot* only "partly enchanted." Of Lerner and Loewe, Taubman said, "It would be unjust to tax them with not attaining the heights of 'My Fair Lady,' but it cannot be denied that they badly miss their late collaborator—George Bernard Shaw." And he said of Guenevere: "In the slim, airy person of Julie Andrews, a lovely actress and true singer, she is regal and girlish, cool and eager."

On the strength of its advance and the drawing power of its stars (and Goulet was hailed as the most exciting newcomer in years), *Camelot* had a respectable two-year run. For Julie, a new bride (she had finally married Tony during the last months of *My Fair Lady* in London), it was an easy eighteen months in a comfortable part, one whose pleasant songs—"I Loved You Once in Silence," "The Lusty Month of May," "You May Take Me to the Fair,"—she could have sung with her left lung only—although of course, she didn't. "It was a very nice time, very pleasant," she said.

Richard Burton, pre-*Cleopatra* and Elizabeth Taylor, centered his amorous attention on M'el Dowd, a character actress cast in the minor part of Morgan Le Fey that was totally missing from the subsequent movie, and later said that Julie was his only leading lady he'd never slept with. "How dare he say such an awful thing about me?" was Julie's retort.

Julie did establish an important new friendship with T. H.

"Tim" White. He introduced her to the peacefulness of Alderney, where she promptly bought a house. He wrote her the poem and said: "Julie Andrews is the most enchanting creature I have ever seen on stage."

III

JULIE MADE HER serious television debut on March 10, 1956, in the CBS ninety-minute musical version of Maxwell Anderson's *High Tor,* just five nights before *My Fair Lady* opened in New York. (She had appeared with her mother on musical programs on radio and TV in England.) The show was filmed in Hollywood the previous November because the stars were available then and to allow time for cutting and scoring the film, which was CBS's first nonlive entertainment special. Bing Crosby played the lead role of a contemporary young idealist, Van Van Dorn, who owned the historic High Tor mountain in the Dutch-settled section of lower New York State, and who loved the ghost of a Dutch girl dead for 300 years. Julie played Lise, the ghost, and Nancy Olson (who had been Betty Shaffer in *Sunset Boulevard* and was later Mrs. Alan Jay Lerner, so petite is the show-business world) played Crosby/Van Dorn's real-life fiancée. Although a second-unit crew went East and climbed High Tor for some authentic long shots, the mist-wrapped craggy mountain was re-created in plaster at the RKO-Pathé Studio in Hollywood, where the actual shooting was done and the fog was strictly from a machine. Arthur Schwartz, the producer and composer of the special, wrote six songs, for which Anderson wrote the lyrics. And CBS spent in excess of $300,000, then some sort of record for a TV show. Crosby had some misgivings: "I've been in lots of features, but nothing like this," he said on the set. "Can you imagine,

59

we're shooting this in twelve days? At a major studio it would take thirty days at least."

Julie, who had had a long rest in England after *The Boy Friend* and whose real stardom was yet to come, had no such misgivings—she didn't know enough to have any. Her seventeenth-century Dutch doll gave her some important firsts and Hollywood correspondents a revealing glimpse of what it would be like to interview Julie Andrews ten years hence. She sat on the set in her Dutch costume, waiting for her camera call, pursed her lips and said to the man from the New York *Times*: "Let's see, first time I've been in Hollywood, first time I've appeared before motion picture cameras and 'High Tor' is my first American television work. And what's more, I love it here. Oh, the shops I've been going through. But I shan't be sorry to get home. I'll be there for Christmas, you know." At that point, a move that was to become painfully familiar took place; a hairdresser whisked her away to check her wig.

The original of Mr. Anderson's play *High Tor*, though sometimes bitter, had been low-key, touching, and fantasy in the purest sense. Anderson, who adapted his play with John Monks, Jr., and director James Neilson had played the musical-comedy version "more for warmth and heart" in Neilson's words, and with none of the bitterness. The key premise of both was that the love between Van Dorn and Lise, across three centuries, was doomed. It was summed up in the scene between Julie and Crosby, where they looked mistily over what was supposed to be Long Island Sound, at the stars. "See the great gulf that lies between the heavy red star down in the west and the star that comes with morning?" she asked. "There's that much lies between us."

The show, despite its being a musical with Bing Crosby, did Julie no particular good—although it did her no particular harm and it had been fun. But the big singing part was his, and he had been wrong for it from the start. The static special looked like the artificial studio-set quickie that it was, and the would-be scene between the boy of the 1950's and the girl of the 1650's was lacking in any feeling.

Julie had better luck a year later with the title part in *Cinderella,* the only full-length original work done for television by Richard Rodgers and Oscar Hammerstein II, on March 31, 1957. She had been established as Eliza Doolittle, a kind of Cinderella character, for almost that whole year, and the public that had been lucky enough to see her onstage at the Mark Hellinger knew exactly what to expect. In terms of her performance at least, they weren't disappointed. Hammerstein had adapted the fairy tale for the ninety-minute musical version with the principal change being that the wicked stepmother and stepsisters were less wicked and more vaudevillian. There was a $385,000 production budget and a supporting cast that couldn't be topped: Edie Adams as the fairy godmother (Julie was later to sign on both her business manager and her ex-secretary), Kaye Ballard and Alice Ghostley as the stepsisters, Howard Lindsay and Dorothy Stickney as the king and queen, and Ilka Chase as the stepmother. Only Jon Cypher, as the prince, was an unknown. The sets and costumes were by William and Jean Eckart, and the show's director was Ralph Nelson, one of the finest directors on early American television, who made the transition to films (*Requiem for a Heavyweight, Lilies of the Field*).

For one of the few times ever, the magic of a Broadway-style musical made it more or less intact to the TV screen, doubly so since the special was one of the first transmitted in color, although only a tiny percentage of Americans had access then to a color set. One critic called Julie as Cinderella, "the best reason yet" to buy one. The musical, with Rodgers and Hammerstein songs like "Do I Love You Because You're Beautiful? (Or Are You Beautiful Because I Love You?)," "Ten Minutes Ago," "In My Little Corner" and "Lovely Night," was perhaps not near their best, but for TV it was a charming, lovely, and unforgettable event. Julie, for her part, was never more beautiful or in more sumptuous surroundings, and *Cinderella* merely confirmed the first impressions of her talent in *The Boy Friend* and *My Fair Lady*. (There was a remake of *Cinderella* in the winter of 1964–65 with the same score but a revised book by Joseph Shrank and a new cast, headed by Lesley Ann Warren, a seventeen-year-old newcomer, who would also go on to a critical success on Broadway and a film career courtesy of Walt Disney. Ginger Rogers and Walter Pidgeon were the queen and king, and Jo Van Fleet was the stepmother. Although Rodgers, as executive producer, oversaw the production, it just wasn't the same.)

In the late 1950's, there were other brief and consequently unsatisfying appearances, as a result of and involving songs from *My Fair Lady*. Julie was on the Ed Sullivan variety show once singing two numbers from the show, "I Could Have Danced All Night," and "Without You." And she and Stanley Holloway, who played her father, Alfred P. Doolittle, signed as a last-minute joint replacement for Ethel Merman in *Crescendo*, a ninety-minute CBS musical special in September, 1957. Miss Merman had withdrawn over dissatisfaction with her part in the pastiche of musical Americana. Rex Harrison had already been signed to star in *Crescendo* as a visiting Englishman who is entertained with a sampling of most styles of American music, blues, country and western, folk, jazz, sacred, Latin-American and musical comedy. Since there was no time to prepare anything else, Julie and Holloway did a medley from *My Fair Lady*.

In 1960 Julie had an entertaining spot on a Jack Benny special on CBS. She sang and sort of danced a 1920's medley that included "Ain't We Got Fun?" and "I'm Just Wild About Harry" and brought back memories of *The Boy Friend*. And she appeared on British TV in typical vaudeville turns. In the spring of 1961 she made a guest appearance on Garry Moore's CBS variety show, where she first met Carol Burnett, a regular on the show, and was such a success that

Moore signed her for five additional visits the following season. Carol and Julie teamed on "Big D," the song about Dallas from *The Most Happy Fella,* a finale number arranged by Ernie Flatt and in such unforgettable fashion that they were inspired and encouraged to do a special of their own, which turned out to be Julie's single most important TV appearance.

The finale had worked better than any number on the *Garry Moore Show* before or since. "Everybody was excited about it," Carol recalled, "except the networks. At the time, although I was a regular on the show, I wasn't under contract to CBS yet. I was fairly new, and nobody had ever heard of Julie west of New Jersey. We went everywhere trying to sell the idea—to NBC, ABC, and XYZ, but nobody was interested." Mike Nichols, then half of a cabaret comedy team, had agreed to write the show, but ironically, in view of his later success, no one was much excited by that potential contribution by Elaine May's partner.

In 1961 only NBC had regular network color telecasts, and Carol used that fact to tweak the CBS management into action. At the CBS luncheon at the Waldorf-Astoria in New York just after Christmas, with Jim Aubrey, then president of CBS-TV, Mike Dann, then East Coast programming vice-president, and Oscar Katz, overall vice-president for network programs, Carol was the only woman at the table. "I was putting the three of them on, and they didn't realize it for a long time. I kept saying, 'It's a shame you boys passed up your chance at Julie and me, but then we do look so much better in color anyway.' They, of course wanted to know what the hell I was talking about, and I told them that Julie and I were going to do a special. Aubrey asked why and I said, 'Because Julie and I have these magical powers.' By then they had figured out that I might be putting them on."

After lunch the three executives and Carol had to walk back to the old CBS Building on Madison Avenue. "Everyone was returning Christmas presents, and you couldn't get a cab," Carol said. "When we got to the CBS Building, the men said, 'We'll wait and get you a cab.' I said, 'Oh, don't worry, with my magical powers I'll probably get a ride.' At that instant a beer truck appeared, and a big beefy driver with a tatoo yelled out, 'Hey, Carol, you want a lift?' The three men helped me into the cab of the beer truck, and I rode off to Central Park West, waving to the three of them standing there with their mouths open."

The telephone in Carol's apartment rang less than an hour later. It was Katz, who said, "You're a witch—you've got your special." "I called Julie at her dressing room at *Camelot* —it was a Wednesday, a matinee day, and there we were." The special was aired on the superhumid evening of June 11, 1962, a little more than a year after Julie's first appearance on the *Garry Moore Show*.

Julie and Carol at Carnegie Hall was just that, a taped hour of hilarity from the stage of the famed New York concertorium, before a live invitational audience, and starring two of the most talented performers ever to appear on a stage in the United States, attractively opposite but completely complementary. The pairing reminded viewers of a similar special featuring Mary Martin and Ethel Merman on behalf of the fiftieth anniversary of Ford seven years before, only in its uniform excellence and in the fact that it was one of those once-in-a-TV-decade inspirations. From the opening number, "You're So London," chronicling the very opposite characteristics of the very American Miss Burnett and the very English Miss Andrews ("You're so 'hi there, how are ya,' I'm so 'how t'y'do' "; "you're so Kensington Gardens and I'm so San Antone"; etc.) to the reprise of "Big D," it was one of those rare exhibitions of pure talent in total top form.

In "The Nausiev Ballet" a Mike Nichols and Ken Welch satire on the endless stream of touring Russian dance troupes that was invading the United States in 1962, Julie proved the equal of Carol in campy clowning, which wouldn't have surprised English audiences but was a first in America. Julie did just one solo, a simply exquisite rendering of "Johnny's So Long at the Fair." She and Carol did an outrageous and devastating parody of *The Sound of Music,* then the biggest hit on Broadway (eclipsing among others *Camelot* and something like the seventh company of *My Fair Lady*). In "The Pratt Family of Switzerland," a prophetic piece that would come back to haunt her, Julie played the Mary Martin/ Maria Von Trapp prototype and Carol played Cynthia, the only Pratt girl among seventeen Pratt boys, and the Nichols-Welch songs were perfect send-ups of the Rodgers and Hammerstein score. Another delicious bit was "The History of Musical Comedy," a duet medley of American musical numbers.

The program showed American audiences a new versatility in Julie, and at that wonderful point in her career with two hit Broadway shows behind her and *Camelot,* her own favorite, running very well, there was no such thing as worrying about a Mary Poppins image. And the material the creative team had chosen held up well on the RCA Victor cast recording, which became TV's only classic sound track and was still stocked by stores seven years later.

The Carnegie Hall special not only gave Julie two extremely close friends, Carol Burnett and Mike Nichols, but was a critical and audience triumph for both its stars, as well as for all concerned with the show. It gave Nichols a big push in his desired transition from performer to writer-director, and producer-director Joe Hamilton (who had done both jobs on the *Garry Moore Show* and who would marry his leading lady) got an Emmy from the National Academy of Television Arts and Sciences. The show itself got a Rose D'Or Award from the Montreaux International Television Festival in 1963, the first American TV program so honored. "We were booed when we won," Carol remembered, "because everyone thought the show was filmed, and of course, it was taped. We convinced the audience we had done it in a single performance, and they quieted down."

Although all her previous TV work had been on CBS, Julie's only solo special was on NBC, with which she had a vague verbal agreement that gave them "first refusal on anything I do." By late 1965 nobody was refusing anything that Julie Andrews chose to do, and if in the United States, there was still someone who had not heard of the bewitching Briton on the night of November 28, when *The Julie Andrews Show* was broadcast, he too was in on the phenomenon. Julie did a faultless full-color hour of singing, dancing, and comedy, featuring Gene Kelly as her chief guest (they did a seemingly effortless soft shoe together), the New Christy Minstrels, and a special number written for her by Ray Charles. She sang "I Could Have Danced All Night," "Try to Remember," "Auld Lang Syne" with its second verse, and of course, "The Sound of Music." The film's scorer, Irwin Kostal, was musical director of one of the best-sounding, from a technical standpoint, specials ever on TV. The show drew 35,000,000 viewers (more than either Streisand or Sinatra that season) and won two Emmys and a George Foster Peabody Award, less known by the public, but considered more prestigious by the industry.

Once she had her choice, however, TV was almost her least favorite medium, and even her tough-minded and usually influential agent, Arthur Park, couldn't change her mind about that. "She just isn't crazy about TV," Park said. "She feels there are too many compromises in time, that there isn't enough time to do anything right." But finally in November, 1969, Julie taped a second special for NBC, *An Evening with Julie Andrews and Harry Belafonte,* directed at her request by her friend Gower Champion and with Michel Legrand as musical director. She agreed to do it essentially because Hathaway House, the home for disturbed boys on the old DeMille estate that constituted her chief charity, was offered the chance in effect to produce the show (Champion was the producer of record for the sake of control) and earn a percentage of the profits. She worked for a minimum fee, but the other three principals got their usual prices.

Julie at age eleven, before her teeth were fixed, practices her high notes. UNITED PRESS INTERNATIONAL.

Below: With "Pop," step-father Ted Andrews, learning lip and tongue control for the Albert Hall concert, July, 1947. PICTORIAL PARADE.

Age thirteen, with Danny Kaye during a rehearsal for the Royal Command Performance.

With "Mum" and "Pop" after the opening of *Starlight Roof*. RANDALL CARLSEN LTD.

Julie in a platinum wig as Polly Browne in *The Boy Friend*, during "Poor Little Pierrette" number, October, 1954, her first Broadway appearance. NEW YORK TIMES.

In her first American TV special, *High Tor,* with Bing Crosby, November, 1955. CULVER PICTURES.

Julie and her mother, Barbara Andrews, arrive at New York International Airport in January, 1956, before the start of *My Fair Lady*.

Julie as Eliza Doolittle and Rex Harrison as Professor Henry Higgins outside Covent Garden in *My Fair Lady*. 1956. FRIEDMAN-ABELES, N.Y.

Julie and Rex Harrison recording "The Rain in Spain" for the Broadway cast album of *My Fair Lady*. COLUMBIA RECORDS.

Below: With Alan Jay Lerner during the *My Fair Lady* record session. 1956. COLUMBIA RECORDS.

A word of encouragement from "Mum" during the recording of *My Fair Lady*. COLUMBIA RECORDS.

Rehearsing the *Cinderella* songs with Richard Rodgers. CBS TELEVISION.

Below: Oscar Hammerstein II, Richard Rodgers, and Julie in costume during a rehearsal of *Cinderella.* 1957. CBS TELEVISION.

Below: Alice Ghostley and Kaye Ballard as the stepsisters, Ilka Chase as the stepmother, and Julie as *Cinderella* in the Rodgers and Hammerstein musical version of the fairy tale for TV. 1957. CBS TELEVISION.

Julie marries childhood "mate," Tony Walton, at Oatland St. Mary Church in Weybridge, Surrey (near Walton-on-Thames, where they both grew up), May 10, 1959. She was twenty-three and took a two-week leave from the London run of *My Fair Lady* for a honeymoon trip to California, where she had to be anyway for a TV show. He was twenty-four and, as a fledgling set and costume designer, designed her wedding dress. WIDE WORLD PHOTOS.

Richard Burton as King Arthur and Julie as Queen Guenevere in *Camelot.* 1961. UNITED PRESS INTERNATIONAL.

Richard Burton, Alan Jay Lerner, and Julie working out a *Camelot* song. COLUMBIA RECORDS.

Tony Walton explains the design of baby clothes as Julie, Mike Nichols, and Carol Burnett open presents for the yet unborn Emma Kate. 1962. COLUMBIA RECORDS.

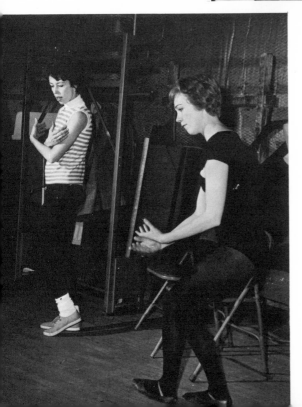

Carol and Julie coping with a tricky dance step in rehearsals for their special. 1962. CBS TELEVISION.

Sending up "The Sound of Music" in *Julie and Carol at Carnegie Hall.* 1962. CBS TELEVISION.

Carol and Julie in the "Big D" finale of *Julie and Carol at Carnegie Hall.* 1962. CBS TELEVISION.

An earnest chat with Mike Nichols.

Julie with daughter, Emma Kate Walton, at the age of one, leaving New York International Airport, November 7, 1963, for Hollywood and *Mary Poppins*—and more or less for good. UNITED PRESS INTERNATIONAL PHOTO.

Above: Julie and Jack Warner congratulate each other on their Oscars, backstage at Santa Monica Civic Auditorium. Hers was for *Mary Poppins,* his as the producer of *My Fair Lady.* Gregory Peck stands between them, and Audrey Hepburn, who played Eliza in Warner's movie and wasn't nominated, tries hard not to look on. WIDE WORLD PHOTOS.

Left: Trying on her costume bonnet for *Mary Poppins.* UNITED PRESS INTERNATIONAL PHOTO.

Julie in her best movie yet, *The Americanization of Emily,* with James Garner and Joyce Grenfell. CULVER PICTURES.

The hills were alive with the sound of Julie—and money— after her portrayal of Maria von Trapp in *The Sound of Music.* This scene was shot in the Austrian Alps in the spring of 1964, and for it Julie learned to play the guitar. TWENTIETH CENTURY-FOX PHOTO.

Julie and a favorite food—vanilla ice cream—during a brief break in the filming of *Hawaii*, on board the converted square-rigger *Thetis* (in real life, the *Greta*), off Oahu, summer of 1965. STEPHEN PALEY.

Julie had first envisioned the show as a solo performance
set at the Los Angeles Music Center with "somebody fabulous" conducting the Los Angeles Philharmonic. After delays
on *Darling Lili,* the symphony hall wasn't available when
she was. Champion remembered that "the really memorable
TV specials had been twos: Merman and Martin, Julie and
Carol . . ." and tried to come up with as dynamic a pairing.
He and she settled on Belafonte, whom Julie had met just
once, at the New York premiere of *The Sound of Music,* but
with whom Champion and his wife, Marge, had worked back
at the beginning, in 1954's bus-and-truck company of *Three
for Tonight.* The special was staged with just the two performers on camera, singing virtually every song together or
to each other, sometimes romantically, as in "Scarborough
Fair." (Except for one calypso number that Belafonte and
his fans were allowed, and a fast finale medley of *My Fair
Lady* and *Mary Poppins* for her and hers, the songs were
modern pop.)

The interracial pairing was somewhat of a breakthrough
for TV. Belafonte, who in an appearance on a Petula Clark
special the previous year had been the focal point of a major
scandale when Miss Clark merely touched his arm, said: "I
had no self-consciousness about how we'd relate and I was
convinced she had no hang-ups either. There was no censorship, and Gower never pulled back because of color. We ca-
vort around the stage holding hands, dance and sing cheek to
cheek—she's biting and kicking me all through the show. It
could have been Frank Sinatra or Robert Goulet instead of
me, or Lena Horne instead of her."

Julie, who picked most of the songs for the special after
several weeks' close attention to the radio in her white Mercedes (and they included "Abergavenny," "Feelin' Groovy,"
and Joni Mitchell's "Michael from the Mountains"), suc-
cumbed to the medley after hearing a "simple and elegant"
Lena Horne special and finding herself "never so happy as
when she finally settled down to singing 'Stormy Weather.'

If I reacted that way to her, maybe some people will feel cheated if I don't sing something of the past." She still found television "rushed and different," despite a self-imposed ten-week rehearsal schedule, a huge budget, and no audiences for either rehearsals or the final taping. She encountered Carol Burnett in a corridor at NBC in Burbank, where Carol was also taping a special, and said, "How do you do it every week? You must have a marvelous nanny."

Although, she said in the midst of taping, "I'd forgotten about the pace, one pleasant surprise was to find that in the four years since the last one, the crew has changed. It's now made up of bright, nice boys—you get to feeling rather old —who are eager, inventive, helpful, and anxious to make it work; I hadn't counted on that. I really didn't expect to enjoy this special at all, and I am. I don't know if it's because I've had a year off or what. I think it's the company. But I wouldn't be in a mad rush to do TV again any time soon."

Thus, except for the 1965 special, which was repeated by NBC in April, 1968, Julie had not been seen on television (apart from in filmed promotional trailers for her movies and for charity) for four and a half years. But she was always part of the networks' wishful thinking. Michael H. Dann, who had survived the firing of network president James Aubrey, Jr., and several other more minor purges at CBS, and became senior vice-president for programming, in announcing to the network's affiliates that the young black singer Leslie Uggams would replace the *Smothers Brothers Comedy Hour,* which had been canceled after disputes over censorship in April, 1969, said wistfully: "Julie Andrews is simply not waiting in the wings to do a one-hour variety show." (A higher CBS official than Dann had said privately that the relatively unknown Miss Uggams was "the right color at the right time and she was already under contract.")

Julie was happier appearing on other people's shows rather than on her own special, about which she felt "diffident," she said. "It seems not right, a little cheeky, to come in from left field to be the star. It's a bit nervy to come in with no real knowledge of the medium"—she laughed— "in contrast to my immense knowledge of every other conceivable subject."

Carol Burnett, who in the years since Carnegie Hall had become one of American TV's few genuine superstars (and with Lucille Ball, the only woman to reach that rank) with her hour-long weekly variety show, did get off at least one good joke at Julie's expense. In the midst of a sketch spoofing fairy tales in general, Carol, as a damsel in distress surrounded by the forces of evil, screamed: "Oh, what would Julie Andrews do in a spot like this? I bet she'd sing. Hit it!"

IV

JULIE HAD HER only screen test when she was twelve, at Metro-Goldwyn-Mayer in London. "They tried to make me look like a child star, but with my buck teeth and bandy legs, I didn't look like much of anything," she recalled in late 1966, after her first three films had put her in the highest ranks of box-office stars.

"There was some interest among a few film executives after *The Boy Friend* and a few very tentative offers during *My Fair Lady*," she said. "But nothing that seemed real or important."

Julie's agent, Arthur Park, of Chasin, Park, Citron, one of the most successful offshoot agencies of the demonopolized Music Corporation of America talent department, remembered: "She was available for movies, but as good as she was in *My Fair Lady,* no one recognized her potential or ran across anything that seemed to be right for her. Until Disney saw her in *Camelot.*"

"I had thought a lot about movies, but never very seriously," she said. "I had *fantasies* that I'd like to make a movie someday, but I had no serious intentions of making them."

She was a West End and Broadway name, and despite success after success in the theater and on television, she was totally untried in movies and therefore worth supposedly nothing at the box office. American moviemakers still thought that way in the mid-1960's (it took some no-name successes like *The Graduate, Bonnie and Clyde, Oliver, Romeo and Juliet,* and *Rosemary's Baby* to destroy that myth completely—and to make "stars" of such unlikely types as Dustin Hoffman, Ron Moody, and Mia Farrow). For it was also Julie's unusual looks that mitigated against her in movies.

Julie herself was sure that the Hollywood executives were most concerned about her not photographing well. "I had not looked too well on a couple of television shows, and I think they were frightened of how I'd look on a big screen," she said. All that changed the spring afternoon in 1962 when Walt Disney went to see a matinee of *Camelot.* Disney never worried about names in his movies because his own as producer meant more at the box office and among the world's children and parents than that of any star, even Donald Duck. He was looking for a Mary in *Mary Poppins,* which like all Disney movies involving any animation had been brewing for some time until all the elements were exactly right. (After Disney's death it took the studio more than three years to complete the all-animated *Aristocats.*) He had thought of Julie Andrews, but sitting in the Majestic Theater watching her—particularly during "What Do the Simple Folk Do?"— he was convinced that she had the right kind of sense of humor. He was also impressed with her whistling ability in that sprightly number, whistling being a helpful asset for most nannies and many Disney characters. He sent word backstage during intermission that he was in the audience and would like to see her in her dressing room after the show. Julie said, in effect, show the gentleman in. Disney, who had discovered Hayley Mills for American movie audiences, discussed the Poppins role briefly and invited Julie and Tony to visit him at the studios in Burbank, to discuss it further, "when you've finished here."

"Since I had never made a movie, the idea appealed to me greatly," she said. And so, three months pregnant with Emma, Julie and Tony went to Hollywood, where they were entertained lavishly at Disney's watchful insistence. They discussed the script, and Tony was offered a designing job on the film so they would be together with their expected new-born child. It was the Robert and Richard Sherman music, though, that did it. "I was sold." She signed, and Tony signed as overall design director, and they returned to London to have the baby.

Carol Burnett, who had become Julie's good friend and was to become the baby's godmother, remembered the enthusiasm and a few self-doubts. "Julie always put herself down about movies, never thinking she would look good enough. When Poppins came up she asked me, 'Do you think I ought to? Go to work for Walt Disney? The cartoon person?' I assured her that Disney did other things besides cartoons, but she was a little worried about it. But when she came out to Hollywood, she became totally enthusiastic. I don't think she ever came out here to be the great big star of the world, but she was very excited about that one movie."

"I must say, I will be forever grateful to that man," Julie said of Disney. "Tony and I flew out after *Camelot,* took a look, and liked it enormously. It was so very easy to see what he was trying to do, and I loved that very slight flavor of vaudeville to it."

Years later, in another context and at the peak of her fame, Julie said to me, in the present tense: "We don't make long movies at the Disney studios—just good ones." And several times, as one of the "Disney ladies," Julie narrated on-camera the Disney Christmas TV show, a compendium of the year's activity at the studio. She didn't enjoy it any more than she did other TV, but she still felt the debt to Disney and the studio long after his death.

For this, her first film role, Julie got $150,000, plus a living allowance, since she was technically a resident of London who had temporarily stationed herself in New York. Tony also got a fee for designing the picture. The family of three settled into a rented house in Studio City, in the San Fernando Valley, with a nanny and a maid. And except for trips to other movie locations, a few vacations in Hawaii and Switzerland, and brief visits to England, Julie never left.

Pamela Travers, the then fifty-nine-year-old author of the Mary Poppins books on which the Disney film was to be loosely based, legally had nothing to say about who played the leading role. "She rang me up in the hospital [the London Clinic] the day after I had Emma," Julie recalled. "She said, 'P. Travers here. Speak to me. I want to hear your voice.' I was still too weak and told her I wanted to recover first. When we finally got together the first thing she said was, 'Well, you've got the nose for it.' I adored her. She was so wonderfully honest and direct. Tony and I had several lunches with her before we came out here to do the movie. Later I wrote her long letters from the set and tried to give her a sort of idea of what we were doing."

The one movie Julie wanted most, of course, was the one she didn't get—*My Fair Lady*. "It may have been that celebrated ill wind," she was able to say years later. "I had *Mary Poppins* to soften the blow." But at the time she was deeply disappointed and hurt, more so because she was British and didn't really understand the Hollywood star system that had worked against her, but that she was to learn all about soon enough. Warner Brothers had invested a record $5,500,000 in acquiring the screen rights to the musical. And Jack Warner was determined to use Rex Harrison, although he then was not a particularly potent box-office name in America; but there was simply no one else who could come close to playing the part, Warner felt. A string of fair ladies, including Sally Ann Howes, Pamela Charles, Lola Fisher, and Margot Moser, had followed Julie on Broadway and had done Eliza incredibly well. There was a feeling at Warner's that although it might have been a difficult role to "get" on stage, any number of stars who were also good actresses could probably get by on-screen, especially under George Cukor's direction. And there was that investment in the screenplay and a total budget of $17,000,000 to think of. Julie stayed in the running, simply because she had been so brilliant in the part for three and a half years on stage in New York and London, but that just made it harder to take when she didn't get it and Audrey Hepburn, then a superstar of the first magnitude, did—for a fee of $1,000,000, and not even to do her own singing. Marni Nixon, the "ghost" voice for Deborah Kerr in *The King and I,* Rosalind Russell in *Gypsy,* and Natalie Wood in Robert Wise's *West Side Story,* would do that, without formal acknowledgment or screen credit, of course.

The morning Julie found out that Miss Hepburn had been signed, she was sitting in her agents' office. They knew already and assumed she did, but she didn't and asked something about how it was going. "Haven't you heard?" said one. "They've signed Audrey Hepburn." "Oh . . . I see," was the quiet, composed reply, as Julie struggled to get hold of herself. After a pause she said, "Well that's that, isn't it?" Later that morning, Julie was riding by the Warner Brothers Studios in Burbank. Out of a protracted, deliberate silence came, in a crystalline, high-pitched voice, "And a good morning to you, Mr. Warner, and the best of luck." That was almost Julie's last word on the subject. She often said that if it had been anyone but Audrey Hepburn, an actress she didn't know but did admire, she "would have been blazing mad."

"Of course, I wanted to play it," said Julie. "Who wouldn't want to play Eliza? But in a way it's a good thing having to play a different role. People at least will know I can do something else." It would have been possible for her to have done both roles, however, because principal photography involving Eliza wasn't begun until Julie's part in *Mary Poppins* was completed. She, of course, could not have done *Emily* or *The Sound of Music.*

Miss Hepburn was held in high repute by most of Hollywood, too, and so after the initial shock of the announcement, talk about it in the industry was short-lived. It was the fans and some of the less mature critics who carried on as if Goldwater had been elected President and who never got over it. Some fans vowed never to see an Audrey Hepburn movie again, much less *My Fair Lady*. Julie had no such violent reactions. While some of her public utterances ("I would have taken the part had Mr. Warner asked me even though I had about enough of Eliza, two years on Broadway, eighteen months in London." "I was more than compensated by three marvelous roles." "I wasn't desperately upset over not getting the role; I didn't hold out much hope in the first place") smacked of stiff-upper-lipping, it was true that she had a chance to show versatility in *The Americanization of Emily* (even if the two nannies typed her for a long time to come) that she just wouldn't have had had she reprised Eliza. Julie went to see the movie *My Fair Lady* and pronounced it "a wonderful film. It was the first time I had ever seen it from the front. Now I know why people are so crazy about it." Of the Marni-Nixon-dubbed singing, Julie said, neutrally, "I think dubbing is fine as long as you can get away with it."

Audrey partly returned the compliment, by slipping in unnoticed at Radio City Music Hall with her then husband, actor-producer-director Mel Ferrer, while *Mary Poppins* was playing. "We were in such a hurry that we could only stay for an hour," Miss Hepburn recounted, "but Julie was simply wonderful, and Mel thought so too."

The freeze between Julie Andrews and Warner Brothers would continue through tentative *Camelot* movie negotiations in 1966 and half thaw at least only when Jack Warner sold his interests to Seven Arts in 1967, whereupon he became a private producer and the studio temporarily became Warner Brothers Seven Arts, which paid $3,000,000 for screen rights to the Broadway musical *Mame* (the second highest price ever paid for a property) and promptly began to consider Julie Andrews for the title part, with no resistance from her.

V

JULIE PLUNGED into the Poppins part with every ounce of enthusiasm and energy she could muster, and as a new mother of a healthy daughter and with six months of rest in Alderney behind her, that was considerable. It was pleasant being on the college-campus-like Disney backlot in Burbank, so unlike any other studio (at 12:30 P.M., each working day, no matter what, all film and TV activity stops for lunch and Frisbee on the well-manicured lawn), even if a mile or less away, also in Burbank, *My Fair Lady* was in preproduction for a new Eliza at Warner Brothers.

P. L. Travers in the original book in 1934 had written that her idea of Mary was: "Shiny black hair, like a wooden Dutch doll, with large hands and feet, pink cheeks and round blue eyes." Thirty years later she said: "My conception of her has changed in some ways, because I've grown and she's grown with me" (the last of four books, *Mary Poppins in the Park*, had appeared in 1952, published by Harcourt, Brace & World, Inc.). "I now recognize a mixture of arrogance and poetry and, underlying both, a certain invincible integrity." The physical appearance had not changed, nor had the character aged in her mind. "She is a plain 27-year-old who obviously has assumed all the prerogatives of a pretty woman, because, if you notice, although I didn't originally intend it to be like this, everybody falls in love with her."

Julie, except for the black hair and the fact that she was in no way "plain," fitted the description admirably, and when she began shooting the film, she was twenty-seven, although she was twenty-nine when it was released for the Christmas trade in late 1964. And P. L. Travers approved. She also did not object to Disney's turning her classic children's stories into a musical. Nor did she mind when the scriptwriters demoted the setting from London in the 1930's back to London of the Edwardian era, which all concerned considered much more photogenic and much less Depression-grim. But she was absolutely adamant that the platonic friendship between Mary Poppins and Bert, the Cockney sidewalk artist (played by Dick Van Dyke) not be expanded into a big-screen romance.

The number of children was reduced from four in the book to two in the film, a wise move in any case, and in retrospect, an essential one for Julie who was to govern seven children in *The Sound of Music* and who might thereafter have been considered incapable of appearing on the screen without a brood of some sort. And the Disney workers conscientiously tried to keep the fans of the book in mind, even as they created a whole new story around the Travers characters. Julie said up front that her own characterization of the acid-tongued no-nonsense nanny would be "a little softer, a little rounder."

The Poppins books, although written and published in England by an "Irish" author (born in the tropics of North Queensland, Australia, of Irish parents) about English people, had always been more popular in America. The Disney studios, having counted on that thirty-year popularity and having set the Christmas release date, allotted $6,000,000 for the picture, one of the most expensive and lavish films the studio had ever produced. And the animation sequences added considerably to the cost.

As in the book, in the movie nearly everyone floated in the air at some time or other, and Miss Poppins could do it at will. The others, like the late Ed Wynn, and Karen Dotrice and Matthew Garber as the children, Jane and Michael

Banks, had to laugh a lot to achieve the heights. At one point, Van Dyke joined the three of them and Mary for a tea party on the ceiling of Wynn's (as Uncle Albert) place. The aerial tea party and most of the other visual fantasies in the script had been described in the books. But Mrs. Banks, the children's mother, played by Glynis Johns, was most certainly not a suffragette who neglected her children in the original, nor was her husband (David Tomlinson) neglecting them because of the pressures of his business. The writers took these liberties, they said, to introduce a bit of "harmless" dramatic conflict, and to allow Mary to arrive, windborne by an umbrella to save the children from this neglect.

Pamela Travers ("Don't call me 'Miss' or 'Mrs.' just P.L.") had described the Banks house, the smallest on Cherry Tree Lane as "rather dilapidated" and needing a coat of paint, but the Disney "imagineers"were having none of it. They were having, instead, a sumptuous, velvety Edwardian mansion, re-created on one sound stage and the whole of the exterior of Cherry Tree Lane on another.

In *Poppins* the live actors were frequently surrounded by cartoon animals, as when Mary, Bert, and the two children disappear into a cartoon land where barnyard animals dance and sing or when they get mixed up on a cartoon fox hunt and ride into the horse-racing derby, which Mary then wins.

The Sherman brothers, Robert B. and Richard M., wrote fifteen new songs for the movie, which was an intricate amalgam of animation and live action, with one twenty-five-minute sequence in which Mary Poppins and the two children dissolve into a picture that Bert has drawn on the sidewalk and with tricks like clothes folding themselves. While the production was pure Disney American, the cast except Van Dyke, was largely English and included Hermione Baddeley and Elsa Lanchester.

Flying on invisible wires was fun for everyone (Van Dyke did most of his own, while the others at times used stuntmen and women). But sometimes acting with the nonexistent animated characters that would be drawn in later was annoying for all but Julie, to whom the whole business (and she was finding out already that it was a business) of making movies was brand-new.

Carol Burnett recalled: "One night I went to dinner at her house and for two hours afterward she played dubs [prerecordings the actors sing along to while the film is being shot—they will usually dub in the final version during postproduction and editing if they are using their own voices] from the film and showed me some of the bits with the cartoon characters, she was so excited."

"At first I missed the live audience reaction," Julie said. "But as I grew accustomed to the medium, I found myself enjoying moviemaking more and more. One thing that appealed to me particularly was the permanence. If your performance was good, it was preserved for posterity. Another wonderful thing about movies, you don't have to be in perfect voice every night."

"She was tense when she went to Hollywood," said Svetlana Beriosova of her friend. "She wondered how she would make the transition to a new medium, where there is no applause, no response from the audience to carry you along."

While making *Mary Poppins,* Julie began what would become her long-standing reputation as an easy thoroughly professional person to work with—and as an on-set cutup.

Bill Walsh, who doubled as writer and co-producer with Disney and who became a friend of Julie's, summed up the experience of having her on the set: "She has sex appeal with dignity. Her sex appeal is subtle but glowing."

Although Tony was costume designer on *Mary Poppins,* he and Julie rarely saw each other during working hours. Most of his work was done, of course, before the actual shooting began. And since they were brand-new parents and the working experience in California was a new one for both, the situation put no obvious strain on the marriage. There was the underlying fact that both of them knew well, though they seldom talked about it: that Tony, essentially a stage designer, would never have been hired to do the picture had his wife not been the star.

During filming Julie took great delight in shrieking the highest note she could reach at the moment like a factory whistle into the microphone hanging over her head. Her co-workers were all amused but one, the sound technician, sitting with his earphones in. "Usually he'd have to go away for almost half an hour to recover," she said, exaggerating.

The prerecorded songs provided another early moment in Julie's saga of clowning on movie sets. When a scene is being shot that involves one of the musical numbers, a scratchy record of the actor or his ghost singing is played with usually only piano accompaniment so the actor can merely mouth the words and concentrate on acting. A final "scored" version is later done with full orchestra, the singer in full voice, and stereophonic sound. One morning as Van Dyke and Andrews were doing a duet, the entire crew stopped, amazed and perplexed. His baritone voice was coming out of her mouth, and her clear soprano was emanating from his. It took the technicians only a moment to figure it out, and then they were in stitches. It had been Julie's idea to have them mouth each other's words.

It didn't take the shrewd businessmen at Walt Disney very long to realize what they had on their hands, and in the summer of 1964, before the late September release, they set an exploitation budget that was "more than for any other picture" released by the company. And they signed contracts for a wide variety of official Mary Poppins merchandise, with thirty-eight separate licensees, which was due to appear in September with the picture. Among the products were girls' dresses, dolls, housewares, and jewelry; a King Features syndicate cartoon series; 4,000,000 books reprinted by various publishers; and several sets of recordings. Advertising tie-ins were established with Kraft Foods and the National Sugar Refining Company. It was the biggest and most lucrative merchandising campaign since television's Davy Crockett had almost every American boy—and many of the girls—under eleven in coonskin caps.

The picture opened in Los Angeles in late August and in New York at Radio City Music Hall a month later, to almost unanimously glowing reviews. A few critics, most definitely including P. L. Travers, took issue with the interpretation, but Bosley Crowther, the able veteran critic of the New York *Times,* was not among them. Said he:

> In case you are a Mary Poppins zealot who dotes on her just as she is, don't let the intrusion of Mr. Disney and his myrmidons worry you one bit. Be thankful for it and praise heaven there are such as they still making films. For the visual and aural felicities they have added to this sparkling color film—the enchantments of a beautiful production, some deliciously animated sequences, some exciting and nimble dancing and a spinning musical score—make it the nicest entertainment that has opened at the Music Hall this year. . . .
>
> This is the genuine Mary Poppins that comes sailing in on an east wind . . . played superbly by Miss Andrews, with her button-shoed feet splayed out to give her an unshakable footing and a look of complete authority, who calmly proceeds to show her charges that wonders will never cease and that there's nothing like a spoonful of sugar to sweeten the nastiest medicine.

Judith Crist, movie critic of the New York *Herald Tribune,* at the end of the year placed *Mary Poppins* tenth on her Top Ten for 1964, just below *A Hard Day's Night* and just ahead of the first of seventeen possibilities for a mythical eleventh place—*My Fair Lady.* Mrs. Crist called *Mary Poppins* "a charming, imaginative and technically superb movie musical, sparkling with originality, melody and magical performances by Julie Andrews and Dick Van Dyke and, through the triumph of Walt Disney's craftsmanship, offering uniquely cinematic entertainment."

P.L., on the other hand was privately annoyed, but having sold out her interest, she would only say publicly, "Let me be silent." She was delighted, she said, that "the character is no longer mine; people think it belongs to them. You used to have to be dead for that to happen."

Julie had not read the Travers books as a child, as she had not done so many things that ordinary children do, but she did read them as preparation for her role in the film. And she understood what Miss Travers and other critics of the film were talking about when they condemned the Disney version, but, she said, "I don't honestly see how I could have done it very differently from what I did, within his framework."

Despite the covert objections of Pamela Travers and the overt objections of some parents and educators to the movie *Mary Poppins,* this fairy tale, like most, had a happy ending. During the making of the movie Julie had been "surprised by the amount of interest in me from the other studios" as a result of Disney's showing the rough cuts and rushes around. She had been signed for *The Americanization of Emily* and *The Sound of Music* as a result of these most unusual previews. When the movie was out, followed closely by *Emily* and the reaction to both was ecstatic, Julie knew she was in movies to stay if she wanted to be. But she was not prepared for what happened next.

A good movie, *My Fair Lady* opened in mid-October, 1964, just a month after *Poppins* and to even more lavish praise. Audrey Hepburn's acting and Marni Nixon's singing got solid notices for their Eliza Doolittle (perhaps not because it was so great but because it wasn't as bad as the critics had feared).

All observers agreed that Julie's debut as Mary and Emily was more auspicious than if she had simply repeated her stage triumph from *My Fair Lady.* But some, particularly the European press, smelling the potential for an old-style Hollywood feud, tried their best to create friction between Julie and Audrey. It turned out to be impossible for two reasons: Both were indeed fair ladies, and that sort of thing was beneath their dignity, and at that point, they had not ever met (they did once, briefly, a year later at a party but one which gave them no chance to discuss their mutual role) . The negotiations for the Eliza movie role had, of course, taken place through agents, with Arthur Park the unsuccessful one and Kurt Frings, who handled Elizabeth Taylor, as well as Audrey Hepburn, and was considered for obvious reasons the most knowing woman's agent in Hollywood, the winner.

But the press and the rest of Hollywood and the moviegoing public were to have their revenge. When the Academy Award nominations were announced during the third week in February, 1965, *My Fair Lady* was nominated in every major category *except* best actress, and Julie Andrews was given a best actress nomination for Mary Poppins that Audrey Hepburn had been denied for Eliza. While Ava Gardner, for *The Night of the Iguana,* was a sentimental selection among a large segment of the more serious and less influential press, with Audrey not in the running, Julie was considered the heavy favorite from the moment she was named. Another, almost unnoticed Oscar nominee that year was an unknown London stage designer, Tony Walton, for best costume designer for his first picture, *Mary Poppins.* The picture was also named for best of the year along with *Dr. Strangelove, Becket, Zorba the Greek,* and *My Fair Lady.*

There was a sort of tacky dress rehearsal for the Academy Awards in those years of the mid-1960's, the annual Golden Globe Awards of the Hollywood Foreign Press Association, a frighteningly large collection of encyclopedia salesmen and seamstresses who managed to free-load meals to add to their meager existences in America by sometimes writing, or claiming to write, for everything from the most obscure trade journal to a real newspaper in their home or anybody else's home country. The Golden Globe nominations and awards, like everything else about the HFPA, could be bought by studios and press agents and cheerfully were. Usually the one stipulation was that the awardee had to promise to show up at the ceremony in February. The proceedings—that is, the presentation of the globes, not the shameless chicanery behind the scenes—were televised each year by a major airline on a major network (both of which had the sense to drop it when the scandal became public). Julie, quite innocent of the awards procedures, was pleased to have been named best actress in a musical for *Mary Poppins* (for the next two years she would be named the group's World Film Favorite, the one more or less honest award that was voted on by a worldwide press corps and announced in advance). At the ceremonies in 1965 she thanked among others, "Jack Warner, for making it all possible." Warner, as a recipient for *My Fair Lady,* "was sitting right there in front of me—it was grand fun." Her press agents swore the whole idea had been hers, and she never denied it. It quite likely had been.

At the start of the Academy Award ceremonies on April 5, in the Santa Monica Civic Auditorium, the high preponderance of foreign, most particularly British nominees, prompted master of ceremonies Bob Hope to quip: "This will be an unusual night—tonight Hollywood is handing out foreign aid." And it did. The Russian-born actress then living in France, Lila Kedrova, was named best supporting actress for her work as the dying vaudevillian in *Zorba the Greek.* Tony Walton lost to a fellow Briton, Cecil Beaton, who had designed the costumes for both the stage and screen versions of *My Fair Lady.*

"Oh, no, Tony," Julie said softly to her husband when Beaton's name was announced. Tony applauded dutifully.

"Chim Chim Cher-ee," from *Mary Poppins,* did win the Oscar as best song, but otherwise it was mostly a *My Fair Lady* night—except that Alan Lerner lost the best screenplay based on material from another medium award to Edward Anhalt, who had adapted *Becket* from Jean Anouilh's play George Cukor, who since 1930 had directed *Camille, The*

*Philadelphia Story, Gaslight, Born Yesterday, A Double Life,
A Star Is Born, David Copperfield, Little Women,* and
Adam's Rib and had won Oscars for many of his stars but
never for himself, finally won as best director for *My Fair
Lady,* surprising no one.

Audrey Hepburn as a previous best actress Oscar winner
(for *Roman Holiday* in 1953) had been picked to present
the Oscar for best actor, perhaps deliberately, certainly ironically. "Rex Harrison!!!" exulted Audrey as she tore open the
secret envelope, and a beaming Harrison bounded onto the
stage to be hugged and kissed by his unnominated co-star,
whom he in turn comforted gently. The ABC-TV cameras
then caught a quick close-up of Julie licking a very dry, very
stiff lip. Harrison said simply, "I have to thank two fair
ladies, I think." "Oh, yes," said Audrey, with that special gra-
ciousness that had kept her the superest of superstars for
fifteen years, until that moment—or the next, when her successor sped to the stage to claim her prize (and the industry's
revenge against Jack Warner) the best actress Oscar for
Mary Poppins. Julie was bathed in smiles, the earlier up-
tightness gone. She too was gracious: "You Americans are famous for your hospitality, but this is ridiculous." Indeed it
was, but a new queen had been crowned that night, in front
of everybody. In post-Oscar publicity pictures Julie and Harrison posed together with their gold-plated statuettes, as
surely as they would have had she played Eliza again. Jack
Warner's acceptance of a best picture award for *My Fair
Lady*—without, of course, any reference to his casting decisions—was an anticlimax, delivered in the self-confident
tones of a successful businessman being congratulated on a
worthwhile $17,000,000 investment. He paid tribute to "the
many people who contributed to *My Fair Lady,*" definitely including George Bernard Shaw, whose *Pygmalion* was the
basis of the musical, and presumably including Julie.

The *Mary Poppins* purists had their final small triumph,
however, when the New York City Parks Departments de-

cided, in 1966, that it wanted to erect a statue of the magical governess in Central Park, in the Conservatory Lake area near Seventy-Second Street. The model for the proposed statue, by an anonymous sculptor, was not Julie Andrews, but none other than P. L. Travers herself, then a sixty-two-year-old writer-in-residence at Smith College, who had posed for a working sketch, she said, "on tiptoe, holding up an umbrella to get the balance right."

Julie stashed her Oscar, once it was engraved, "in a box in the attic at home with some other memorabilia, waiting until I find a suitable place to put it." It stayed there for some years, Julie being the rare kind of movie star who didn't even want pictures of herself around unless they were good art as well.

VI

STRAIGHT FROM *Mary Poppins* and while most of the animation work on the Travers piece was still to be done at Disney, Julie went right into *The Americanization of Emily,* the story of a young English war widow during World War II who works as a motor-pool driver for American Navy officers in England during the day and who sometimes out of kindness plays in bed with them at night, especially if she thinks they're doomed to be killed in battle. Paddy Chayefsky had taken a novel by William Bradford Huie and embellished it with an antiwar message of his own in the final screenplay. Julie, who had never had an acting lesson in her life (she was then twenty-eight) or a part that didn't have a song or a dance to hide behind, scored heavily as a dramatic actress.

She admitted she was "scared to death" at the prospect. "I was at a loss without songs at first—at least in *Mary Poppins* I would always take comfort in the knowledge that I would be doing a song and would feel secure eventually," she said. "But in *Emily* there were no songs to hang on to."

Marty Ransohoff, the rotund, baldish chairman of the board of Filmways, the company that produced *The Americanization of Emily* (but only after making his and its bundle with *The Beverly Hillbillies, Petticoat Junction,* and *Green Acres,* the hit television series), was an incongruous friend for Julie—except that he, along with Walt Disney and Robert Wise, had believed in her as a movie actress when no one

89

else did and that he, along with her and most of the people around her, had uncanny show-biz instincts.

Ransohoff had been a small-time businessman in Connecticut, nobody and nobody's son. He had come to Hollywood and built his production company in five years, making no major mistakes (even his three less successful TV series, *The Addams Family, Henry Phyfe,* and *The Trials of O'Brien* —this last highly acclaimed by critics, but ranking one hundred and sixth of 106 evening shows in popularity at the end of its one truncated season—made money as segments strung together and released as feature films in Europe). By the summer of 1966, as *Emily* was about to be rereleased under the shorter title, Ransohoff, then a chubby whirlwind of thirty-nine, had made six films—all of which made money (he was soon to release two that did not) —and was grossing $30,000,000 a year.

And he was still small, carrying most of the business around in the baggy khaki army pants and shirt he always wore—or in his head. He had two associates in Hollywood, one essentially for movies and one for TV, and there were five executives in New York. Most corporate secrets were his alone, and that summer, when a proposed merger of Marty's Filmways and Seven Arts (which later merged with Warner Brothers) that would have created a new major Hollywood studio, with Marty as head, fell through just as it was about to be consummated, there was hardly a shred of industry gossip about it. No one had any information about which to gossip, for Marty had kept it in his head, and he wasn't talking. "It just isn't gonna be," is all he would say at the time, and he has said nothing more since.

John Calley, later executive vice-president for production at Warner Brothers (when it merged into Kinney National Services in mid-1969 and dropped the "Seven Arts"), was then Ransohoff's chief deputy, executive vice-president of Filmways, the associate producer of *Emily,* and a man who helped encourage Julie toward analysis. (There was a time when it was impossible for anyone to make a lunch date with John Calley because he spent each lunch hour with his psychiatrist.) Calley was part of Julie's small social set and had even been linked with her romantically. He called Ransohoff "an L. B. Mayer without overhead."

Ransohoff even had the advantage of Mayer's original overhead, without any of the headaches of keeping it up: Most of his films, including *Emily,* were released through Metro-Goldwyn-Mayer, and Marty kept his Filmways Hollywood offices on Metro's Culver City lot, where some of the films (and *The Trials of O'Brien*) were shot and where they were often the only studio activity in those lean and runaway production years of the mid-1960's.

He was the most independent of the independent producers, a highly selective man (though many quarreled with his standards), who estimated he had bought only two film scripts out of every hundred he had read. He was willing to meet any terms to get the stars and directors he wanted; he was the first to pay the Burtons $1,000,000 each for a movie, *The Sandpiper* (it was to become their standard asking price). Ransohoff's deal with Miss Taylor in the fall of 1964 was actually for $1,000,000 against 10 percent of the gross receipts, then a record, which Julie herself would break with *Darling Lili* four years later. The contract with Burton called for only $800,000 against 10 percent, then also a record for a male star. Since the picture *The Sandpiper,* even before the sale to CBS television, had grossed more than $10,000,000, Richard caught up to Elizabeth, and they stood to split at least $2,500,000 for three and a half months' work. Ransohoff had given total creative control of *The Loved One* to Tony Richardson (something he and Calley later regretted) because he was so anxious to have the young English director of *Tom Jones* working for him on the Evelyn Waugh story. (Another producer described the undisciplined, self-indulgent, but often savagely funny and surprisingly successful end result as "thirty-two faggots doing their bits.")

"We had many differences with Richardson during the editing period on *The Loved One*," Marty recalled, "but he had the controls. It was the only way we could get him, and John Calley and I had decided he was the only one we wanted for the film. He seemed ideal."

Richardson turned out to be somewhat less than ideal, at least as far as Calley was concerned. "*The Loved One* is a reflection of the director's taste, not mine," said the then-thirty-five-year-old Filmways executive and the producer of record on *The Loved One*. "We shot four hours and forty minutes of movie, and the movie I wanted to make we shot. We thought we could do no wrong with Richardson, that we were safe when it came to taste, that we had a good shot at commercial success, as well as quality. It was in the final cuts that we disagreed. All it proves is that emphasis in selection controls the overall look of a comedy film. In comedy you shoot as many choices as you can. In that film you had a lot of weird actors doing elongated entrances and funny asides [among them John Gielgud, Margaret Leighton, Jonathan Winters, Robert Morse, Anjanette Comer— and Ruth Gordon and the late Jayne Mansfield, who didn't survive the cutting room and were never seen in the final version]. We shot fifty of those secenes to get five that would add to the film. I'd say forty-five are in the final version. Richardson thinks it's just great; I don't."

Although Ransohoff said he would give that kind of total creative control to a director again "only if I really have to," when it came time to sign Mike Nichols to direct *Catch-22*, Marty was willing to do it again. ("Nichols is a unique talent; you do what you have to do to get him," Calley said. Besides, by then, after an Oscar as best director for only his second film, *The Graduate*, and a near-miss for his first, *Who's Afraid of Virginia Woolf?*, on which, to his great chagrin, he had not had the final say, Nichols was used to it.) Still, Marty's flexibility, which was only one of the eccentricities the Hollywood Establishment, the "Bel-Air Circuit," resented him for, was one of the very qualities that Julie liked so much in him.

"He speaks for himself; he stands or falls by himself," was the star's way of putting it. "He didn't depend on anybody to achieve his success, and so if he stands or falls, it's on his own. And if you don't like it, he couldn't care less."

Julie of course had reason to be grateful for that quality in Ransohoff. Not only did he take a long chance on an antiwar story way before being antiwar in America was the least bit fashionable—just as he took on *The Loved One* before being anti the American way of death was trendy—but "he certainly took a chance on me. He also chooses very interesting properties, and I think he's very courageous in that respect," she said.

Even Marty dismissed his first two features, *Boys' Night Out,* with Kim Novak, and *Wheeler Dealers,* with Lee Remick and James Garner, as strictly formula comedies he had to make to get a sound economic foothold in films, although he contended they were better than average, and they were. But then he got artistic aspirations, or at the least artistic pretensions, just as the first two appeared on television. "I hated to sit there and see them jumping out of the set at me," he said, shuddering. And while *The Cincinnati Kid* (Norman Jewison's first big break) , *The Loved One,* and even *The Sandpiper* could only be put in the "good-try" category, *Emily*—at least until *Catch-22*—was Filmways' masterpiece.

It did take several kinds of courage to do it. Apart from the antiwar script (which did cop out at the end) , Ransohoff took a noted nonactor, James Garner, who subsequently turned in the performance of a lifetime, and two unknowns, Julie and James Coburn, as the leads, although he did have Joyce Grenfell, as Emily's mother, and Melvyn Douglas, as a mad American admiral, in strong support. And in an era when Metro, like all the other major studios, had an eye on the lucrative television sales and was beginning to make every kind of movie, even the cheapest B cops-and-robbers story, in color, Marty was determined that a serious film of this kind should be made in black and white.

Marty, like Robert Wise and others, had seen some rough-cut footage of *Mary Poppins,* just forty minutes' worth, six months before the musical opened. Walt Disney had taken this unusual step of setting up screenings for other producers simply because he was so excited about Julie's work in it. And the other producers and directors who saw it were excited, too. Yet so many girls in Hollywood have had sensational screen tests and washed out on the screen in a real movie, and still so many others have had a part—usually the first one, thanks to typecasting departments—that was perfect for them and then gone on to do nothing. But when Marty first saw the *Mary Poppins* footage of Julie he knew he had found at least his English ambulance driver, Emily, if not a star. "After three minutes of the stuff I knew Julie was our girl."

He immediately signed the then movie unknown to play the title role in *The Americanization of Emily.* "I took just that one look and knew she was right for *Emily,*" Ransohoff said. "She did not generate obvious, overt sexuality. She is not a sex symbol, but she has a classic sensuousness. She also had a certain refinement—another classic quality—rather than an overabundance of physical equipment, which gave her a great deal of sex appeal, slightly more refined and highbred than most."

Garner, as the nominal star of the film, by virtue of prior film success at the box office, if not at the hands of critics, had co-star control written into his contract with Filmways. He could have vetoed the Hollywood unknown but didn't since he had starred in *The Caine Mutiny Court-Martial* on Broadway at the same time as, and just up the street from,

Julie in *My Fair Lady.* "I didn't know her, but I had seen her in it," he recalled, "and that was enough for me."

And when Marty saw the first footage of Julie in his own film, he was positively ecstatic. "She was a revelation," he said.

Julie read the script of *Emily* and agreed enthusiastically. "I had heard about the film but didn't think I had much chance to get it," she recalled. "When my agent suggested I read the script, I got very excited." And enormously grateful to Marty Ransohoff. "A lot of people told Marty that he was out of his mind to pick me."

At the time of shooting she said, "I am worried about the absence of an audience, but I suppose if I get enough movie work, I'll get used to it. But the audience gives you a push. It makes you realize you've got to do it right. There will be no second time. Still, I love the feeling in movies of doing something fresh every day instead of the same thing. I find movie work much more exhausting than I had expected. I suppose my own nervous tension has a good deal to do with it. And the only way I can ease the tension is to sing, hum or whistle. I wonder, sometimes, what will happen when I do something in the theater again. Will I feel nervous in front of an audience?

"I chose *The Americanization of Emily* for my next film after *Mary Poppins* because it proposed another challenge. It was a straight dramatic role with no singing or dancing to fall back on. I'd have to act. It would also give me the chance to prove to myself and the public that I could do something besides musical comedy," she said. And afterward she allowed: "I absolutely adored playing Emily. I had never done a straight part before—no singing—and it was a huge challenge."

Ransohoff had almost equal praise for other members of his company. "Arthur Hiller, who had replaced William Wyler after a dispute over the concept of the film, was a fabulous director. Garner was never better. The decision to go black and white was the right one, and the invasion scene worked. Joyce Grenfell and the other supporting characters were great. The chemistry between all the people on the picture was right; we were loaded with the right dynamics, and you didn't have anyone mad at anyone. To produce a film, there are at least eleven or twelve key elements that represent a marrying together of highly specialized, creative, and sometimes temperamental people. It's not a question of adding two and two together and getting four; its more a question of adding one hundred and eleven and getting two hundred and twenty-two. It is a constantly frustrating thing, and it doesn't always come out right. Most times it doesn't, but this time it did."

So far as the final result was concerned, *Emily* was Julie's own personal favorite, too. *The Sound of Music* had been even more fun to make, *Mary Poppins* was the most exciting in some ways because it was the first, *Star!* had been the most stimulating, and *Darling Lili* the easiest—and the hardest—because she was with "Blackie." But *Emily* proved to her, and then to the world, that she could act without singing, dancing, a stage, or living color and stereophonic sound.

Emily cost only $2,700,000 to make, and it grossed more than $4,000,000 in the first release in 1964-65, another million in the second go-round in 1966-67, and was sold to television for the 1968 and 1970 seasons for another $1,000,000—an incredible total take for a black-and-white antiwar film devoid of marquee names.

Marty, who had done it both ways, from Liz Taylor to Anjanette Comer, did believe somewhat in a star system, and he kept using proven names even as he created new ones—the late Sharon Tate was a Ransohoff discovery. "The day of any star's guaranteeing a successful picture is gone, it's a joke, and that goes even for Taylor," he said. "It's great to have a star if the picture's good. On the other hand, anyone who says you can make a picture without some stars is nuts. Most of the top male stars are also good actors, so that's no problem. But when it comes to choosing between a great actress and a star who's a good actress, I'll take the star every time. Distribution costs are so high that you have to have a cushion against the bombs. The stars provide that cushion. Stars can also boost the gross of any given picture. If I had had Doris Day in the two comedies, I would have doubled the gross."

Bored easily by details ("I'm not an on-the-set guy"), Ransohoff relinquished more and more of the traditional producer's functions to Calley, who said, "He has a low boredom threshold. He just won't do that picky shit that producers do." Ransohoff and Calley, who collected a low $150,000 to 175,000 production fee for each movie, made maximum use of $500-a-week production managers, who kept the costs down (only *The Sandpiper,* which cost $5,500,000, and *The Loved One,* which cost close to $3,000,000, went over the budget) and things running smoothly. Still, while he never bought a property by the cover or unless both he and Calley had read it and agreed it was good, and while he was often content to leave the making of the film in other hands, he was often obsessed by the most minor of details.

"I had just one sexy gown to wear in *Emily* [when she goes to the admiral's ball on her first date with Garner]," Julie recalled. "And he spent a lot of time just worrying about a pair of shoes to go with it."

Julie also remembered being unhappy about one scene in the film that was already in the can. "We were watching the rushes together, and I was not happy about it at all. He had them set it up again the next day and let me do it all over again. I'm not at all sure that it was any better the second time, but it was completely my whim, and he indulged it."

Marty recounted the incident a little differently, but after it and because of it, his admiration for her was as great as hers for him:

"Arthur Hiller and I thought it worked well, but Julie thought it could be done another way. So I gave her and the crew a day to restage and reshoot the scene her way. When we saw a rough cut of the whole movie a few weeks later, her scene wasn't in it. I had used the original scene. She burst out laughing. She just couldn't understand why I would redo the scene and spend all that money if I was so sure I was right. I told her that it was just that the values in the original were the ones we wanted. Instead of having a big ego attitude, she just laughed. It's never a question of ego with her. She completely respected my position, but the shock of realizing 'Oh, my God, we've thrown a day away' sent her into hysterics."

Marty and Julie stayed friends, but it was more "a business friendship and not so much a social one," she said, which is not so surprising since they both hated large parties and he hated even small ones. "I called him for advice on various projects, and I must say I found him always to be fair and to give very good advice indeed. I suppose if you looked at it head on, we would have been the unlikeliest of friends. We are quite unalike. But at the very beginning we cut through all the preliminaries, and we seemed to be honest and frank with one another from the very beginning."

As a result of the reshooting experience and others like it, Marty allowed that "Julie is always cooperative and anxious to help. She seems to care more about the effect and outcome of a scene than about money or her own part. She has an infectious humor that has a great effect on other performers and a great positiveness both behind the scenes and in front of a camera. A film can be damaged by a growler, but Julie, by her cooperative and uncomplicated nature, her dignity and class, lifts up a production. She's a clown, but her humor is always in good taste and fun, and her effervescence is contagious. She is a big star because she is big—in every sense of the word, in personality and in makeup. She is totally lacking in the kind of ego that says she knows it all and is always right."

Another firm fan, as a result of working with her in *Emily*, was James Garner, who had been somewhat upstaged and who had reason to resent her. He didn't. "We did the first love scene she'd ever done in a movie and the first real love scene she'd done anywhere," he recalled, "and she knows only one way to do something, and that's right. She's marvelous. In reality she's not like what she's like on screen—certainly not in *Mary Poppins*—but nobody does it better than Julie can. Julie's a little bit more natural at anything than anybody else.

"Nobody knows the depths of her talent or personality. She's so fresh she opens her mouth and the whole world blooms. The things about Julie on screen and off camera that make people like her are her warmth, levity, and sincerity. That's what makes her the star she is. Throughout the history of films, people have succeeded because of their marvelous human qualities. These people had something on the screen that make people want to see them and come to them. She has that. Yet you can't be much of a screen personality without being a pretty damn good actor. Julie is a person that the camera does not affect. She does what she does without being affected by all those lights and forty people around her. Some stars can only do it with all that; some can't do it with any of that. She is a personality who became a superstar. An actor working with a young superstar like Julie opposite him might worry about being acted into the draperies. I wouldn't and didn't compete with Julie on those terms for two reasons: I might lose, and I wouldn't care.

"I admire Julie in the way I admire Audrey Hepburn. It would be unthinkable, people would hate themselves for being jealous of, or mean to, either Julie or Audrey. They give you no reason to. And yet Julie is a very strong-willed girl. But she manages her life so you are never offended by her strong will." Garner found Julie and Miss Hepburn (with whom he starred in *The Children's Hour*) "similar in their attraction. They are both professional, warm and friendly, hard-to-know, and complex. It is not a façade. They don't give to anybody past a certain line, but they give to everybody up to that line. They don't give people their problems and make them feel bad. If something is bothering them, they don't show it to everybody else."

Arthur Hiller, *Emily*'s director, was not to be left out of the encomiums: "She's utter perfection," he said. "She's got great compassion—on the screen and off."

Marty Ransohoff summed it up this way: "She's the most exciting thing I've seen in ten years. There's an open honesty in her face that's like magic. It lights up the screen. She is a dream to work with. She is cooperative and has ideas. All conversations with her are on an intellectual level. She brings quality to a project. She's infectious around the set." And when *Emily* was over, he said, "I'd like to do another picture with her next year. I shudder to think of the price."

Julie didn't stop singing when she made *Emily;* it was just that when she sang, the cameras and recording equipment were not on. The singing (and sometimes it was whistling or just a high note held as long as possible) was a tranquilizer for her taut nerves, brought on by *not* singing in the film.

One day during shooting, as a camera was being reloaded, Julie apparently decided to use her most common method of calming herself, and she broke into a chorus—her notes and enunciation faultless as usual—of "Melancholy Baby." Garner and Hiller were delighted to suspend the work on the set in favor of a free Julie Andrews concert. But she was totally oblivious to their watching her, and even to her own singing, because she was so internally preoccupied with the role of Emily.

Garner played Lieutenant Commander Charlie Madison, nominally an aide to a rear admiral in the American Navy, played by Melvyn Douglas, but actually a "dog robber," a procurer of everything from perfume to the people who wear it, for Douglas and the rest of the American Navy brass in wartime London. Madison is also an admitted advocate of open cowardice, a doctrine of self-preservation that he says is opposite to the prevailing one, especially in England: "As long as valor remains a virtue, we shall always have soldiers." He is a most difficult and untypical suitor for Emily, but they are equally nervous about his ending up in the first wave on the beach at Normandy on D Day, as he does.

The film contains romance, high humor, cool sarcasm, and biting satire that did not let either the Americans or the British down gently, in a rare combination. They all come together in scenes like the one between Emily and Madison in his bedroom of the admiral's hotel suite in London, which looked more like the central clearing house for a Continental black market, with nylon stockings, silk scarves, cigarettes and every kind of liquor known to man. Emily makes caustic comments about the avariciousness and rule bending of Americans, and he takes down the English for their anti-American ingratitude, their self-imposed stiff-upper-lip martyrdom, and their unconcealed jealousy. This is the beginning of their romance.

When *Emily* opened, unfortunately and accidentally, or at any rate coincidentally, in the winter of 1964-65, smack in between *Mary Poppins* and *The Sound of Music* and overshadowed by both, the reviews were mixed. Many critics were confused by the intent of the screen play, the apparent seriousness of the antiwar theme, and others, who liked the film intensely, were annoyed by what they considered a sellout ending. (Charles as an unarmed photographer doesn't die in the Normandy invasion but returns to England and Emily.) A few critics found Julie's performance bland and stereotyped, but most agreed with one New York magazine critic who said: "Her mastery of drama and comedy . . . promptly indicated that if she chose never to sing again, she'd still have a solid career ahead."

But of the favorable reaction to her in the sophisticated and caustic *Emily* Julie merely said: "It wasn't that I was so good; it's just that it was such a surprise to see me in it.

"I don't think of myself as any great shakes as an actress.

That's why I consider myself lucky when an *Emily* comes
along," she said several years later. "I'd love to do more serious roles like that. But films like *Emily* aren't available too
readily. The script was so good. It had something to say. But
today, with road shows and films costing so much, one must
commit oneself years in advance to guarantee to the studio
the film will start on time."

Blake Edwards, ironically, once thought she was wrong for
Emily. He had only met her once, casually, at that point.
William Wyler had walked out as the director, something he
also did with *The Sound of Music* and *The Sandpiper* that
year, only to end up doing *The Collector* and opposite Robert Wise and *The Sound of Music* at Academy Award time.
Arthur Hiller had not yet signed to take Wyler's place, and
Edwards was in on some casting discussions; asked about
Julie for the lead, he said, "No, I don't think she's right."
Several years later he said, "And she wasn't right, in terms of
the screenplay. I would have bet you against her doing it
well, which is interesting now [like most of her friends and
responsible critics, Edwards considered it her finest movie
acting]. But she brought something to it that changed Emily
without changing the screenplay, and it worked."

VII

IN 1963 JULIE did not greet the prospect of making *The Sound of Music* with the kind of unalloyed joy that audiences would receive it with two years hence. "After all," she reasoned, "what can you do with nuns, seven children, and Austria?" And then there had been that mean swipe in the TV special the year before: "We were always putting *Sound of Music* down," Carol Burnett recalled. "And she always made fun of that happy nun. I'm not sure Richard Rodgers was awfully pleased when she was offered the movie. And I think she was concerned about being Gwendolyn Goodie Two-Shoes. Later when she did make the movie, from Austria she sent me pictures of her in her nun's habit, which was a big laugh. But she made her real; the way she played Maria she had guts."

"I thought it might be awfully saccharine," Julie said, "but Bob Wise and Saul Chaplin decided to get rid of the sugar—no filigree, no carved wood, no Swiss chalets—and they stuck to their guns. We all felt the same way. It helped that it was a motion picture because they could do such sweeping things visually."

Robert Wise, the short, sixtyish, gray-haired Academy-Award-winning director (*West Side Story*), accepted the directing assignment only reluctantly—after William Wyler walked away in a cloud of indifference. "I had great reservations," Wise said. "I didn't jump at it at all. The play was very, very saccharine, and obviously we haven't eliminated that for all people. But we tried to tone it down. We didn't go in for too-cute costumes or turreted castles, and we were careful not to overdo colors." Wise finally agreed only when Fox let him bring Saul Chaplin in as associate producer.

Screenwriter Ernest Lehman, who also had written Wise's *Executive Suite* and *West Side Story* and Twentieth's *The King and I* and who would go on to *Who's Afraid of Virginia Woolf?* and *Hello, Dolly!* as a producer, as well as writer, recalled "a sugary curse" on *The Sound of Music*, which nonetheless did not dim his enthusiasm for the writing job, since he knew the director and the studio.

In the movie industry the Rodgers and Hammerstein piece—still enjoying a healthy run on Broadway—had "a certain—well, stink is not quite the right word—about it," Lehman said. "I saw Burt Lancaster, who was doing *The Leopard,* in the cafeteria one day, and he just looked at me and said, 'Jesus, you must need the money.' " Need it or not, Lehman got it, 2 percent of the profits, which came to $1,000 a day for the first three years of the picture's run and could reach $2,000,000.

Even the studio was hesitant. "It was a gamble for us," recalled Richard D. (for Darryl) Zanuck, Darryl's son and vice-president in charge of production at Twentieth Century-Fox, "because eight million two hundred thousand dollars, which is what it cost to make, was a lot of money; it was not the most distinguished show Rodgers and Hammerstein had ever done, and our cast was relatively unknown."

Once the production package was assembled, it was up to Wise to cast the principals, although in retrospect Zanuck and Lehman both took credit for Julie Andrews and for having the good sense not to cast Doris Day or Debbie Reynolds (there was never the slightest thought of asking Mary Martin, who was then fifty years old, to re-create her stage triumph) . Wise saw the Disney rushes from *Mary Poppins,* and that decided him. Wise also insisted on casting Christopher Plummer, a distinguished Canadian actor but not known for musicals and not a major movie marquee name, as Captain Georg Von Trapp. "I wanted the character to have bite, incisiveness, and real dimension. I felt we must go on the basis of the story, and not bastardize it with just big names." And so Peggy Wood was picked as the mother abbess; Richard Haydn as the supposedly roguishly unscrupulous impresario who ends up planning the Von Trapp family's exit from Austria and thus saving their lives (even the villains were good villains in this one) ; Eleanor Parker, a still-lovely screen star from the 1940's and 1950's, as the baroness that Von Trapp doesn't marry; and Charmian Carr, a part-time fashion model whose only previous acting was a bit in a high school play, as the chief juvenile and eldest Trapp child. All the actors were on modest salaries (even Julie got only $225,000), while Wise (and his Argyle Enterprises, Inc., in which Chaplin participated) was working toward 10 percent of the profits—which as it turned out would eventually be something like $10,000,000, more than enough to allow Wise an early retirement.

Fox had bought *The Sound of Music* for $1,250,000 against 10 percent of the gross in January, 1962, the year *Cleopatra* had cost the studio $31,000,000. Spyros Skouras had been deposed as president of Twentieth, to be replaced by the Zanucks, who took over an empty studio, with a closed-down commissary and a minimal maintenance crew. When Lehman checked in to write the screenplay and asked where his office would be, Dick Zanuck said, "Where would you like it to be?" "It was like calling a theater and asking, 'What time does the movie go on?' and they say 'What time would you like it to go on?' " Lehman recalled. Forging ahead with *The Sound of Music* just when things seemed most hopeless saved Twentieth at least temporarily. The studio made money for three years running—1965, 1966, 1967 —mostly from the one film and again became a major force in American TV production for a while, before it declined again.

The four producers of the Broadway version, including Rodgers (who was among those who assumed Doris Day would be cast in the lead), the estate of Hammerstein, and Richard Halliday, Mary Martin's husband, collected 10 percent of the gross instead of a mere $1,250,000, netting each of the four 10 times what Julie got.

The real Baroness Maria Von Trapp, who then operated an Alpine ski lodge in Stowe, Vermont, and the members of her family, whose life story *The Sound of Music* was, received a comparative pittance: three-eighths of 1 percent of the profit to be split among them, about $375,000, based on the first five years of worldwide release. She wisely retained a lawyer in Cleveland to try to help increase the percentage. The baroness, who happened to be in Salzburg during the filming, was used in one scene as an extra, for which she got the standard wage for an extra on a foreign location, about $20 a day. "We certainly aren't rolling in millions," she said, "either as a result of the play or the movie," both of which she liked (she liked the movie more but emphasized that "one can't expect accuracy from Hollywood").

"It was never planned as a documentary of the Trapp family," said Robert Wise. "The large bones of it are true, but the way it was put on are renditions of the truth." By the time filming started in the spring of 1964, nobody else was worrying about historical accuracy either, except that there did seem to be a general determination to do at least some of the work on location in Austria, and Lehman had spent several weeks there, "just soaking up atmosphere, looking for locations, and becoming thoroughly familiar with the locale of the Trapp family story."

"A crucial decision for us was taking it on location in Salzburg," said Richard Zanuck. "We could have approached it à la *My Fair Lady*, where it was all done in the studio [those were the days when everyone was knocking the still-unfinished *My Fair Lady* and by implication supporting

Julie's prior claim], but I think a lot of the value would have gone down the drain."

They ended up splitting the difference, which bothered many critics, but the audience either didn't notice or pretended not to: Of a twenty-two-week shooting schedule (short for a major musical), eleven weeks of *The Sound of Music* were spent in the Alps. It was supposed to have been nine, but Alpine rains caused a fortnight's delay in filming (and the picture to go $1,000,000 over budget, according to Zanuck). And lost baby teeth on the part of the younger children caused slight delays; in one case a local dentist stayed up all night making a false set of children's teeth so the shooting could continue without great big gaps in the wrong places on the wide screen. "It wasn't nearly as much of a challenge as *West Side Story*," said Wise.

Julie, as might have been expected, in spite of her earlier reservations about *The Sound of Music*, had "a larky time." Wise recalled that she "always enjoyed a good laugh with the kids. She had humor, marvelous fun in her, and in addition to humor she had warmth and understanding." The first sequence shot was of Julie and the children bundled up in Maria's bed during a bad thunderstorm, with her singing "My Favorite Things." "I was having trouble getting the proper reactions from two of the kids during this sequence," Wise said. "All of a sudden I heard this shrill laugh in back of me. I turned, and it was Julie putting on an act to make the kids laugh. She did it without announcing it to me or anyone else, but she put the kids at ease and made them easier to work with."

In her own attempt to desweeten *The Sound of Music* Julie focused on the "My Favorite Things" sequence. "It occurred to me that Maria *couldn't* be sweetness and light with seven kids on her hands all the time. Seven kids would have to get on one's nerves, at some point or other, so I tried once in a while to show that I might be slightly exhausted by them. For instance, on the bed when they ask me to do this or that and say, 'What kind of things do you mean?' just before I go into 'My Favorite Things,' I thought, 'Oh, my God! Children always *do* ask questions like that.' Maria must have had moments when she bordered on being tired and cross."

The film gave her a chance to cut her hair very short, "something I'd always wanted to do, though having to bleach it blond was a bit of a shocker, especially my first sight of it." And in it she could experiment with variations on resurrected vaudeville bits she hadn't tried in fifteen years, like catching her guitar case crosswise in the door of the bus Maria took from the convent after being told by the mother abbess that she must become at least a temporary governess for seven children, in what was supposed to be a solemn moment. At another solemn point Julie deliberately walked into a post. Wise rejected that Buster Keatonism but allowed a variation of it in the final version: when she turns away from the mother superior, dejected but determined to make a go of it, the gangly novitiate sees the post in time and sidesteps it—thereby giving the character a tiny added sympathetic dimension of confusion and tugging at the audience's heartstrings early on in the action. Little scenes like that prompted at least one admiring member of the crew to remark: "She must have eight thousand bits."

Off-camera she was even wilder. One day to clear tension before a complicated camera move, she did a deliberate trip and fell flat on her face, and she was versatile enough on another tense occasion to pratfall on the other side. For the part of Maria she had learned to play the guitar, and one day she flung it aside to fly into an impromptu flamenco dance— still wearing her postulant's habit and high-button shoes. Scheduled to drive to Munich one weekend to see her friend Svetlana Beriosova dance with the Royal Ballet on tour, Julie instead chartered a bus, took thirty chums from the cast and crew, and throughout the entire sixty-mile bus trip from Salzburg to Munich did an imitation of an English sight-seeing bus conductor, sometimes lapsing into bits of Cockney left over from *My Fair Lady*. (Berioslova, as it happened, was not performing the night they went but met their group for dinner.) On the return trip to Salzburg Julie led group singing and soloed on some Cockney songs.

During the shooting of the opening sequence of *The Sound of Music,* where the helicopter-bound camera swoops down over the summertime Alps to catch Julie dancing bareheaded in forbidden fields singing the title song, was when the rain was at its worst, and there were several days when she couldn't go tripping across the mountains. Julie and Saul Chaplin and Marc Breaux, the co-choreographer, would sing songs on the rainy hillside for hours. She thought the trio's harmonies so good, particularly on the "Hawaiian War Chant," she named the group the Vocalzones. She favored the others who had to wait with solos, of "The Bell Song" from *Lakme,* in pure operatic style, exquisitely on every note —but with the mannerisms and facial expressions of a twelve-year-old child surprised at the power of her own voice —or of the "Indian Love Call," slightly off-key at strategic points. "These things," said Julie, "were all spontaneous, and they related to the situation at the moment. If the situation is getting depressing, or people are getting pesky or touchy, a little fun always helps. I'll do anything I can think of to relieve any kind of tension."

The costume designer on the picture, Dorothy Jeakins, summed it up for most of the cast and crew: "She's extremely pure, extremely human. Julie has great zeal and spirit. She's ethereal, yet down-to-earth. Everything she does is fresh and impromptu—and gone—like a whistle or a laugh."

There were quieter generosities, too; when a member of the company was hospitalized, Julie was the first to visit. She stayed an hour and came alone. It was characteristic of Maria and maybe Mary Poppins and definitely of Julie Andrews, but no one but the injured and the nurses was there to notice. Emma's nanny had a birthday during shooting, and

Julie gave a party. The children in the cast got a party, too. And one tough veteran grip, who had been in movies for twenty-five years, allowed: "I never worked with anybody who said 'thank you' so much."

Not all was constantly sunny on the set of *The Sound of Music,* however. Other members of the crew were muttering, "She may be a nun, but she's a nun with a switchblade." And co-star Christopher Plummer called her "terribly nice but terribly nervous" and told his then wife that working with her was "like being hit over the head every day with a Hallmark card."

Plummer was having problems with his part, and not just because he was being overshadowed by his co-star. He had expected to do his own singing, but he was told his numbers, "The Sound of Music" and "Eidelweiss," twice each in the film, would be dubbed, and Lehman recalled that he said he would feel castrated and walked out on the part. Leslie Bricusse, the composer (*Pickwick, Dr. Dolittle*) and a friend of Plummer's, was called from Palm Spring to try to talk him into returning. By that time, said Briscusse, Plummer "was so fed up that he began calling it *The Sound of Mucus.*" Plummer did continue and sang for himself during the filming, but the songs were dubbed in later by Bill Lee, who also did commercials for, among other things, chewing gum.

Marni Nixon, the busiest and best-known ghost singer in movies, was on hand, and on-camera, for once. She played one of the nuns and did her own singing in "How Do You Solve a Problem Like Maria?" and dubbed for some of the other sisters, most importantly Peggy Wood.

Julie and Peggy Wood even caused one minor bit of friction—and Julie fought hard for her point of view in a display of what would later be termed her "temperament" but then was only her tenacity and total professionalism—toward the end of the picture, when the company had returned to Hollywood for its very Hollywood-looking interiors. In the scene between Miss Wood and Miss Andrews in the abbey when Maria confesses that she loves the captain and the mother abbess says that it is all right, that the love of a man can be holy, too, urges her to return to the captain, and then moves her lips while Marni Nixon bursts into "Climb Ev'ry Mountain," both the principals felt uncomfortable. They had strong feelings that the whole scene as written was wrong, that some of the lines, in Julie's words, were "too on-the-nose, too corny." "We took some time, the three of us," Wise recalled, "and thrashed it out. They gave some, and I gave some. But Julie knew how a character should be played, and she would fight to have it played right."

The same sort of competitive spirit showed through the day Wise and Darryl Zanuck and several other Twentieth Century-Fox executives entertained Julie for lunch to discuss the part of Maria. Wise pointedly announced that the film versions of *The Sound of Music* and *My Fair Lady* would be showing in New York at the same time on opposite sides of Broadway—and then sat back and awaited the reaction. "She looked at each of us in turn without speaking," he said. "Then she threw her head back and laughed. 'All right then. Let's show them, eh, fellow?' That was the new Julie Andrews talking."

Wise was most surprised by "the range of her talent, the depth of it, especially in emotional scenes," and most pleased to discover "she was the most unaffected player I'd ever worked with. She was so down-to-earth, pleasant and natural, it was hard to believe she was really Julie Andrews. She had an open, warm response to work, but then she was used to working, to getting on with the job."

The Sound of Music had its first public preview in the winter of 1965, in Minneapolis, of all unlikely places, "because we wanted a totally fresh audience," in Dick Zanuck's words. "The weather was miserable, and we thought nobody would show up." But the Mann Theater in downtown Minneapolis was filled to capacity, and "at intermission the whole audience stood up and applauded for five minutes,"

Zanuck said. "They did it again at the end, and these were people who had paid to see the preview. Bobby Wise and I looked at each other, shell-shocked."

In view of the subsequent success of the film, Fox was so grateful to the discerning preview audience in Minneapolis that they decided to preview all future musical road-show films there, at the Mann Theater. But the Minneapolis audience proved to be so equally discerning about the dreadful *Dr. Dolittle* that after the sneak preview and its lukewarm response (shared by the audience at a second preview in San Francisco) and the subsequent disaster of the $17,000,000 musical, the practice was abandoned. By the time *Star!* was ready the guinea-pig cities were Cleveland and Denver.

The Broadway premiere at the Rivoli Theater on March 2, 1965, was a star-studded klieg-lighted event in the old style. Julie was there with Tony (having flown in from California with Emma and Nanny), and besides Wise and Darryl Zanuck, others attending included Helen Hayes, Beatrice Lillie, Harry Belafonte, Salvador Dali, Samuel Goldwyn, Adlai E. Stevenson, and, of course, Richard Rodgers, the composer (who had written two new songs, "I Have Confidence" and "Something Good," both of which Julie liked, to replace the four that were dropped for the film version) and the widow of lyricist Oscar Hammerstein II, with her stepson, William Hammerstein. The evening was sponsored by the March of Dimes, with proceeds going to the Mary MacArthur Memorial Fund of the March of Dimes (Miss MacArthur, the daughter of Helen Hayes and the late Charles MacArthur, had died of polio). And Mrs. Hammerstein accepted a posthumous Humanitarian Award to her husband at a postpremiere dance at the Americana Hotel.

The premiere and dance, coming as they did within a fortnight of the Oscar nomination for *Mary Poppins* and Audrey Hepburn's nonnomination, were Julie's unofficial coronation as the new Queen of Hollywood. Dali allowed that she might even be as good an actress as he was a painter, and Bette Davis called her "one of the loveliest things I've ever seen." Julie and Harry Belafonte met for the first and only time until they taped their joint special for NBC four and a half years later. Clutching a mink stole uncomfortably, she said the film was "my most difficult yet; the hardest thing was the eleven weeks we spent in Austria—it rained nearly every day and did terrible things to our nerves."

None of it showed, according to Mrs. Hammerstein. "I'll have to drag out all those old superlatives about Hollywood," she said. "It's as close to perfection as any movie musical I've ever seen. The beauty of it is you really see Austria; the streams, valleys and mountains are the real thing. I know Oscar would have loved it."

And so the Zanucks, Julie, Wise, Rodgers, Mrs. Hammerstein, Fox in general, and the manager of the Rivoli Theater went to bed—albeit very late—in triumph. They woke up the next morning to disaster.

In case there is any student of American journalism or the American cinema left who believes that movie critics can, in a moment of pique or indigestion, thwart the will of the American public and destroy a Hollywood work of art, let him consider the case of *The Sound of Music,* which one critic's headline writer called "The Sound of Marshmallows," and too many people since have called "The Sound of Money." All the major American film reviewers found considerable fault with this one; there was not, as in the case of *Cleopatra,* even one or two raves to temper the general lack of critical enthusiasm. But as we, and Twentieth Century-Fox, were to find out years later, they were powerless to stop it.

Judith Crist, writing in the New York *Herald Tribune,* said:

> One star and much scenery do not a two-hour-and-fifty-five-minutes-plus-intermission entertainment make, and the issue must be faced. Squarely. That is the way to face "The Sound of Music." This last, most remunerative and least inspired, let alone sophisticated, of the Rodgers and Hammer-

stein collaborations is square and solid sugar. Calorie-counters, diabetics and grown-ups from eight to eighty had best beware.

The other daily critics that day and magazine movie reviewers in the next few weeks were hardly less livid. *Playboy* said: "Rarely has such a mountain of molasses avalanched over such a wide, wide screen" and called the film "pure Trapp-clap throughout." Pauline Kael, then writing in *McCall's*, the monthly woman's magazine, asked: "Whom could it offend?" And she answered: "Only those of us who, despite the fact that we may respond . . . are aware of how self-indulgent and cheap and ready-made are the responses we are made to feel. The best of all possible worlds, that's what 'The Sound of Music' pretends we live in . . . it's the sugar-coated lie that people seem to want to eat . . . and this is the attitude that makes a critic feel that maybe it's all hopeless. Why not just send the director, Robert Wise, a wire: 'You win, I give up'?"

"How could they do this to us?" was what Wise said when he had read the first reviews. And Zanuck said: "I was very depressed, too. A lot of kind of intellectuals attacked us for being too saccharine. We'd taken a lot of that out of the original show, but it still didn't appeal to some of the reviewers and some of the snobs. The public answered them in a big way, though, around the world."

Indeed it did, for despite the reviews, the advance ticket sales at the Rivoli, already substantial as they would have been for any "Easter attraction" movie musical that was based on a preproven property, instantly began to increase in a geometric proportion even greater than that of the negative notices. And the pattern was repeated in city after city: Within the first week of opening, seats were sold out for the next three months. (In some major and medium-size U.S. road-show cities, whose chief movie critics a year before had been flown by Fox to the Salzburg location, where they had

had full access to the star and the creative personnel, the reviews tended to be kinder.) In less than eighteen months in Salt Lake City, admissions totaled three times the city's population of 190.000.

In Atlanta, Syracuse, Colorado Springs, Cedar Rapids, and Orlando, attendance at *The Sound of Music* in those same eighteen months exceeded the town's total population, as it did in at least twenty other places.

Among the towns in which it had record runs was Moorhead, Minnesota, where it ran more than a year in the town's lone movie theater, prompting a demonstration by students of Moorhead College, who picketed under the banner of POOIE (People's Organization of Intelligent Educatees), carrying signs reading 49 WEEKS OF SCHMALTZ IS ENOUGH, WE WANT SOMETHING NEW, and DON'T GET CAUGHT IN THE VON TRAPP).

And that was just in the United States during the first run, one theater to a town, 275 towns (all on a reserved-seat basis). In 1965 and 1966 the movie was seen at 3,200 theaters in the world—almost one-tenth of only a possible 35,000. In Great Britain it grossed more than £6,000,000 ($14,400,000), twice as much as any other film in that country, although the stage version was in its sixth year in the West End and still running strong. It broke box-office records in twenty-nine countries, including Thailand, where it was called *Charms of the Heaven-Sound* (at the Bangkok premiere, King Bhumibol, whose predecessor was the subject of the best of all Rodgers and Hammerstein musicals, *The King and I,* played "Do Re Mi" on his clarinet), and Italy (*All Together with Passion*), Egypt (*Love and Tenderness*), Hong Kong (*Fairy Music Blow Fragrant Place Place Hear*), and Argentina (*The Rebellious Novice*). It was dubbed in Parsi, for Iran and India, and in four other languages (in other countries subtitles were used), and the lyrics to the songs were rewritten in German, French, Spanish, and Italian.

Only in Germany, whose ruler of twenty-five to thirty

years before had been the villain of the piece, and, surprisingly, in Salzburg itself (in both places it was *My Song, My Dream,* and maybe that had something to do with it) did *The Sound of Music* not do well. In Germany it simply did not bring them to the box office in droves, but in Salzburg, where nearly everyone went to see it, the people just didn't like it. "That was really rather nasty of them," said Julie. And downright ungrateful. The company had spent $900,000 there during its eleven weeks of locations and had left behind enough for some local citizens to charge $20 per person for a tour of *The Sound of Music* sets. And then there had been a special commemorative postage stamp, a tribute that also brought additional revenue to the Alpine city.

There were individual tributes unequaled in the annals of moviegoing, even by religious fanatics seeing things like *The Ten Commandments.* The woman in Wales who went to see *The Sound of Music* every day at least once clearly was the champion. There were others, like the sailor in Puerto Rico (75 sittings); Elizabeth Pick, the fortyish Los Angeles typist who hit more than 100 viewings, at from $2.50 to $3.50 a throw, spending more than $300 ("It makes me feel good," she explained); the man in Oregon who saw it 50 times or more, often enough to send the studio a complete script he had written from memory; Jesús Alviola, a Filipino who saw it 50 times in Manila and kept the stubs to prove it ("Each time I found it more enchanting and engrossing," he said) ; and the articulate Manhattan surgeon who logged only 9 screenings, but after nine significant personal depressions: "It's my psychiatrist's couch and an undrugged high at the same time," he said.

That it was cheaper than, and sometimes a substitute for, therapy did not surprise the psychiatrists, particularly the Bedford-Drive-in-Beverly Hills-based variety, who also opined that its positive, constructive kind of fantasy with moviegoers could identify with and at the same time escape into was responsible for the success of *The Sound of Music.* Wise and Zanuck were not so glib with their theories on why the film had grossed $120,000,000 worldwide by late 1969. "Who knows?" said the director, when asked what was responsible. "If we knew the answer to that, we'd know the answer to a lot of things," said Zanuck. Most movie-industry theories paid lip service to the music, the parent-child relationships, the everything's-going-to-be-all-rightness of the screenplay, and the location scenery (but Lehman countered: "Nobody goes to see a picture because they love the Alps so much"). And all gave credit to Wise. He won almost every award it is possible to win as a producer and director, including the Directors Guild of America's Best Director Award in 1966, awards from the Roman Catholic and several other churches, and the Producers Guild of America's Best Picture Award, two Oscars (one in each capacity), and a Motion Picture Academy Irving Thalberg Award in 1967, ostensibly for creative service to the Hollywood film industry, but really for packing them in. But the real answer, if there was one, was the essential sunniness, hard-won professionalism, and sheer talent of Julie Andrews, summed up in the helicopter-shot opening sequence over the Alps, of the young novice escaping her nunnery for a few moments to sing the film's title song. Julie and the film were a word she would come to loathe: wholesome.

Julie herself said the reason for the movie's popularity might be that "it's very joyous. It's refreshing and not too complicated, a love story with children and music. And I think, from the enormous amount of mail I got, that word 'joyous' has an awful lot to do with it."

Wise was willing to speculate on her success in the film, and perhaps that was close to the whole story: "It can't be all just talent; a lot of talented people don't begin to make it the way she's made it. There is a genuineness about her, an unphoniness. What you see on the screen is an extension of Julie herself. She goes right through the camera onto film and out to the audience. Julie seems to have been born with that magic gene that comes through on screen; this magic gene, whatever it is (that Audrey Hepburn also has) coming through commands you to react abnormally to her."

Escape and reassurance were seen as the chief ingredients in the success of *The Sound of Music* not only by its makers ("Everything comes out right, the Nazis aren't *really* Nazis, and it's happy-ending time," said Lehman, who was in a better position to know than anybody), but also by its imitators—MGM came out with *The Singing Nun* and Debbie Reynolds finally did play one, and Columbia brought out the nonmusical *The Trouble with Angels* and a sequel to it, *Where Angels Go, Trouble Follows*.

"I wasn't trying to say a damn thing in *Music*—no message —that's as good a face as I can put on it," Wise said. "People just feel good when they see it; there's a sense of warmth, of well-being, of happiness and joy. And then, perhaps, it's come out at a time when people around the world want to get away from their problems."

When it came time for the Academy Awards in April, 1966 (although Julie's first three movies had been made in rapid succession, and *Mary Poppins* and *Emily* had been released in late 1964, Twentieth Century-Fox and Robert Wise had been shrewd enough long in advance to schedule *The Sound of Music* opening for March, 1965, as an "Easter Picture," making it eligible to compete in a different academy year), the movie was well on its way to making barrels of money. Although it already looked a good bet to place second to *Gone with the Wind* as an all-time box-officer grosser, no one yet was predicting it would pass the long-standing champion, and it would be almost a year before it actually did. Still, just on the basis of the box-office receipts so far, it was a sure bet for a slew of nominations, and considering the relatively weak competition (*A Patch of Blue, The Collector*)—except for *Dr. Zhivago,* also a box-office blockbuster that had received better, though not entirely satisfactory, reviews than *Music* had—the film had a good shot at the best picture Oscar. The nominations in February confirmed the general optimism. *The Sound of Music* got ten nominations (to *Dr. Zhivago*'s eleven), including one for Julie as best actress, Wise as best director, and one for the picture. Peggy Wood's citation in the best supporting actress category confirmed the eagerness Hollywood had to heap gratitude and accolades on this picture; a venerable and justly acclaimed actress, best known for *I Remember Mama* on early American live television, this time out she had walked through the part of the mother superior of the abbey in which she was miscast (and which Patricia Neway had sung so brilliantly on Broadway), understandably turning her face from the camera—or having it turned from her—every time she tried to move her lips to the dubbed much younger voice of Marni Nixon singing "Climb Ev'ry Mountain" in her stead.

Julie's nomination, surprising no one, gave her a good chance to become the first (and only other) actress to win two Oscars back to back since Luise Rainer, in 1936 and 1937 for *The Great Ziegfeld* and *The Good Earth*.

Actually, a slow reaction to the *Poppins* win the year before was setting in in Hollywood, a slight feeling that maybe we Americans had been "hospitable" enough and that while we had perhaps given Julie the Oscar for the wrong film, one was enough. And Julie Christie was nominated for her brilliant portrayal of the title part in *Darling*, providing tough competition from the first, even tougher after she won the Best Actress Award and *Darling* won the best picture award from the New York Film Critics later in February. Yet it boiled down to a battle of the two British Julies (Elizabeth Hartman, for her fine performance as the blind girl in *A Patch of Blue*; Samantha Eggar, for *The Collector*; and Simone Signoret for *Ship of Fools* were never considered much competition), and Julie Christie's win was the last for a British actress (Paul Scofield the next year, for *A Man for All Seasons,* was the last British actor) in the mid-1960's cycle of British dominance of Hollywood (ten of the twenty nominees in acting categories in 1966 were British, while many of the top films were made in Britain or at any rate in Europe).

Monday, April 18, the night of the awards, at the Santa Monica Civic Auditorium, was one of those coolish California evenings that academy members and nominees always hope for on Oscar night because they are required to wear formal clothes and floor-length dresses. The fans, some of whom had driven from as far away as New Jersey, were in place in 3,000 bleacher seats outside the auditorium by 6 P.M. and another 2,000 or so stood by to cheer their favorite stars. Mrs. Mamie Washington, a local young woman whose husband was a soldier in Vietnam, had arrived with her two infant children, twenty-one and nine months old, at 4:30 that morning, to claim the first seats, and Mrs. Washington's mother had brought fresh diapers and food throughout the day. Other fans began arriving at 8 A.M. and came steadily throughout the day.

Julie Christie, whom press agents hired by Avco-Embassy, the distributors of *Darling*, had been touting as a house guest of the other Julie, had opted instead for the Beverly Hills Hotel ("Our schedules for the weekend were both so hectic," Julie Christie offered as the reason for the "switch"). The two Julies had planned to arrive at the Santa Monica Civic Auditorium in the same limousine, but Avco-Embassy and Julie Andrews' two studios, Twentieth and Universal, where she had spent much of the day doing scenes in *Thoroughly Modern Millie* and dictating letters to her then secretary, Bea Hopkinson, insisted on separate cars for maximum publicity. So the actresses arrived at Santa Monica two minutes apart at 6:42 and 6:44 P.M. They were the twin favorites in the best actress Oscar derby and the favorites of the assembled fans, except for only the blond Shelley Winters, who would go inside and become the first woman ever to win two Oscars as best supporting actress, this second one as the slatternly mother in *A Patch of Blue,* and for Miss

Lynda Bird Johnson, of the then Washington, D.C., Johnsons, who arrived at 6:50 on the arm of actor George Hamilton, followed closely by two Secret Service men.

The President's daughter had called Hamilton, then a steady beau, just a few days before and invited herself to the awards simply by announcing she was coming and that it would be necessary for George's secretary, Charles Malcolm, to submit the usual list of people who would be at the Hamilton mansion, permanently or temporarily, for White House security clearance. George was livid at first (not so much at her coming out as at her steamrolling and his losing the initiative), but since he had to be at the ceremonies as a presenter (which Lynda Bird knew), he was trapped. Hamilton then decided to make the most of the intrusion and even agreed to have the Oscar show's scriptwriters insert a feeble joke about his escorting Miss Johnson. For the occasion Lynda, who recently under the influence of George Hamilton and of George Masters, the brilliant Beverly Hills hairstylist and makeup expert, had become an attractive, slimmed-down, well-dressed beauty, reverted to a gown of her favorite color: tacky orange. But it was a mink-hemmed brocade gown that held its own in the Hollywood crowd.

For twelve years, the Academy Awards ceremony had been televised in black and white, but this year, 1966, it was to be Hollywood in living color for the first time. During the twelve black-and-white years, Edith Head, the Motion Picture Academy's fashion consultant for the awards and a three-time Oscar winner herself, had tried vainly to get some of the actress presenters and nominees to wear plain white gowns. Not a chance. "They wore green, yellow, pink, red, orange, and pumpkin—anything but white," Miss Head observed. That Monday night in April, 1966, with the ABC color cameras grinding away, no fewer than nine lady presenters and nominees, of only twenty-three, wore white gowns—most in last-minute costume switches. Had Sophia Loren made it to California, as planned, to present the best director award (director Charlie Chaplin kept her on the London set of *A Countess from Hong Kong* instead), she would have worn an all-white Dior, and that would have made it ten, including Lana Turner in a white Jean Louis and Virna Lisi, who wore something by an anonymous Italian designer.

"I looked at all those white dresses, and I thought we were doing a reprise of *White Christmas*" was the reaction of Edith Head. "If we had frozen the fountains, we could have had a snow queen ballet." Worst of all, the white dresses came out a garish green on many color TV sets, especially those that had not been properly tuned.

Neither of the Julies was among the nine, however; in fact, they were responsible for two of the most colorful costumes seen on all televison that season. Julie Christie, who was escorted to the awards by Don Bessant, her English beau (whom she was then living with in London), had designed a pair of gold lamé pajamas for what was to be her night of triumph at the thirty-eighth annual Academy Awards. "How did I know she was going to get dressed up as an Oscar until she got up onstage?" snapped Miss Head the next afternoon. Her reaction to the outfit that showed beyond the shadow of a smile that the talented Miss Christie's talents were not as a designer was one of the kindest. "Some people are just so independent that you expect them to dress differently," Miss Head said. "If she had come out in some proper little black dress and a string of pearls, we would all have been disappointed."

The nonwhite gowns had only their length and their appallingness in common. Kim Novak, as she had for several previous years, slinked off with the booby prize for the worst dress: a tight-fitting red, white, and blue sequin number that had to be seen in living color to be believed. But Julie Andrews came a close second. About to be separated, by agreement as well as by physical fact, from her husband (although it was not publicly known), she came to the ceremony with

Saul Chaplin, the safe associate producer of *The Sound of Music*. Chaplin, who had a married daughter almost Julie's age, was divorced and not yet remarried, and he was a legitimate professional associate. Tripling as nominee, presenter (of the best actor award to Lee Marvin, for *Cat Ballou*), and substitute acceptor for Robert Wise, Julie was one of the most conspicuous of the movie people present. She wore a dress of reddish-orange imported lightweight wool, with a discothèque back, a deep-V "wrapped" front, and long, narrow sleeves. The dress had a waistband of changeable silk, shading from pale pink to red, that was fastened to it by a thirty-carat topaz pendant. It was designed by Dorothy Jeakins, a previous Academy Award winner (for *Samson and Delilah*, *Joan of Arc*, and *The Night of the Iguana*), who was also nominated for her costumes for *The Sound of Music*. Occasionally it was mercifully covered by a white mink stole.

Apart from the color consciousness of the fashions, and the unusual attendance of the first President's daughter in anyone's memory, there was little to distinguish at that year's Oscar festivities. Most of the predicted winners won. Lynda Bird was conspicuous, but her usual untalkative self. "It's my first Academy Awards show, and I'm just very thrilled to be here," was all she had managed in her soft Texas accent on the way in, and during the show she just sat wide-eyed, as did most of the other guests in the 1,700-seat auditorium.

The nominees were more nervous than wide-eyed, however, and Julie was no exception. In her ninth-row aisle seat on the right side of the hall, she kept wringing her hands together. Saul Chaplin smiled a lot and tried to make little jokes to cover his nerves and soothe hers. Just behind Julie sat Rod Steiger, a best actor nominee for *The Pawnbroker*. He did his best to ignore the tension he felt, and his then wife, Claire Bloom, helped by holding his arm in her kid-gloved left hand. He choked visibly when Marvin won. Marvin, seated just in front of Julie, gazed sullenly at the floor the entire time until his name was called. When it was, he raced to the stage to claim his Oscar, managed to look surprised, and properly gave half credit to "a horse somewhere out in the [San Fernando] valley." To Julie, who as the previous year's best actress winner presented it to him, he said: "It's kind of wonderful when it happens to you." She knew that already. Later, clutching his Oscar in one hand and longtime girlfriend, Michele Triola, in the other, he said simply, "Well, that's over."

But it still wasn't over for Julie, who had several minutes to go to find out she wasn't going to do a Luise Rainer. At one point, when presenters George Hamilton and Patty Duke announced the best editing award—to William Reynolds for *The Sound of Music*—Julie shouted, "Oh, boy," and clapped so wildly that she knocked her white mink onto the floor. Reynolds, in accepting the award, returned the compliment by saying: "When in doubt, cut to Julie Andrews."

Julie happily accepted the best director award for Robert Wise, who was in Hong Kong directing *The Sand Pebbles*, and then waited quietly backstage for the best actress announcement, which was next (there wasn't time to return to her seat). Rex Harrison, in another of life's little coincidences, as the prior year's winner for *My Fair Lady* strode to the rostrum and ripped open the envelope. "Julie," he said with lips pursed, then paused for an agonizing and perverse split second, "Christie . . . for *Darling*." Miss Christie, who had been trying to sit calmly through it all, dissolved the minute he said it, and she stayed dissolved for three days. She kissed Don Bessant, ran to the stage, cried a lot, and clutched her Oscar and Harrison at the same time. Backstage and off-camera she asked him, "Why isn't my name on it?" Harrison replied coolly and a bit condescendingly: "My dear, they didn't know you were going to win. They'll take it from you and put your name on it, and then you may put it on your mantel." Julie Christie continued crying, and said, "But I haven't got a mantel," and cried some more.

The previous year's winner and that year's unofficial

runner-up had watched this scene quietly, waiting for a
chance to say: "Julie, doesn't it feel good?" Julie Andrews
bravely tried to hide her disappointment at not being tapped
a second time and was helped moments later when *The
Sound of Music* won the Oscar as best picture of 1965, for a
total of five Academy Awards (to six, but lesser, ones for *Dr.
Zhivago,* which had also starred Julie Christie, and just two
for *Darling*) . "Oh, boy," said Julie Andrews again, broadly
smiling. "We did it. Isn't that great? Now I'm happy."

The next day Julie Christie was asked about the battle of
the two Julies. She said with modern British candor: "At the
time, believe me, I didn't think of anybody but myself. I
can't say I'm sorry, of course. She won it last year, after all."
She claimed she never really thought of the Oscar before—
"that was for great big film stars." Later that next day Julie
Christie took off with Bessant for Palm Springs to spend a
few days at the home of Mr. Blackwell, a dress designer. Following the car she rode in was a separate limousine full of
congratulatory flowers she had received and wanted to take
to the desert with her. On top of the heap was a two-foot-
wide pink paper rose from Julie Andrews.

The Sound of Music was withdrawn from its initial release
on Labor Day, 1969, four and a half years after it had opened
in New York. At that point it was estimated to have brought
in $120,000,000 worldwide. In America, however, the re-
ceipts were "only" $68,000,000 and *Gone with the Wind,* in its
sixth rerelease, had surpassed that figure with a $76,000,000
domestic sales total (but lagged badly on the foreign
market). *The Graduate,* which had been released at the end
of 1967, was third in U.S. grosses, with $42,000,000 and the
ten-year-old *The Ten Commandments* was fourth with
$40,000,000.

VIII

AND THUS, eight and a half years from the opening night of *My Fair Lady*, Julie Andrews, at twenty-nine, was finally an old-fashioned big-time movie star, with an Oscar and everything, including a small critically acclaimed arty film and the blockbuster movie of all time. She was turning down movie parts as fast as her film actress contemporary—also British-born and also a former child star—Elizabeth Taylor. She was still happily married and a relatively new mother, with a new home in Wimbledon that she and Tony had had several months to work on and rest in between finishing her first fast three films in a row (although she had done her first TV special in the meantime) and the night she won the Oscar. (The only danger was "that I'll be considered the nanny of all time.") But now, in April, 1965, with the Oscar out of the way it was time to go to work again. And there was nothing left to do but marry Jesus in New England and go to Hawaii on a long honeymoon—and to do it all for a real movie-star price, $400,000.

Max von Sydow, the Swedish actor, had played the character of Christ in George Stevens' *The Greatest Story Ever Told*, precisely because he was unknown to American audiences (no chance for humorous or distracting identification between a deity and a well-known face, the theory went), but as a result of having done that, he was well known enough to star in a major American movie opposite

Julie and Richard Harris. The film was *Hawaii,* based on a third of the rambling James Michener novel, and Von Sydow had the major part of a Fundamentalist missionary, Abner Hale, who leaves his New Hampshire home to convert the Polynesian natives in Hawaii to Christianity (only virtually to extinguish them), taking a somewhat unwilling, arranged wife, Jerusha Bromley, played by Julie, with him. Julie liked the whole idea of another straight nonmusical character and working with Von Sydow.

"Oh, marvelous publicity—can't you see it?" she chortled just before the start of shooting. " 'Mary Poppins married Jesus.' Gorgeous! She must have flown up to him and said, 'Listen, with my magic and your talent, we'd make a great team. I can fly. You can walk on water. What more do we need?' Actually, come to think of it, who else could she have married? It's the classic mother and father image for all children."

She found less to laugh at once the film was actually under way. It started in Sturbridge Village, a reconstructed Colonial town in southwestern Massachusetts, a location site Julie and Von Sydow couldn't get to because of a spring snow in New England that stopped all air traffic. A chauffeured limousine drove the two of them up from New York instead. (There had been a week in a fjord in Norway of staging external scenes of a storm at sea, footage that was almost entirely scrapped and reshot in Hollywood and off Honolulu later, not involving the principals.) In Sturbridge, a paid-admission park which was playing the part of Walpole, New Hampshire, of 140 years before, Julie learned the meaning of the word "superstar."

"That little place," Willard "Daddy Bill" Buell, her long-time makeup man, recalled, "that's where she learned what she was." Prior to *Hawaii* there had been a few incidents, mostly in department stores when she was shopping, mothers poking their children and saying, "Look, dear, there's Mary Poppins!" But nothing like the clutching and clawing of the grasping fans on Patriots' Day, a unique Massachusetts and Maine holiday held on April 19, in Sturbridge. (The company had paid $10,000 a day for the use of the site, but it was not closed; the portions being filmed were merely roped off.) Julie just remembered that "it was some sort of public holiday. We were in a kind of park. It was not like Hollywood. Hollywood is good about these things—one is asked for one's autograph or perhaps someone in a shop tells you of having enjoyed your performance in a film, but it's not a rush, not a mad thing. But in Sturbridge the police had to rope off the set. People started to converge as I was walking to my trailer with these rather nice husky policemen. These very sizable policemen were around me, and people would be on one side being pushed back, and then they would circle around and come in from the other side. You could hear them saying, 'Look, it's Mary Poppins', to their children. They didn't mean any harm, it was a lark for them, but then I got into the trailer and I was alone in eight square feet of space, alone in this island. You could hear them outside giggling and joshing and pushing. And the trailer was swaying. They were scratching at the walls. I pulled down the shades and sat there alone. I thought, 'My God, how alone I am. I can't send for anybody. I can't get out.'"

On another occasion a zealous fan stole a costume bonnet from her trailer dressing room, a bonnet that had not yet been used, that was not recovered, remade, or in the final film. Whenever and wherever she went to eat around Sturbridge, she was mobbed by adoring fans, and when the weekend came and Tony arrived for a visit, she requested a small, cheaper-model, older car so that the two of them could go sight-seeing unrecognized. The move worked, and they spent a quiet Friday afternoon and evening driving through the Sturbridge area. They spent the rest of the weekend in New York, at the modest Wellington Hotel, where a superstar was not expected to stay and so was not bothered; they saw the new hit play, *The Odd Couple*, directed by Mike Nichols.

From Sturbridge the *Hawaii* company went to Hollywood to shoot some interiors. The film was under the auspices of the Mirisch Company, particularly Walter Mirisch and United Artists, headquartered at the Goldwyn Studio. Also at Mirisch-UA at that point was a writer-producer-director named Blake Edwards, who was preparing *What Did You Do in the War, Daddy?* (usually shortened to simply War Daddy). Edwards and Julie would pass each other on the Goldwyn lot and say brief hellos. And then from Hollywood the company went to Hawaii, to the island of Oahu and the Kahala section of Honolulu, where Julie, Von Sydow, Richard Harris, and director George Roy Hill all had large houses. (The picture, except for the abortive sea storm sequence, was filmed more or less chronologically, from Abner Hale's graduation from divinity school, to his marriage to Jerusha, to on board ship to Hawaii, to the arrival in the islands, and straight through to twenty years later.)

"I fell in love with Hawaii," she said, referring to the state, not the film. "There had been Sturbridge, all cool and New Englandish, and then there was Hawaii; it was quite a change. To watch the dawn in those islands is one of the memorable experiences of a lifetime. Hawaii is gorgeous and fabulous. Where else could you drive up to a roadstand and get a paper plate with hamburger, French fries, mustard, and an orchid?" she asked. Julie, in fact, became so infatuated with Hawaii that she bought an interest in a macadamia nut orchard and returned to the islands twice within the next three years for vacations. Emma Kate stayed with Julie at the house in Hawaii "every moment of the time," and Julie's half brother Christopher and Nanny Kay were there most of the time, too. Visitors to *chez* Andrews included Jessica Mitford and Linus Pauling, Jr., and on the odd weekend Julie would return to Los Angeles, no one was quite sure for what.

The cultural life in Honolulu was not what it could have been as far as Julie was concerned, although she did go to the ballet when it was in town with whoever was at hand. She supplemented this with screenings of movies at her Kahala home, including a 16-mm print of Godard's *Breathless* and, solely out of loyalty to the Mirisch Company, *The Magnificent Seven,* another of its products. She gave parties, including one for all the nannies, tutors, and other household help in the company. And during the shooting day, when she had some time off, she would relax alone on the secluded beach near the village set, in a bikini.

"Although I loved the islands unashamedly, it was ten times harder working there, and six months was too long," she said. And as the working days wore on into August, September, and October, she began looking forward to returning to California. In particular, she remembered hot and long, uncomfortable days on the Oahu beaches and three weeks in the boat offshore filming the sea-voyage scenes. (The ship was the 150-ton schooner *Grethe,* built in Denmark in 1936 and converted into an early nineteenth-century two-masted brigantine. Alan Villiers, the author and seaman, had sailed it with his wife and a crew of nine from Copenhagen to the islands in about three months.)

Conditions were somewhat unpleasant and tense because the picture was falling behind schedule, and it was costing the Mirisch Company extra money (the budget was $12,000,000)—money that it appeared not at all willing to spend. Mirisch executives came out from Hollywood, found Hill spending most of his time working with the Polynesians, most of whom were totally untrained as actors but crucial to the action, particularly in the early Hawaii location scenes. Julie felt that she was not getting enough of the director's attention, and when Walter Mirisch, who had been preparing the picture since 1959, finally fired Hill as director, she was on the Mirisches' side mostly by staying silent.

The Polynesians, led by Jocelyne La Garde, a French-speaking Tahitian, standing six feet tall and weighing 300 pounds, who was making her acting debut as Malama, the Polynesian queen (so effectively that she won an Academy

Award nomination in the supporting category), and Manu Tupou, who played Keoki, her consort, went on strike and refused to work until Hill was reinstated. Ultimately, he was, although the Mirisches meantime tried to substitute Arthur Hiller (who had worked with Julie so well in *Emily,* another reason why she did not spring to Hill's defense). Julie thought Miss LaGarde and Manu Tupou "had their nerve" leading a strike, and she would have no part of it. The twin ironies of the situation were that once he was back on the picture and had time to devote to her, Hill and Julie became the fastest of friends and colleagues (and she requested him as director on *Thoroughly Modern Millie,* despite his relative Hollywood inexperience), and that it was Hill, a bright young veteran of Broadway and the film *The World of Henry Orient*—which he later redid as a Broadway musical, *Henry, Sweet Henry*—who had fought to cast Julie as Jerusha in the first place.

"Of course I wanted her," Hill said. "It's awfully hard to get a girl who can play a convincing young lady of breeding of the eighteen twenties in New England. What other names spring to mind? The people of the eighteen twenties— particularly in New England—were closer to the lands of their birth than to the Americans of today. There was a great stillness in the people of that time. That is what I tried to get and that is what she has. She is reserved, yet warm and aristocratic."

Julie did not entirely agree with that assessment. "At first I thought I was miscast as the missionary's wife. Miscast may not be precisely the right word. I didn't think I was in total sympathy with the lady. I wasn't as subdued as she was. My personality is more bubbly. And I felt I wasn't doing anything, just repressing myself and being her. I had never met anyone like Jerusha. She left her home, turned away from the man she really loved to stay with a husband she didn't love, to suffer the hardships and deprivations of a missionary's wife on an untamed island. I don't think I would have

done that. But George was patient with me, Max was lovely
and a marvelous actor to work with, and finally I loved the
work and the part."

Shortly after she arrived in Honolulu, Julie went to visit
the wax museum, "and I almost dropped in my tracks. There
was a wax figure of the first lady missionary, and if that lady
isn't the very image of me! I had an eerie feeling that I was
destined by fate for this part."

As usual, she had "read the novel, I confess, only in connection with the movie. I was dismayed at the amount of
work it seemed to involve. But it was wonderful for once to
go home looking deliberately dowdy and to take off my
makeup and look better. I did quite a lot of reading and
talking with George about the characters. There was one
book I found particularly fascinating, a sort of family tree of
the missionaries who went over and their descendants. In
Hawaii the history is all so recent." She and Hill and the others met and talked with some of the descendants of the missionary families. "They hadn't liked the book" (and they
weren't too enthralled with the movie, it turned out).

The storm-at-sea scenes in Hawaii were done for the first
two days without Julie. "The actors playing the sailors all
got seasick and they came back to shore and said, 'Dose up, it's
going to be hell.' So the morning I was to go out, I ate nine
pancakes for ballast, took six Dramamines, and belted down
a large scotch. I was so drunk I was the only one who wasn't
sick. The bananas scene, which I didn't prepare for, that's
when I really did almost get sick."

Julie's most important scene in the picture was the one in
which she gave birth to a child. It was shot in the converted
Navy warehouse in Honolulu that was serving as a studio,
and it took "seventeen hours over six days, and all I produced
was a lump of celluloid. I don't think I could have done the
scene without having had a baby myself. There was a real
doctor counseling on the set, and after every take he would
put his hand on my head and ask if I felt all right, just as if I

were having a baby. Opening night in New York I noticed that women were fastened on the screen during that scene. The men, I think, rather didn't like it." And Blake Edwards later said admiringly of the birth scene: "When she had the baby, it was almost like being in [Actors Studio director Lee] Strasberg's class and being told to have a baby [it was so out-of-context, he felt], but boy, she had one!"

The peripheral casting of the epic even apart from the Polynesians, was interesting. Dorothy Jeakins, Julie's great friend and the costume designer on *The Sound of Music,* not only performed the same function on *Hawaii,* but made her film debut as a very touching Mrs. Hale, Abner's mother, in a part that was shot much larger and including a moving farewell scene with Von Sydow, but reduced to almost a silent walk-on in the final cutting, and Von Sydow's two small, platinum-haired sons, Henrik and Clas, played the parts of his sons in the film. Gene Hackman, John Cullum, George Rose, and Michael Constantine played tiny parts, as did Caroll O'Conner and Heather Menzies, who had played the second Von Trapp daughter, Louisa in *The Sound of Music.* As for the Polynesians, Julie said, "It was a mutual love affair; I adored them and I believe they were rather fond of me."

Despite the delays, being over budget, several script changes (there were three separate writers, including Hill himself, Daniel Taradash, and Dalton Trumbo, but only the last two got screen credit), and the early contretemps over Hill, the rest of the summer went smoothly enough. "We talked about a death scene for Jerusha [who died before the end of the picture but off-screen], as well as the birth scene, but decided it would be a bit much, what with Malama's death, too," Julie recalled. Before Richard Harris, who as Rafer Hoxworth, the spurned lover, had the smallest of the three star parts, left the islands, he and Julie and Von Sydow gave the cast a dinner party at the posh Kahala Hilton. Don Ho, contemporary Hawaii's best-known entertainer, was brought in to sing. He and Julie did a duet of his hit, "I'll

Remember You," with Julie repeating each verse as he sung it because she didn't know the words. Asked to sing a solo, she said: "I'm sorry, but of all the songs I've sung, the only one I can remember all the words to is 'I Could Have Danced All Night.' " And so she sang that hit from *My Fair Lady* and nothing else.

Julie during *Hawaii* developed two most satisfying professional relationships. One was with Hill; the second with Von Sydow. She and the Swedish star respected each other enormously, and with a little prodding she later admitted that he was her favorite leading man. "He was the unqualified front-runner, the most generous man I've ever met. And he had such a lovely, light sense of humor. I consider it a privilege to have worked with him."

Von Sydow found that "she made fun of herself and her part in a marvelous way, and yet she is so goddamned professional even in the most difficult situations. She doesn't behave like the cliché star. She has a temper, but she is also a disciplined lady, and she does not use her temper just because she feels like it. She is nice with people, but she is determined to do things right, and she will stick up for what she thinks is right. She doesn't show off.

"I learned a lot from her about movie discipline. I have a tendency to tenseness all day when I'm on a picture—to stay with my part the whole time—which made me too exhausted too early in the day. She, on the other hand, has a great ability to walk into a part and then out of it again, to do her part one minute and then relax the next—to do other things, write letters, see people, listen to music, sing and laugh, and then go right back to being Jerusha."

In the midst of filming in Hawaii, Julie told a visitor: "I'm working harder—and I'm basically lazy—because, of course, it is a straight dramatic role [there was one minor song for Julie, "My Wishing Doll"] in a very important picture. I love to do drama. There's more joy to doing musicals, but there's not as much depth. It's because I know I can always sing, but acting is something else again. I have to keep chugging on all engines."

The world premiere of *Hawaii* was not in Honolulu, but once again in New York, on October 10,1966, at the DeMille Theater. It was the first of no fewer than fourteen black-tie charity premieres, a new world record for one picture, and the first time Julie had seen the film all the way through. She wore a Jean Louis dress (thereby being temporarily disloyal to her friend Dorothy Jeakins, who had left the Hawaiian locations early but had sent special-delivery airmail letters to Julie at Kahala almost daily). And although they were already estranged, she attended with Tony Walton. (On that same New York visit, she and Tony saw a paid public preview of the musical, *The Apple Tree*, which Mike Nichols had directed, Tony had designed, and Julie had turned down. She thought it and Barbara Harris in the lead role "just fabulous.")

Of her own efforts in *Hawaii* she said, "I did have reservations about myself—one always does—but I do like little bits in the film that I did." Julie's father, on seeing it, said *Hawaii* convinced him for the first time that his daughter could really act, too.

The critics were kinder to her than to the film, which offended mostly by its epic length and slow pace.

It did only medium well at the box office but was rewarded with eight Academy Award nominations, basically for its big effort and all but one in technical categories, only one, for Jocelyne La Garde as Malama, in an acting classification. It got no Oscars. It was just well enough received that the Mirisches went ahead with their plans to film a sequel, *The Hawaiians*, four years later, with Charlton Heston picking up where Richard Harris had left off. Julie, since she had died in the earlier film, was not ever involved in the sequel.

IX

WITH BARELY A WEEK in between, Julie went from Honolulu and *Hawaii* to Hollywood and Universal City for *Torn Curtain,* the action-spy picture that was to be (and it was proudly touted as such) producer-director Alfred Hitchcock's fiftieth film. Julie had read the script (by the normally talented Canadian novelist Brian Moore, who wrote *The Luck of Ginger Coffey* and *I Am Mary Dunne* and who had been signed after a host of others, including James Goldman, had turned it down) on location in Hawaii, and she announced that it was anything but golden. But her agents had convinced her that working with Hitchcock and co-star Paul Newman was the best (meaning the most lucrative) thing she could do at that moment, and she desperately did want to work for the distinguished past master of movie mystery. She didn't realize just how past that was and plunged ahead, despite a large case of fatigue brought on by the islands.

Torn Curtain had waited for her, and she had been held up in *Hawaii,* so the day production started in November, 1965, the film was already behind schedule. It was finished in February and was first shown to the press at the Directors Guild Building in West Hollywood in June—and although made after, *Torn Curtain* was released before *Hawaii* which opened in October. The setting of the story was Copenhagen and East Berlin, but the shooting involving the stars took place entirely on the good old Universal backlot. Although it was not a big budget film, what money was spent (about $5,000,000) went to Hitchcock's and the stars' salaries—her agents had been right, Julie got $750,000 against 10 percent of the gross, more than Newman who was billed first—and not to production values. Perhaps that was why everybody, including Hitchcock, seemed to walk through it. (The one exception was Lila Kedrova, who had won her Oscar the same year as Julie, for *Zorba the Greek,* and who played a desperate Polish woman who wanted to escape from East Germany to the West and who kept calling everything Communist "deeskosting." She stole what there was of the picture to steal from the stars.)

For the first and only time in her life on stage and screen through 1969, Julie was playing a contemporary woman, Sarah Sherman, secretary-mistress to the American scientist Michael Armstrong (Newman) who has supposedly defected to the Communists. She stubbornly follows him from Copenhagen to Berlin, although he has told her not to complicate both their lives. (Newman isn't really a defector, of course, as any child would know from the mere fact of his being in the film. Oskar Werner or James Mason or even David Niven a defector, possibly; Paul Newman, never.) The most memorable—and clumsiest—scene is one in which Newman and an East German *Hausfrau* savagely kill a secret agent who has followed him to her farm. They use a shovel and a knife in juicy detail before finally sticking his head in an oven.

Hitchcock, as usual, had almost no exposed film left over at the end of shooting *Torn Curtain*; he had shot every scene just the way he wanted it (except one in which he said Newman was too methody and therefore eliminated) and edited in his head as he went along, printing only absolutely the takes he needed. That three notorious perfectionists like Hitchcock, Newman, and Andrews could have made this slipshod bundle of clichés was a minor wonder. That it made large amounts of money on its release as a "summer picture" (Universal, more than other studios, tend to think in terms of seasonal releases) was a major miracle, but a tribute to all three names and their combined potency at the box office despite the critics' acid.

Hitchcock said he got his inspiration for the film from the story of British diplomats Burgess and MacLean, who defected to the USSR. "I said to myself, 'What did Mrs. Mac-Lean think of the whole thing?' and the first third of the film is more or less from a woman's point of view." That technique does not work, unfortunately, because the audience was way ahead of Julie on each aspect of the action.

The film opens with an in-bed, albeit far from nude, sequence between Julie and Newman as Sarah and Michael, who are not married and not too seriously contemplating marriage. This was a shock to many admirers of Mary Poppins and "the image" and entirely unacceptable to the National Roman Catholic Office for Motion Pictures, the successor to the Legion of Decency, which hadn't yet lost the last vestiges of its power to the Motion Picture Association of America's code and rating system. The Catholic office condemned the picture as "morally objectionable in part for all," for its "gratuitous introduction of pre-marital sex between its sympathetic protagonists." It also said the movie's "detailed treatment of a realistically brutal killing" was "questionable on moral grounds" and concluded with a warning: "Parents should be aware that the 'Mary Poppins' image of the female lead (Julie Andrews), shattered in this film, cannot serve as any criterion of the film's acceptability for their children."

Julie, of course, took a different view: "As it was necessary to the story to establish our close relationship, I saw no harm in it," she said. "Paul Newman was such a nice man; we didn't take it seriously and had a lot of giggles over it. It didn't last long, so I don't see what all the fuss is about. I prefer to be known as an actress, not an image."

Making *Torn Curtain* had not provided either the fun or

the professional satisfaction Julie's other projects had, and it was not entirely the fault of the film. At that time in Julie's life, there was a new house she herself had bought that Tony had never seen, still unfurnished and a constant preoccupation; there was Tony himself, absent and still in love with her, and a permanent separation to be arranged. And there was a still-secret affair with Blake Edwards then under way. On the set, Newman was nice enough (he called her "the last of the really great dames") but there wasn't a close friendship. Edith Head, the costume designer, was helpful even on outside projects, like the Theater Owners of America convention in Los Angeles, at which Julie accepted the Star of the Year Award. Miss Head had designed an off-white silk and wool French brocade with long sleeves and a matching stole for the event and worked hard in odd moments on the set to get it just right. But there was not the chumminess Julie shared with Dorothy Jeakins or Tony and not the immense professional respect she would later have for Donald Brooks.

Even her clowning during shooting was less funny and more forced. When Hitchcock complained at one point of a spotlight "making a hell of a line over her head," she put her hands on her hips demurely and said, "That's my halo." She was lying on the bed in what was supposed to be the Copenhagen hotel room, and suddenly she said to the director, "Won't the camera be looking up my skirt?" Newman squatted down next to the camera and looked. "Yeah, that's the idea," he said. "Oh, you beastly thing," she retorted. "I say, did you see the cartoon about Mary Poppins? She is sailing through the air with her umbrella and there are two little boys on the ground looking up and one says, 'Coo, you can see right up her skirts.' " Everybody on the set laughed, but dutifully.

In talking about the experience of making *Torn Curtain*, she tried, as always, to be discreet, but some of her resentment came through. "I did not have to act in *Torn Curtain;* I merely went along for the ride," she said. "I don't feel that the part demanded much of me—other than to look glamorous, which Mr. Hitchcock can always arrange better than anyone. I did have reservations about the film, but I wasn't at all agonized by the final result. The kick of it was working for Hitchcock. That's what I did it for, and that's what I got out of it. So that's that."

She was privately so upset by the film that she urged her good friends not to see it. That fact appeared in the *Time* cover story, causing Hitchcock such apoplexy that Julie wrote him a note saying she hadn't meant that the whole film was bad, just her work in it.

X

FOR ALMOST TWO YEARS Julie had been looking forward to making the movie version of *The Public Eye*, Peter Shaffer's one-act play, with her good friend Mike Nichols as director. It was to have been for producer Ross Hunter, who had made many films with Doris Day, Lana Turner, and Sandra Dee, and also at Universal. But Nichols was tied up with his film debut, *Who's Afraid of Virginia Woolf?*, and committed to direct the three-part Jerry Bock-Sheldon Harnick musical *The Apple Tree* (which was then called *Come Back! Go Away! I Love You!*) in that summer of 1966. And meanwhile, Hunter had produced the movie of the other half of the Shaffer Broadway bill of two one-acts, *The Private Ear*, which was called *The Pad (And How to Use It)*, featuring three unknown actors, and which proved to be a large bore and a total critical and box-office failure that was sold to television quickly to try to get back some of the investment. And so *The Public Eye* dissipated, but Julie still had a commitment to Ross Hunter and Universal, at another $750,000 against 10 percent of the gross.

Hunter recalled that he had talked to Julie as far back as *The Boy Friend* about doing a 1920's movie. He wanted to do *The Boy Friend* itself, but the property was owned by Metro-Goldwyn-Mayer, which would not sell it to Hunter's company. When *Thoroughly Modern Millie*, which was first conceived as a comedy about a young career girl in New York in the 1920's and not a musical, came along, "I read the script [by Richard Morris] as a favor to Ross Hunter," Julie said. "I thought it would be the last chance I'd have to do the ingenue. After all, when you're thirty-one, how many more chances can you have? So I thought I'd have a last fling at the part." She was so enthusiastic about it she canceled a vacation and put off all other pictures, including *Star!*, which wasn't ready yet anyway. She got Hunter to hire George Roy Hill, who worked with Morris on the conversion of the script to a musical, largely by using existing songs of the 1920's, like "Baby Face," "Poor Butterfly," and "Japanese Sandman." Sammy Cahn and Jimmy Van Heusen wrote four new songs, including a title number, "Jimmy," "Trinkt Lechaim," and "The Tapioca." Carol Channing, James Fox, and Beatrice Lillie were signed in support, and the budget was boosted to $8,000,000.

Julie found herself "very excited about Millie; it had great style, it was wild and wacky and had a marvelous cast. The way the script was written the character was a fine line between a selfish, tough, ambitious girl and a fine lady. The challenge in Millie was to be that whole person. I hope one didn't fall one way or 'tother. The picture was *very* twenties, high style, not high camp. It didn't scream, 'Oooooohhhh, I'm just *so* twenties' [here she did a Pollyish vo-de-o-do movement]—it just said, 'I am the twenties' [here just a slightly vampish flip of the wrist]."

And in the title role of Millie Dilmount, an essentially sweet girl who tries to be a flapper but is so naïve that she is surrounded by a ring of white slavers (led by Miss Lillie) and rich people (led by Fox as her romantic interest) and doesn't realize it in either case, Ross Hunter found, he said, "a new Julie. She has a lot of sex appeal, a clean look. I've never worked with anyone like her and I've worked with them all. She is probably one of the greatest stars ever in the business."

Millie was filmed with black, white, and gray backgrounds and one or two bright dominant colors in the foreground, what Hunter called "very Art Nouveau and very twenties," together with some subtitles, wipes, and iris-ins giving it the look of an early silent film in color.

Andre Previn, who served as musical director on the film— he arranged and conducted the twelve musical numbers, but Elmer Bernstein scored the instrumental-only portions of the film, in a unique but workable arrangement necessitated by neither man's complete availability—agreed that "it was a perfect twenties farce and she was perfect in it." But despite the fact that Julie once again was "Julie Andrews as You Love Her—Singing, Dancing, Delighting," as the Universal advertising campaign put it, and *Millie* could have been a romp, she was going through a difficult personal period: the separation from Tony was effected, she began appearing with Blake at dinner parties around Hollywood, and having done three *more* movies in a row without a break, she was tired.

There were professional worries as well: She was contending with two film debuts, Miss Channing's and Mary Tyler Moore's, with Hill's debut as a movie musical director, with James Fox's as a movie musical actor, and with a studio that was finding its most financially successful film in *Torn Curtain* and was determined to better its and her own record. All of them needed her help, and she knew it and responded. (Hill didn't need it as much as she thought he did; during one scene between her and Mary Tyler Moore, the two girls objected to his direction, and he said he would walk away and let them do it themselves. They tried for an hour with no success and pleaded with him to come back.)

Julie was secure with Andre Previn, as a good friend and from having worked closely with him so recently on an album of Christmas carols for RCA Victor. She worked doubly hard on the musical numbers, both because she found satisfaction in working with Previn and as if to compensate for other possible lacks in the film. They worked often at night, especially on the dubbing of her songs after filming was completed. That work was done at Twentieth Century-

Fox instead of at Universal, for Julie knew from *The Sound of Music* days that the sound facilities were vastly superior. Dory Previn would usually be there watching, and Blake would meet them at the end of the evening, which was sometimes topped off by the four of them going for ice cream.

She did not stint on the help she gave her co-stars, however, and one day, when she was not needed on the set at all, she came in just to read her lines off-camera for Carol Channing, on-camera, to react to, instead of having her stand-in do it. Hunter and Miss Channing were flabbergasted. "I never had anyone help me the way Julie did," said Miss Channing. "That would be unheard of for any other star," said Hunter.

Miss Channing told her after the incident: " 'Julie, if it had been your stand-in, I wouldn't have spoken the same way to her.' She said, 'Yes, I knew that, that's why I'm here.' I always played to Julie. She was the one who was listening. She grabbed the words right out of my mouth."

Julie was superprofessional and businesslike on the set, according to James Fox, who "stood in awe" of her, and, like most of her other young leading men, beginning with Burton, fell a little bit in love. ("I didn't fall the least bit in love with her," snorted Rex Harrison. "I was fond of her.") Miss Channing, who learned how to do a close-up ("which has nothing to do with reality—it's like having your head in a vise") from Julie and found in her a friend, could only agree. She would also add that Julie was determined and dedicated.

"There was a fly on the set during one close-up," Miss Channing remembered. "Julie jumped up and said, 'Well, we are going to get that fly, damn it, we are going to get it.' The director had a flyswatter, and he was just going to swat it when she grabbed it right out of his hand and swatted the fly and killed it. Well, now you know you can't do that to a man, and I laughed and said, 'Julie, you are the kind of woman who pushes the elevator button first when you are standing there with a man,' and she said, 'Oh, why not, for heaven's sake?' "

(A year or so later Miss Channing, who had ten years before lost her triumphant Lorelei Lee role in the stage version of *Gentlemen Prefer Blondes* to Marilyn Monroe for the movie, again lost a Broadway-to-film transfer, *Hello, Dolly!*, to Barbra Streisand. Julie wired her: "Don't worry, Carol, you'll get your *Mary Poppins.* "Now wasn't that just the right thing to say," said Carol.)

George Roy Hill, now having directed her in two movies, and not at all emasculated by the loss of his flyswatter, was effusive in his praise of Julie. "There was a period when she seemed a little too good to be true, but she has at last gone beyond that. If I had searched anywhere on earth for a different movie for Julie after Jerusha in *Hawaii,* I couldn't have come up with a better one than *Millie.* Jerusha was subdued—she had to be, by nature. Millie was so alive that Julie came in every day with a thousand ideas of what to do. She fell completely into the style of the picture. She was damn good-humored and great fun on the set. *Millie* was not like making a movie; the set went absolutely to pieces. We were hysterical and helpless with laughter most of the time."

But Hill, who had been through that firing and rehiring in Hawaii, also paid tribute to her professionalism and business sense: "She is a fantastic businesswoman. I'd put a production in her hands before I'd give it to the so-called businessmen in the studios. And the tremendous professionalism of someone like Julie is a willingness to give, experiment, try. That is the hallmark of the really talented people. She is an enormously gifted girl who has done an extraordinary job with everything she has attempted."

Universal executives late in 1966 took one look at the rough-cut footage Hunter showed them before tearing the film apart again for the piece-by-piece editing, dubbing, and scoring and decided that *Thoroughly Modern Millie* should be a hard-ticket spectacular road show to open as either the Easter or summer big picture for 1967 (Easter was pushing it, but they compromised by making it a spring opening in New York, summer in London, Los Angeles, and elsewhere). The decision distressed Julie, Hill, and Previn who had thought they had a very good, possibly even great, "little" picture on their hands. To be a road show, long enough for an intermission (to allow exorbitant prices to be charged), almost all the footage would have to be left in, including the gratuitous and cynical "Trinkt Lechaim," which Millie sang at a Jewish wedding solely as a sop to the Jewish theater party and matinee trade. Julie had a list of seventy grievances about *Millie*, mostly having to do with length, and she pleaded with Universal to cut the film (particularly the Jewish wedding song) and release it as a regular movie.

But her opinion was based on artistic merits, and that of Lew Wasserman, president of MCA, which owned Universal, and others who saw a chance to cash in on the big trend to road shows in 1967 and on Julie's popularity, was based on money. Money won, and they were having none of her cuts. It was the biggest battle Julie had had with a studio, and it left her cool to Universal. "I wish they had cut just twenty minutes and not made it a road show," she said. "It wasn't planned as a road show, and I think it was blown up too far out of proportion from its original conception." But the picture was released long, and Wasserman was proved right at the box office. *Thoroughly Modern Millie* grossed $30,000,000 and broke *Torn Curtain*'s record as the top grosser for Universal. It also established Julie as the only star who could guarantee the success of a movie (the Burtons had already proved that they could make a pretty good movie do even better, but then even they could not save a true turkey).

The critics rather liked the film. (Crowther in the *Times* said it was "a thoroughly modern burlesque . . . a thoroughly delightful movie. It's hard to say which of the ladies comes out ahead in the end." He finally opted for Carol

Channing, but said Julie "is absolutely darling, deliciously spirited and dry as she picks up the fashions of the period . . . learns the latest dance step, [hits] the right expressions of maidenly surprise and dismay, the right taps in a flow of nimble dances, and the right notes in a flood of icky songs."

Bea Lillie had had a ball, living at the Chateau Marmont, walking down Sunset Boulevard in outlandish outfits, making a twenties musical again (although at dinner parties around town she would repeatedly lament, "Don't you think I should have had a song?"), sometimes having great trouble remembering her dialogue. George Roy Hill became firmly established as a movie director, and Julie made it as a big box-office star and not just a flash-in-the-pan phenomenon. But Carol Channing came out best; she got her *Mary Poppins* in the form of an Oscar nomination, one of seven for *Thoroughly Modern Millie,* including one for the title song and one for Elmer Bernstein for scoring. Bernstein won, but Channing might have pulled a Julie Andrews on her first film (she lost to Estelle Parsons for *Bonnie and Clyde*), and it would have been because she hadn't got *Hello Dolly!*.

Despite the Universal blurb, Julie really didn't dance in *Millie* except in the improvised "Tapioca" number with Fox. "It's just that so many of my movements were choreographed—and so well—that it seems as if I did," she said.

Just after *Millie* was made, but months before it was released, a second but smaller storm cloud gathered over the Warner Brothers Studios in Burbank. Casting was under way for the screen version of *Camelot,* and Jack Warner was personally producing the film, as he had *My Fair Lady.* Warner let it be known that he would like Julie to re-create Guenevere in the film, a tacit admission that he had made a mistake the first time around. He called Arthur Park, who later said that money was not discussed, but that Julie "said she would be interested in being in the film and Warner's said they would submit a script to her." If she ever got the script (she would only say, "There were some tentative feelers, but we couldn't make it work out"), it quickly became academic because Burton, working in a succession of pictures with his wife, was not available and not really interested, and Julie was reluctant to repeat her role without his repeating his. Stories circulated that Julie was asking an outrageous sum (some said as much as $1,200,000) for *Camelot* just to get even, a highly unlikely occurrence. It was doubtful that the negotiations ever got that far.

Instead, Warner signed Richard Harris and Vanessa Redgrave as King Arthur and Guenevere, for comparatively small prices (although the production managed to cost $18,000,000 with lavish sets, costumes, and some location shooting in Spain). Harris and Miss Redgrave (who said, straightforwardly, "I'm sure if Julie Andrews had wanted to play this part, she'd be playing it") did their own singing. Director Josh Logan, for one, couldn't have been more delighted with the casting for the movie, which had been overhauled completely by Alan Jay Lerner, particularly of Vanessa Redgrave—the only one of the *Camelot* principals he liked before, during, and after shooting *and* on the screen. "Can you see two men and two armies going to war over Julie Andrews?" he said, sneering.

XI

IT COULD HAVE BEEN and probably should have been one of the best Hollywood movies ever made: The subject, Gertrude Lawrence, was a glamorous one, if not as universally popular as nuns and children and the Austrian Alps; the star, Julie Andrews, was the most beloved and best paid (and one of the hardest-working) in the world at that time; the director and producer, Robert Wise and Saul Chaplin, had merely made the most successful movie of all time and certainly knew or should have known from *The Sound of Music* what audiences did and did not want; and the studio, Twentieth Century-Fox, out of gratitude and hope was prepared to spend and did spend whatever Wise and Chaplin said it cost ($12,000,000 was the final tally). There was expensive location shooting in London, New York, Cape Cod, and the South of France and even more expensive shooting at the studio. There were songs from George and Ira Gershwin, Kurt Weill, Noel Coward, and Irving Berlin, jewels from Cartier's, clothes from Donald Brooks.

And yet *Star!* was a total failure, artistically, critically, and commercially. It was a big reason for Julie's fast fall from public favor, and it hastened in number and bitterness the attacks on her by the press. It raised new general doubts about the ability of Wise, who had started as a film editor and worked on *Citizen Kane* and *The Magnificent Ambersons* with Orson Welles (despite an Oscar nomination in the

151

editing category, *Star!* was one of the worst-edited films of 1968 or any other year, and Welles later had said of *The Magnificent Ambersons* that "it must have been cut by the studio gardener"). Wise had won Academy Awards as the director of *West Side Story* and *The Sound of Music* and made some of the finest "little" films to come out of Hollywood, like *Executive Suite* and *The Haunting*. But *Star!* had come on the heels of the unsuccess of *The Sand Pebbles*, and the short memories in the movie capital were talking him down.

Wise had spent a good part of three years just getting ready for *Star!*, but Julie spent a year of her life as Gertrude Lawrence. She looked back on the experience as "the most stimulating thing I've ever done—and the most exhausting. And I think it put me off rhinestones forever." (Although Cartier's kindly supplied, in exchange for public exposure, the use of more than $3,000,000 worth of diamonds, rubies, and other jewels, and $200,000 of it was kept at Twentieth for a time, in the charge of the studio police, sometimes lesser stones and even total fakes photographed better. "Jesus, real jewels, as if we didn't have enough problems," Louis "Doc" Merman, Fox's assistant head of the production department, had said at one production meeting during the filming of *Star!*, reported John Gregory Dunne in his excellent book-length exposé of Twentieth, *The Studio*. "The director says it makes the actors feel good, and you can photograph that feeling. That's a load of shit. The main thing you got it for is the publicity.")

Whatever it was for the movie business and the moviegoing public, *Star!*, the musical film biography, more or less, of Gertrude Lawrence, was for *its* star, the biggest British musical-comedy star since, a fascinating study, leading to a generally sympathetic understanding of a woman she never knew or even had seen and revealing the often eerie parallels in their two lives and even "one or two rather unpleasant things about myself that I'd rather not think about."

Julie had been born in 1935, past the midpoint in Miss Lawrence's three-and-a-half-decade career, and way past the midpoint of *Star!*, which took Gertrude Lawrence from the age of six to her triumph in *Lady in the Dark* in 1941 at the age of forty-two. Julie was not yet seventeen when Miss Lawrence died in 1952, and she had never seen her in person. "I'd heard some scratchy old records of hers a few times, but that was about it," Julie said. Yet she was the first and only choice to play "G" or "Gertie" from her vaudeville debut at Brixton at age sixteen, through 95 percent of all the scenes in the movie (a succession of child actresses portrayed the stage star from ages six to fourteen, the first 5 percent of the film, all done in black-and-white neodocumentary style).

Robert Wise had decided that he wanted to make another film with Julie even before *The Sound of Music* was begun, and he was wise enough to sign her for a second film at the same price, a comparatively meager $225,000 with no percentage of the profits. Max Lamb, Wise's story editor and a longtime Gertrude Lawrence enthusiast with a large collection of her records, was assigned to find another vehicle for Julie, and he convinced Wise that Gertrude Lawrence's story was just the thing. "I had Max spend six months digging into the Lawrence legend to see what was possible," Wise recalled. "Then I took it to Julie. I wouldn't have made the picture without her; if she hadn't wanted to do it, I'd have been busy on something else. The great drive was not to do the Gertrude Lawrence story, and we were interested in it only as a starring vehicle for Julie. She was always in it."

Lamb and Wise did not assign a screenplay writer, although stars almost invariably ask to see scripts before they commit themselves to a property. Wise did not want to invest in a writer, buy up the rights to all the books about Gertrude Lawrence (not to mention the rights to all the songs she had sung), "and then have Julie turn it down, leaving me stuck with the Gertie Lawrence story." Instead, Lamb interviewed friends and associates of the late star to see what he could add to the existing literature, which was long in quantity, short on depth and insight. As part of his research he flew to London to see Noel Coward and found him "enormously warm and easy to talk to."

Wise recalled his own nervous meeting with Coward in London: "It would have been impossible to tell Gertie's story without including the important part played by Coward. If he didn't agree, I knew we'd have to give up the whole idea. We'd already been turned down by Beatrice Lillie [who, of course, was an important person and fellow performer in Miss Lawrence's life, had worked with Julie in *Thoroughly Modern Millie,* and was not portrayed at all in *Star!,* just one of the more notable omissions of the movie]. But the first thing he said when we met was, 'Who's going to portray me?' Dan Massey was actually his choice, too. We'd been considering him on a list that included Robert Stephens and Peter Cook."

With Coward's promise of cooperation, Wise was eager to go ahead with the project, although after *The Sound of Music* and with *The Sand Pebbles,* another period—albeit nonmusical—costume drama (the United States Navy in China in the 1920's) coming up next, he would rather have done a smaller picture. Apart from the fantastic rapport among himself and Julie and Saul Chaplin, associate producer of *The Sound of Music* and the full producer of *Star!,* already evident on the Austrian location of the Rodgers and Hammerstein film, Wise sensed the impending success of his still-untried star in the trio's first film, and he and Chaplin could hardly wait to get on with the second. Besides, Wise felt that Julie would be right as Gertie:

"Their lives are somewhat similar; Gertie was a product of music halls, a broken home and stepparents too. Physically there's a certain resemblance, although Julie's a far better singer than Gertie ever was. She was the proper age, too; we were taking Gertie from a young girl into her forties, and Julie can go either way. Both Julie and Gertie had great senses of humor. Gertie was a great clown and had a great love of gagging—Julie does, too."

"Actually, I was first asked to do a [stage] musical about Gertrude Lawrence when I was in *My Fair Lady*," Julie recalled. Wise and Chaplin broached the possibility of their Lawrence story (even then tentatively titled *Star!*) in Austria in April, 1964, during a luncheon lull in the filming of *The Sound of Music* made longer by an Alpine rain. When Wise first mentioned Gertrude Lawrence, Julie thought; "Oh, there it comes again." But Wise sketched in the basic details of Miss Lawrence's life and Julie said, "that sounds a lot like me." When he outlined Lamb's research, she got "terribly enthused," and she agreed to the project before the rain stopped, as her second picture under the $225,000-per contract with Wise.

"He fired my imagination by saying he didn't want to do the usual glamorous backstage sort of story," she said. "Somehow the way he spoke about the theater, how he wanted the draperies to be green velvet and how he wanted to use old-fashioned theaters that Gertie used to play in, got me very excited." And so Wise went ahead and bought the books, including *Gertrude Lawrence as Mrs. A.*, by Richard Aldrich, her husband, and Miss Lawrence's own memoir, *A Star Danced*; he also obtained the rights to all the songs she had ever sung in public (like "My Ship," "Someday I'll Find You," "The Physician," and "Jenny") and to her diaries (which indicated that the books and even some of the friends' and co-workers' memories were exaggerated and embroidered). An Englishman, William Fairchild, was assigned to write an original script that would not be based on either book but would suggest a flavor of the stage star and her on- and offstage personality between the two World Wars. But the film was three years off, since Julie was committed to *Torn Curtain* and *Hawaii* and Wise was involved in *The Sand Pebbles*, which would be shooting on location in Taiwan and Hong Kong.

Finally, in February, 1967, Julie reported to Twentieth Century-Fox in Hollywood to make film quality tests and for fittings on the first of ninety-four separate costumes by designer Donald Brooks that she would wear in the film. The thirty-nine-year-old Brooks was designing for only his third film—after eight Broadway shows and a prestigious private business—and the first in which he did the costumes for the entire cast ("between twenty-five hundred and three thousand designs," he estimated). "I didn't try to make replicas of the clothes of any particular period. Instead, Saul and Bob and I all immersed ourselves in the various periods and I tried to make the clothes believable. The author establishes the character, and then it must be established visually. Bob looks for character in the face and setting. I look for texture, pattern, and color." Brooks was rewarded with an Academy Award nomination, although he lost the Oscar to Danilo Donati for *Romeo and Juliet*.

With *The Boy Friend* and *Thoroughly Modern Millie* in her past, Julie was no stranger to the fashions of the 1920's. But she was eagerly looking forward to her first fling in the 1930's. "Almost everything I've ever done has been set in some different period and that makes it all the more fun," she said—and in the case of *Star!* all the more difficult. Wise and his creative crew insisted on tight adherence to hair and makeup styles of the street and the stage during the Lawrence era. And Gertie Lawrence had changed both frequently.

In those preproduction months of February and March, 1967, at the studio, tests evolved into thirty-six different sets of makeup for Julie and twenty different wigs, each of which could be reset significantly at least once. Armed with these, during the actual shooting, Julie could be forty first thing in the morning, twenty-two at lunchtime, and sixteen at sunset, and one day she actually was. To accommodate the wigs (which were also to be a major factor in her next film, *Darling Lili*), Julie cut her short hair even shorter—and in the process, since almost no one would see it, let it go from her lightened blond back to her natural brown.

In preproduction, Julie also rehearsed dances with choreographer Michael Kidd (despite her days in vaudeville, she is the first to admit: "I don't really dance; if they give me lots of fancy movements, I can make it *look* like I'm dancing") and recorded six of her fifteen songs in which she soloed—she appeared in twenty-one of the twenty-four musical numbers in the film.

Actual filming began in mid-April, 1967, and Julie actually started wearing the largest single wardrobe ever fitted onto an actress for one work. Shooting took 149 days, and Julie was on camera for all but 17 (mostly when Wise and his crew were in London filming childhood scenes with the six juvenile actresses). Of 1,400 separate camera setups, she appeared in 1,372. Wise defended this use of his star by saying, "When a biographical story is being told in film, it is best to have the character be up on the screen nearly all the time rather than having other characters talk about her." Richard Crenna, who played Richard Aldrich, put it another way: "The rest of us are window dressing."

The film set another record—that for the most sets ever assembled for one movie, 185 in all. There were twenty filming sites in London, fourteen different locations in New York (which were shot in only eighteen days) , and historically important visits to the Cape Cod Playhouse in Dennis, Massachusetts, and to the South of France for several scenes at a private $2,000,000 seacoast villa called Medi Roc (it was there that Miss Lawrence attempted unsuccessfully to reconcile with her daughter, whom she had neglected in favor of her career) .

In New York, the company worked in the theater district, in Washington Square, at Tibbetts Brook Park in Yonkers, at the Algonquin Hotel, and, of course, at Cartier's, surrounded by Brink's men. Onstage at the Cort Theater, empty but for a piano and lights, Julie mouthed the words to a prerecorded "My ship has sails that are made of silk; the decks are trimmed with gold," as Miss Lawrence rehearsing the Ira Gershwin-Kurt Weill song. For a week the cast, abetted by 900 extras, simulated the 1926 opening of *Oh, Kay!* at the Lyceum Theater, and Julie sang "Someone to Watch Over Me." It had been almost six years since she had sung on a Broadway stage, and Julie felt "tingling all over, and suddenly realizing I'm having the best of both worlds in one movie."

From New York, the *Star!* company went to Dennis, Massachusetts, where in 1939 Miss Lawrence had worked with Mr. Aldrich, who was producer at the Cape Cod Playhouse, on the tryout of *Skylark,* and married him on her birthday in 1940 (they had met in New York at a party). Julie and Richard Crenna did three days of scenes at the famous theater, which was built in 1790, and at the private home in East Dennis where the Aldriches were married and where he had lived briefly.

Aldrich himself paid a visit to the locations and his first visit inside the house since the wedding twenty-seven years before. He watched Crenna and Julie run through a rain of rice, in the scene of his wedding, to a waiting 1935 Rolls-Royce. And he watched the scene of their first encounter inside the playhouse, she playing the temperamental big star, and he playing the cool small-town businessman who was not impressed. He would make no public comment on Miss Andrews' portrayal of Miss Lawrence or on Crenna's of himself, but watching Julie do the scene in the playhouse, he was heard to whisper, almost to himself, "Remarkable, how much . . ."

The part was great. "When I got into the role and read the script, I couldn't wait to get my hands on all the things she had done," Julie said. "She was an incredibly multitalented lady. What we'd come up with was a rattling good story, credible rather than realistic. Our voices are different, but I suggested inflections and cadences here and there."

But the routine was unbelievably rigorous. "It was like going into training. I had to take care of myself or I'd be dead. I got up at five forty-five every day and had to be on the set by seven, and sometimes I didn't get home until eight. There were only three mornings when I wasn't needed for that first call." (Even rehearsal days, with no shooting, Julie had to be in at nine and stay until six. Because the shooting schedule depended so completely on her, there had to be three separate shutdowns for rehearsing song-and-dance numbers.)

Her only respite in the grueling business of being Gertrude Lawrence was Julie's daily lunch break, usually from about one to two thirty, more often than not taken up with costume fittings, press interviews, out-of-town visitors, and her agent, press agents, business manager, and secretary. But invariably she would clear out her dressing room for fifteen or twenty minutes of "putting my feet up," a nap which would seem to get her through the rest of the day. On rare occasions, daughter Emma Kate Walton would appear, and Julie would visibly brighten as she bounced onto the set. At the end of almost every workday, Blake Edwards would arrive to take her home. And during almost every working day a doctor would arrive to give her a vitamin shot.

During the filming of *Star!* Julie finally divorced her husband of eight years, Tony Walton, deepened her already-fast relationship with Edwards, and enjoyed a long visit from her "real Dad," Ted Wells, and her stepmother, Win. But her real and almost sole preoccupation was Gertie Lawrence. "I can't converse on anything outside this movie," she told me one day in the middle of filming. "I just manage to read the morning paper every day; when I go home at night I collapse. I'm very stale I'm afraid."

Toward the end of the shooting, when Julie was doing musical number after musical number, from "Jenny" to "Limehouse Blues," she said, "The whole thing is so fast and furious it's like a gloriously dangerous game which hopefully one will win." "Jenny," an overproduced, supercinematic, and circusy version of the Kurt Weill song from *Lady in the Dark*, would be on-screen for just over four minutes, but it took two weeks to film, involving as it did acrobatic choreography and singing precision from dozens of performers. And "Limehouse Blues," although in the picture it appeared before the intermission, was the last number filmed, just before Christmas, 1967, and it was heavily choreographed. The principals were exhausted, but the perfectionism of Julie and Wise required retake after retake. If he was satisfied, she was not, but finally after several days, they both were, and the multimillion-dollar musical was finished (but for five more months of scoring and editing before the first sneak preview).

Although Julie found the pace of the film "unrelenting and merciless," there was the time and the need to think about Gertrude Lawrence. "I found myself reflecting on her a lot," Julie said. "And I realized that in many ways she was a sad and lonely woman. Sometimes I get muddled—where does Gertrude leave off and where do I begin?"

To help her tell the difference, Julie kept a file on her desk labeled "Impressions of Gertrude Lawrence—Confidential." And she avowed that as Miss Lawrence was "definitely a kook, eccentric, glamorous and witty," all that was an acting challenge for her. "This was not an attempt at a totally truthful portrait of Gertrude Lawrence, and I didn't feel I was *doing* anything like her," said Julie. "I certainly was not trying to sing like her. I don't think her voice was particularly strong or pretty. The result was part me, part script, and part her. I was not trying to be faithful to the way people remember her—I don't think I could be."

The black-and-white newsreellike movie-within-a-movie technique that Wise used in *Star!* at times made it seem more like an attempt at a documentary than it was intended to be. Julie defended it. "It doesn't go by the book in every episode. But I think each thing in the picture is a genuine possibility."

Walking "the fine line between caricature and tribute and avoiding impersonation" was not easy for Julie. "In some ways trying to be a character like her is not as good or as solid as doing something right from *Private Lives*. When you try to *be* someone, the temptation is to lay it on with mannerisms and speech. But if I did that, I'd only be applying it rather than feeling it myself."

Wise, who normally would have nothing bad to say about Julie's abilities, was troubled during production by her failure to apply the more flamboyant aspects of Miss Lawrence's personality to her portrayal. "If Julie has anything, it is a quality of honesty and truthfulness," he said, "and that has made her doubtful and given her difficulty with some of the theatricality of Gertie's behavior. If she has had to work hard on anything, it has been on the volatile and hammy aspects of Gertie. She doesn't quite realize yet how many things she can make her own."

Daniel Massey also had some reservations about his performance as Noel Coward. John Gregory Dunne quoted him in *The Studio* as saying: "I'm going to be pilloried. There's no doubt about it. People are going to say I'm just imitating Noel. I'm not you know. I could imitate him of course. But that's going the Frank Gorshin route. That's all right for night clubs, but I'm not a mimic." When the film opened, no one thought Massey was imitating Coward, and he even got an Academy Award nomination.

As an actress who up to that point had played only fictional heroines (with the one exception of the semifictional and highly romanticized Maria Von Trapp), Julie found that "what was really fascinating for me was when the application of certain things in her life [as seen through the screenplay] and truthfulness in mine blended."

For openers, there were "the obvious biographical facts,

like separated parents and starting in vaudeville" (to say nothing of a brief first marriage ending in divorce, one daughter, and a love affair with a producer). Miss Lawrence had debuted at the age of sixteen, singing "Piccadilly" with her father and his woman partner (and lover) at the Brixton Music Hall. Julie had also played Brixton, when she was fourteen, with her mother and stepfather, Barbara and Ted Andrews. (On the same bill then was Beryl Reid, who played Gertie's father's partner in the Brixton scenes in *Star!*).

Both actresses also played Swansea, and much later in their respective careers both achieved significant success playing Eliza Doolittle, Miss Lawrence in George Bernard Shaw's "straight" *Pygmalion*, to Raymond Massey's Henry Higgins, and Miss Andrews in the musical version, *My Fair Lady* (Julie didn't get to play Gertie playing Eliza because that production, by Richard Aldrich, was in 1945, and the film ends with the *Lady in the Dark*, opening in 1941). Moreover, both Gertie and Julie were directed by Moss Hart, Julie in *My Fair Lady*, Gertie in *Lady in the Dark*.

Julie along the way discovered several traits she and the star had in common: "We both whistled a lot, and we both were always lapsing into bits of Cockney. She had a habit of singing a high note to relieve the tension. I do the same thing, sing as loud and as high as I can.

"She was extravagant. I am too—even more so after I played her. She would fill her dressing room with flowers; she once bought a large cherry tree because it was in bloom." Julie likes plants and flowers too, but said, "I'm certainly not as extravagant of gesture. But I think I understand her quite well. I think I know how she felt. When you're in the theater on matinee day from noon until midnight, you don't see daylight. You want some living thing in your room."

At picture's end, in December, Julie was trying to buy Christmas presents the way she bought pretty much everything except food when she was working: by having the stores send items out to her dressing room on approval. Between Donald Brooks and his costumes and the best that Jax (as in Jax Slax) and the other Beverly Hills boutiques had to offer, that second-floor cottagelike "star" dressing suite at Fox (which Rex Harrison had also had for *Dr. Dolittle*) looked somewhat like a store itself. And Julie was buying expensive presents for all. "I'm spending more money now," she told me at the time. "I figure, what the hell, since I'm playing her, I might as well spend like her. I went berserk for Christmas. Whether it will disappear when the next movie comes along, I don't know."

The extravagance parallel had a limit: Miss Lawrence at her peak was earning $3,500 a week onstage (Julie in a good week made $30,000 or more in movies) but went $75,000 in debt and drove to bankruptcy court in a Rolls-Royce. Julie has a careful, conservative business manager, who during *Hawaii* wouldn't let her buy a Mercedes Benz and insisted she keep her Ford Mustang compact, perhaps with a new set of tires, and who had to approve the purchase of every painting or major piece of furniture.

One more certainly permanent result of her playing Gertrude Lawrence was that Julie, never one of Hollywood's (or New York's or London's) best-dressed women, renewed her interest in expensive clothes, became interested for the first time in jewels ("I wish I could have kept them all"), and found happiness in the design boards of Donald Brooks. He went on to design her clothes for *Darling Lili* and for her closet. He made the stunning long and billowy gown she wore to the 1968 Academy Awards—where she presented the best picture Oscar to Walter Mirisch, her old *Hawaii* producer, for *In the Heat of the Night*—and it was the first time she had ever looked good in black.

The "hateful" things Julie found she and Gertie had in common were "an absolute fear of any kind of commitment" and "always putting on an act. She would play at being a mother one minute, a gardener the next, a shopper the next.

I'm rather like that." She told me this in her dressing room
one day just as we were about to have lunch. And in a perfect and probably unconscious illustration of her last point,
she called out to the kitchen to "Mom," Mrs. Lorraine Roberson, her adored hairdresser and chief fusser: "Is there anything I can do to help?" Julie had no more business in the
kitchen at that moment than I did and almost certainly had
never helped "Mom" make lunch for company, but the moment, because it involved a hard truth, had become uncomfortable, calling for her to shift gears.

Julie most disliked Miss Lawrence's outbursts, being intensely controlled herself. "I'm not as fiery a temperament as
she was," she said. "She was not a terribly nice person; in
fact, she was a real bitch at times." But Julie loved not being
Millie Dilmount, Maria Von Trapp, or Jerusha Hale. "This
feels like the first *character* I've ever done," she said with a
touch of laryngitis in her voice at the end of filming *Star!*.
She and Emma and Blake were about to depart for a month-
long ski holiday in Gstaad. "It's been very pleasant to play—
to be—somebody like that for real for once."

At the end of every film in Hollywood, no matter how bad
those involved expect the product to be or how much they
may hate one another, there is a cast and crew party on the
very last day of shooting. *Star!*, where there was great optimism and mutual respect and liking, was expected to have
one of the better movie-closing parties, and it did, although
the proceedings were strangely muted, probably owing more
to exhaustion than to a lack of enthusiasm. These affairs can
be simple or elaborate, catered by Chasen's or cooked up by
the studio commissary (Barbra Streisand reportedly had
flown in hot dogs from Nathan's on Coney Island at the
finish of *Funny Girl* in Hollywood), and they don't necessarily, but usually do, involve supper. The *Star!* party was medium elaborate, served right on the "Limehouse Blues" set
on Stage Seven, the last set to be used in the picture. It
started on a Friday, at six thirty, and was planned to be over

early, since Christmas was a week from the next Monday and
no one on the picture had had time to get ready for the holiday. Normally members of the press are never invited to these
functions (often even wives and husbands of cast and crew
can't come). I asked the morning of the party if I could this
once, never having been to a closing party and having a special interest in this film, and as an old friend of the family, so
to speak, I was admitted.

An elderly Dixielandish band tactlessly played "Hello,
Dolly!" the title song from Twentieth Century-Fox's other
big musical in the works, and other numbers dancier than
Star!'s "Burlington Bertie" and "In My Garden of Joy,"
which Saul, sometimes called Sollie, Chaplin had written
himself because he couldn't find an existing number awful
enough for Julie as Gertie to misperform with a catty clutch
of chorus girls. I asked Robert Wise how he felt at the moment. He answered, "Marvelous and nervous," and he
looked both. Michael Kidd, the short, dark-haired dancer-
choreographer, and his friend and assistant choreographer, a
pretty brunette named Sheila Hackett, just looked nervous.
They were to repeat their jobs on *Hello, Dolly!* beginning
rehearsals the very next week. The cocktail hot dogs and
cold shrimp were an enormous success, and the food tables
were almost as crowded as the bars when Julie walked in
in a white mink jacket and with her secretary, Joan Mansfield, shortly after seven. Somebody told the band to forget
the dancing and at least to play the new Jimmy Van Heusen-
Sammy Cahn title song from the picture at hand in honor
of the lady who had arrived.

The London (and world) premiere of *Star!* at the Dominion Theatre, originally scheduled for July 4, 1968, which
would have been Gertrude Lawrence's sixty-seventh birthday, had been postponed until September 11, then pushed
back to July 18, in both cases owing to the availability of royalty, the Duke and Duchess of Kent, who were the patrons of
the premiere, for the benefit of the National Advertising Be-

nevolent Society. Twentieth Century-Fox executives adjusted and readjusted their schedules, and when the night came, Chaplin and Wise with their wives, both Daryl and Richard Zanuck, Richard and Penny Crenna, Donald Brooks, William Fairchild, and David and Helen Gurley Brown (he being the vice-president of Fox in charge of story operations) appeared. So did others, like Noel Coward, Dame Edith Evans, Natalie Wood, Lord Louis Mountbatten and Cathleen Nesbitt (who had played Mrs. Higgins onstage in *My Fair Lady* with Julie)—and Julie's mother, her father and stepmother, and two brothers.

Coward had a prepremiere cocktail party at his river suite in the Savoy, for some of his friends who remembered Miss Lawrence for one reason or another. Among them were Miss Nesbitt, Anna Massey, whose father had played Higgins in *Pygmalion* opposite Miss Lawrence and whose brother played Coward in the film, and Margalo Gillmore. Although he had contributed heavily to the screenplay, writing his own dialogue for Daniel Massey (and thereby assuring some shred of accuracy in at least his own screen image) without screen credit but with a sizable stipend, Coward was skeptical of the final result. As his group was leaving the Savoy for the Dominion, he said, "It will unquestionably be a marvelous commercial film, and Julie Andrews and Danny will be marvelous; so will all those nostalgic, unforgettable songs. But it won't bear the slightest possible resemblance to the Gertie we knew."

And thus *Star!* arrived—but its star didn't. The airplane that had been chartered to stand by at Heathrow Airport to fly to Brussels to fetch Julie from the *Darling Lili* location had never left London. The flower-packed suite at the Dorchester held in reserve for her would not be used. At the last minute, word came from Paramount's people on *Darling Lili* in Brussels that night shooting involving thousands of extras would keep her there. The Zanucks were furious and blamed it on Blake and Paramount and professional jealousy in no particular order. Wise and Chaplin who knew Julie very well by then were upset because it was unlike her not to appear at something so important to all of them when she had promised to do so. The crowds, both inside and outside the theater, did not get the word immediately and unbelievingly, in vain, searched for the star. They were shattered when she did not show up. Even the Duchess of Kent asked: "Where's Julie?"

Without Julie, the film was shown to the public in England for the first time, and the premiere audience came down firmly on two sides: Those who had known Gertrude Lawrence or even remembered having seen her just once or twice on stage were likely to resent the portrait of her as written and played; those who didn't remember her were likely to have been as charmed by *Star!* as by any other Julie Andrews musical. And the popular London critics divided approximately the same way, although the serious Sunday critics were harsher with Wise and Fairchild for taking such liberties with a recent life. The film nonetheless did well at the box office in its first weeks in London, well enough to keep reserved-seat selected cities plans in force in the United States, and the critical reception was regarded as positively enthusiastic compared to the ones that were to follow in the United States.

When the film opened at the Rivoli Theater on Broadway in New York on October 22, 1968 (again without the star, who had pleaded pressing scenes on *Darling Lili*), the reviewers' welcome was the chilliest of all. Even the New York *Daily News*, whose readers could be expected to be among the most ardent fans of the movie, tempered its usual uncritical enthusiasm for big-budget "family" films. Renata Adler, who had succeeded Bosley Crowther as the *Times* movie critic, devastatingly dismissed *Star!* in four icy paragraphs, which was less space than it took some of her critics to dismiss Miss Adler.

Miss Adler and others complained of the excessive length

of the 174-minute-plus-intermission movie musical, but
none so violently as WCBS-TV's Leonard Harris, who said
the night of the opening, on the eleven o'clock news: "The
only reason I can think of for making big pictures so long
nowadays is to justify the hard ticket prices, which in the case
of *Star!* go as high as four dollars and fifty cents. *Star!* would
not be any better if it were shorter, but it would let go of
you an hour sooner, and that would be a substantial bless-
ing.

"*Star!* is a sort of gentile *Funny Girl* and not nearly as
good. It is a clichéd cataloguing of the life and hard times of
Gertrude Lawrence, with Julie Andrews as Miss Lawrence,
and it compounds its spurious attitudes toward show business with its terrible handling of the actual performance
numbers."

Star!, which Richard Zanuck termed "my Edsel," was not
the horror most critics made it out to be, but it was less than
very good. It bore little relevance to Gertrude Lawrence, it
was too long, and the "Jenny" number from *Lady in the
Dark* that serves as a semifinale was grossly overproduced.
Julie was extraordinary in terms of attempting to cope with
an impossible part that was probably wrong for her from the
beginning, but this was one place where energy and verve
(and a quite good sound track) couldn't overcome a lack of
inspiration in script and direction.

It ran at the Rivoli until March, 1969, and played to piti-
fully small audiences. The pattern was repeated in other
road-show cities in the United States, and the picture was
withdrawn and rereleased, after some cutting, as a regular
feature at regular prices. Still, even the hard-core Andrews
fans didn't go to see it, and Twentieth recalled it altogether
on July 1, 1969. Further cuts were made, from 165 minutes
to 2 hours, without consulting director Robert Wise. Twentieth changed the title to *Those Were the Happy Times*, hired
a new advertising agency, and reissued it in October, attempt-

ing to prove—against all previous experience—that expensive failures cold be salvaged.

Once *Star!* was actually out, Julie had very little to say about it. As usual she would not criticize for the record the director, any of her fellow performers, or the final product itself. She felt reasonably good about her own performance, although "there were a thousand little things I would like to have changed, like the Jenny wig and the shape of Gertie's mouth in her and the early twenties." And one hot August day in 1968, outside Paris at the Château d'Anet, the sixteenth-century home of Diane de Poitiers, in the middle of making *Darling Lili* and after the London opening, she said of *Star!:* "I feel like I'm still making it." She explained the razzle-dazzle of the "Jenny" number: "Everything we did in the film was tied to the theater: It was about a woman of the theater, and all the numbers were performed on a stage of some sort. This was the one song we felt we could do as a *movie* musical number, not a stage one, and we were all longing desperately to break out and so we did. If it didn't work, that's too bad." Also Julie didn't like the "Jenny" lyric any more than Gertie did (both termed it "lousy"), "and so we really wanted to do *something* with it" (since it was essential as a semifinale). In her trailer dressing room outside the château Julie talked of her nonappearance at the London premiere in the most pleading terms: "Of all the premieres, this was the one I really wanted to go to. This was home, one's family, royalty and all one's chums. I'd had a dress designed in Dublin, and of all the movies I'd made, this was the one I cared about most. But they had changed the date twice—it was in my contract with Paramount that I would have the night of July fourth off no matter what—and we were in Belgium, behind and with hundreds of extras involved in night shooting. Up until three hours before the time of the premiere I thought I was going to make it. Blake had figured out how to use a double for me in a long shot.

But as the time got closer, we realized that even with using that long shot—which he didn't really want to do—and having the cast and crew wait another hour or so, I could still only fly to London just in time to get to the theater, walk through the front door, and walk right out again. I wouldn't even have got to see my family or friends. And so I didn't go."

Both she and Blake were embittered by the reaction of the British and American press to her failure to show up, and he even more because of the behavior of Twentieth Century-Fox executives who had called their counterparts at Paramount in Hollywood and begged them to call Blake in Brussels to get him to let Julie have the night off. "How could anyone doubt that she wanted to go to the opening and that I wanted her to go?" Blake asked. "It would have been good for Paramount and for us, too. But it was just impossible." Both studios in turn were angry with Edwards for having what they considered an evil influence and final authority over her (particularly since he was spending Paramount's money hand over fist and way over budget anyway, what was one night, even with 900 extras, more or less?). No one involved doubted that Gertrude Lawrence, faced with the same situation, would have told her producer-director (even if he had been her lover or husband) to go to hell and flown to London for at least two days.

XII

ON MAY 10, 1959, Julie married Tony Walton at St. Mary's village church of Oatlands, Weybridge, Surrey, fifteen miles southwest of London. Two thousand fans turned up outside the church. Noel Harrison, the somewhat-estranged son of Rex, was best man; he had gone to school with Tony. She wore a white organza silk dress that he had designed. The reception was held at the Mitre, a 300-year-old inn opposite Hampton Court Palace on the Thames River bank. A portent of the success that was to overtake both of them, her on a more sensational scale, was the fact that the wedding took place during a three-week vacation from the London run of *My Fair Lady*, and for a wedding trip they went to California where she had to tape a television special anyway. The twenty-three-year-old bride returned to *My Fair Lady* on May 25.

Since that first day eleven years before on the train to Walton after *Humpty Dumpty*, when Tony and his three friends had asked Julie for her autograph (and the next day "he came around himself and asked for photographs, and later he wrote me from school—that's the way it began, I guess"), he and she had been what Tony described as "sort of mates, we saw each other at vacation times, and whenever we could."

Despite the work-tinged wedding, there were some indications that Julie had meant it when she said, during the New York run of *My Fair Lady*: "I'd like to work for another two years, awfully hard, then marry, then have lots of children. I really wouldn't mind retiring; it doesn't matter that much to me. I could work locally or in London and do one thing a year. If you can get it all done and settle down, it's worthwhile. I'm sure it may not work out that way, but I hope so." She had said that or something like that so many times in New York, all the while disclaiming any particular plans with Tony. Her engagement to Tony, she recalled, had "just evolved—I don't remember one glorious night on bended knee. We were—and here's the cliché—just good friends for a very long time, and then it grew into love. I guess you could say we were childhood sweethearts, and I'm very glad we were. On the day we got married I was glad I had known him so long. It's a big step to take, and it's better to do it with someone you know."

The day before the wedding she had spent the morning at her apartment on Eaton Square, in a cotton housecoat answering the deliveries of wedding presents. The afternoon she divided between her dressmaker, a theatrical costumer in a dingy building in Soho—while Tony waited outside. He may have designed the dress, but he wasn't going to see her in it until the wedding. She had a late-afternoon sitting for a portrait with Pietro Annigoni and, typically, dinner with her business manager ("to talk about money"), and equally typically, she stayed up late writing thank-you notes for presents.

For the first few years the marriage was an extremely happy one. She did *Camelot* on Broadway, which did not put too many demands on her or him or them, and they lived in a seventeenth-floor extreme East Side apartment overlooking Welfare Island with a gray French poodle named Shy; then came *Mary Poppins,* which, despite its being a new experience for both of them, meant they could be together in the rented English countryside cottage in the somewhat Waltonish (if hotter and browner) San Fernando Valley. Emma Kate came on November 27, 1962. Julie had mothered her younger brothers, particularly Chris, who was eleven years younger than she, and she attributed her notable whistling ability to the fact that there were three younger boys in the house. She had long wanted children of her own, and she wanted more than one. "I'd like a family of three or five boys, weather and tide permitting, as we say in England," she had said many times. "Tony wants girls. I just want a family of little Tonys."

Marriage, according to Julie "helped me stand on my own two feet," and until *The Americanization of Emily* there were no separations longer than two months. But even as success overtook her in Hollywood, it overtook him in New York and London, where he became one of the most successful and best-regarded costume and set designers in the theater with *Valmouth, Golden Boy,* and *The Apple Tree*. After *Mary Poppins* Arthur Park, Julie's agent, had found another movie job for Tony, but he had turned it down to go back East and carve out his own career in his own way. (After the marriage began to crack, he returned to movies, but not in Hollywood. He designed *Fahrenheit 451*, based on the Ray Bradbury story and starring Julie Christie, *A Funny Thing Happened on the Way to the Forum, The Seagull,* based on the Chekhov play—all European productions—and *Petulia,* another film starring the other Julie, directed by Richard Lester and shot in San Francisco.)

Even in the early years of their marriage, Julie made more money than Tony, "but this has never made any difference," she said in 1961. "I get mine in chunks; he gets his regularly, and I expect he'll work far longer than I will." In later years, as the disparity became even greater, Walton ignored his wife's income, instead of being humiliated by it. The salaries were kept separate, and by mutual agreement money was seldom discussed. "It was mostly pride on my part—no, almost entirely pride," he said. "I couldn't conceivably afford the sort of house Julie has in Hollywood, so that sort of expenditure falls entirely on her." (A house in Wimbledon that they lived in together less than a few months was a joint project.)

"If Tony minds my being Julie Andrews, he certainly

doesn't let me know it," she said in 1961, and the only time he resented being called Mr. Julie Andrews was on Alderney in 1964, at a dinner party. "A speech was made by someone which referred in a pleasant enough way to 'Mr. Julie Andrews,' " he recalled. "It got to me like a shot, I don't know why. Maybe because Alderney is such a private, defended sort of place for us."

But Hollywood is anything but a defended place, and the Waltons' separations became longer and longer, aggravated by their "rule never to work on the same thing at the same time," in Tony's words. "There are enough risks without imposing further ones. If I were to decide just to go to Hollywood whatever happened and be with Julie, it would be a way of being together. But the few times I have been there and not been able to get on with the work that I find satisfying I've become impossible to be with. And that's as dangerous as not being there at all. Some husbands of stars can fit into the 'agent-manager' role, but I'm not agently inclined, and there's pride involved too."

Julie had also rejected their working together as a solution. During *Hawaii*, when Tony was working on *A Funny Thing Happened on the Way to the Forum* in Spain, halfway around the world, she said: "We are apart a lot, and it is a problem; it's not easy at all. If he were to follow me around and be Mr. Julie Andrews, that wouldn't solve anything. We have periods of being enormously lucky, when we can work it out to be together. The rest of the time we have a sort of joint agreement, not to make any demands on the other and a kind of freedom which I find rather marvelous. It isn't easy, especially with Emma. She adores Tony, and one can see why. He is endlessly patient, very kind, a loving father, rock solid."

One obvious solution would have been for Julie to quit her career, which Tony thought would have been possible in the first two years of their marriage, "because we were both in the theater, and it was never so hard to be together. And she's never been that passionate about the theater." But as she became a movie star, she felt that to retire "would probably lead to a dreadful resentment in me." And Tony agreed that Hollywood stardom had really involved her for the first time, "because despite all her years in the business, this was the first time that she had any real self-confidence, a real feeling that she has a firm grip on things. I don't think she'd like to drop that feeling, not yet anyway. This confidence is the most marvelous and valuable thing about her success, and I wouldn't want to be responsible for taking that away from her."

Julie acknowledged that Tony bolstered her newfound self-confidence, and Elsie Giorgi, Emma's doctor and a friend of both Julie and Tony, said, "Tony was very important to her, and she would be the first to say so whatever happened." Tony felt that one of the great strengths of their marriage was that they were each capable of taking the pressure off the other, particularly when they were both in the theater. "At times I'd find myself taking on an almost feminine role, trying to calm, soothe, protect or whatever," he said. "And then as soon as I was deeply involved, the roles would be reversed. I think if I were an overly dominant kind of male, I'd find this situation harder to cope with. But neither of us is overpoweringly masculine or overpoweringly feminine, so this switching of roles is a way of making a difficult situation work, but it's hardly the final answer. I think it's very hard for many women to feel really happy about it. They're grateful that this is possible so that they can work and be independent, but ultimately they resent a man easing up on his dominance for a second."

For a time, Tony and Julie kept in touch by daily tapes, "Julie saying how frightened she was of acting, how unreal the whole thing was. But we got too good at the tapes and a bit too tricky. Every once in a while I'd get one from Julie saying, 'It's midnight, and I'm just dragging in from rehearsal,' and I could hear the birds singing in the background."

But even as late as the winter of 1966–67, after the separation had become permanent, Julie went out of her way at times to bolster Tony's career and temporarily submerge hers. She went with him to see *The Apple Tree* and praised his work, and she told anyone who would listen that *Fahrenheit 451* was the best thing Tony had ever done. Still, it was only faintly reminiscent of the time she went especially to Oxford for the opening of a stage version of *A Funny Thing Happened on the Way to the Forum.* Two women dimly recognized her face in the foyer of the theater, and one asked her: "Would you mind telling us if you have anything to do with this production?" Julie Andrews smiled and said, "Certainly. I'm Mrs. Walton. My husband designed the scenery."

It was in October, 1966, that Tony and Julie decided to make their physical separation a permanent one. It was not to be a trial separation in the usual meaning of the word— there had already been enough trials in separation for that— but it was not a legal separation either. The Waltons stayed legally married for another fourteen months. "We just decided to try it this way and see what happens," Julie told me at the time. The split was not, she said, "brought on by any one particular rift—there were many reasons, all of them intensely personal. But we have known each other much too long to fight. We are very good friends, as corny as that sounds. He is the best counsel, friend adviser I have. I really do value his advice more than anyone's. He is one of the biggest influences in my life. I can't put my finger on it exactly, because it's in so many areas. But he's terribly bright, a very intelligent boy. His general help has been fantastic. And his parents are the best bloody in-laws anyone could ever have. They're a very 'family-family'—extremely close."

The Tony Waltons at their happiest had never been a

"family-family," and both Julie and Tony regretted it, on Emma's behalf at least. Even before the separation Tony complained that he had seen his daughter only about a third of the time she had been alive. "I've been overprotective about that, I know," Julie admitted, "but to see him would involve some kind of upheaval for her, a trip to New York or something like that. She talks to him on the phone two or three times a week, and she sees him whenever they can get together."

At the time of the separation, Tony appeared to be much more in love with his wife than she with him, and much less willing to let their twenty-year relationship go by the boards. In early 1967 he was scheduled to be in San Francisco, working on what was then called *Me and the Archkook Petulia*, and he talked of being within "striking distance" for a reconciliation. He told Elsie Giorgi: "Julie is the only girl for me, the most important thing in my life," and Dr. Giorgi said, "He had this marvelous daydream that they'd get back together again, but that's what it was—a daydream." Julie, of course, had already been linked with John Calley and was by then allied with Blake Edwards (she would allow at the time that both men were "very good friends"). Her friendship with Mike Nichols seemed to be a platonic one, although they sometimes went out together, and during *Torn Curtain* she had been hostess at a party he gave at The Daisy, in those pre-Factory days the "in" place in Beverly Hills. Lorraine Roberson and Bill Buell had stayed late in her dressing room the night before to prepare her. "Like Cinderella, all fixed up for the party with pants and a big scarf. That's the sort of thing that should happen to you when you're eighteen—a lot of fuss and a glamorous party. I'm thirty." The guests had included Richard and Elizabeth Taylor Burton, Lana Turner, Sean Connery, and Rock Hudson, and of course, the party made news. Julie, whose all-purpose Watusi and passable frug were as tentative as those of Lynda Bird Johnson in her George Hamilton salad days, said the next morning, "I do hope they didn't send shots of my wriggling rear end all across the country." (They didn't.)

While the flashy dates with Nichols got the headlines, it was the talented director of *Breakfast at Tiffany's* and *Days of Wine and Roses* who was really making the scene with Mary Poppins. They were having dinner together most nights, often at such public places as La Scala, in Beverly Hills. They took weekend cruises together and held hands under the table at a dinner party for eighty at the Bel Air home of the Anthony Newleys, prompting one male nonfan to sneer: "She even conducts an affair like Mary Poppins!"

During this period Julie would go out with other people, like Roddy McDowall, who was Mordred in the stage *Camelot*, "whatever's needed, whenever," as she put it. Her father, Ted Wells, visited her, and "I had a splendid field day with the gossipmongers. I went everywhere, clinging gaily to his arm. I enjoyed it, thinking what the fan magazines might be making of it."

Julie had met Blake Edwards at a party given by Peter Sellers at the Beverly Hills Hotel in 1963, at the completion of *A Shot in the Dark,* in which Sellers had starred and which Edwards directed. "It was a cursory meeting with just the usual bullshit," Blake recalled. " 'I admire your work.' 'I admire yours, too.' " They saw each other infrequently after that, in passing at Goldwyn Studios during *Hawaii* and *What Did You Do in the War, Daddy?* or at parties or in the homes of members of their overlapping sets of friends, which included Nichols, Calley, and the Previns. But it was a less than complimentary remark by him that got back to her that started the romance in earnest. Talking with a group of men at the Mirisch Company at Goldwyn Studios one day, Blake said offhandedly that Julie was "so sweet she probably has violets in between her legs." When Julie heard about it, she sent Blake a bunch of violets and a note, and the romance was officially under way.

Blake Edwards, a small man with a full head of brown hair, had been born in Tulsa, Oklahoma, but was third-generation Hollywood. His grandfather had directed Theda Bara in silent movies, and his father was a production manager. He himself started as an actor, playing the local boxing champion who was floored by Cameron Mitchell in Richard Quine's *Leather Gloves*. He wrote for radio and then wrote and directed B movies. He created the television series *Peter Gunn* and made a succession of movies of varying merit and success, including *The Great Race, The Pink Panther,* and *The Party*. He was charming and intelligent and, like anyone who had spent his life in Hollywood, surrounded by enemies—perhaps by more than his share.

"I have always—whether at a distance or in early cursory meetings or now—felt that this lady was one of the most unusual ladies I've ever been near," Edwards said. "She has an aura about her that I'm tremendously impressed by. I have a natural ambivalence about actresses. I usually withdraw from them instinctively at the beginning. They're fine in their place but I can't have any kind of relationship with them. She's different. She's vitally professional. Her instincts are so damn good. You'll never see her throwing her weight around or being competitive past normal competitiveness, and she seems to be aware of the pitfalls of this business more than most."

Edwards and Julie started dating, "in a very discreet way, trying not to hurt anyone, least of all ourselves," and yet he slightly contradicted himself when he recalled their first date. "I had a Rolls-Royce convertible then, and as we were driving down Sunset Boulevard, I turned to Julie and said, 'This is a hell of a way to be anonymous, driving down Sunset Boulevard in an open Rolls-Royce with Mary Poppins.'" He was legally separated from his wife of fourteen years and close to a final divorce. His wife, a nonprofessional, lived in London with their two children, Jennifer and Jeffrey. Edwards lived alone in a large old-style movie director's house in the Hollywood Hills, not more than fifteen minutes from Julie's.

Long before they started going together on a serious basis, Julie and Blake decided to do a picture together, a property that he, a writer turned director and producer, had written. And since Paramount agreed to assume the production of *Darling Lili, or Where Were You on the Night You Said You Shot Down Baron von Richthofen?* Blake said, "While Julie and I are not irrevocably bound together in the deal, we can't really turn back. I think it's risky, our working together or working with friends in general. I'm determined to keep my personal life apart from my business life, and they inevitably get mixed up if you work with friends. If I had it to do over again, I would, based on our friendship, try to get out of it. But knowing her and myself at this point, if any two people stand a chance of working together and getting away with it, I'd say we do."

Edwards' separation and divorce had been long in the works and were not instigated by his friendship with Julie, and he was affronted by anyone who suggested that the star was a home wrecker. "It is as wrong as it can be, and unfair to all concerned, particularly to my wife and children, to say that Julie had anything to do with my marriage breaking up," he said. "It was a combination of a lot of things, and my wife and I are trying to organize our separate lives. But that has nothing to do with Julie."

Edwards, who was forty-three to her thirty when they met, after the violet incident developed nothing but unbridled and genuine admiration for Julie, personally and professionally. "I feel certain that whatever it is that makes that girl what she is is profound and unique. I told her very early in our friendship that she was an unusual girl. She said, 'I'm not, and don't be surprised to find out someday that I'm not.' Whatever Julie is does come through on-screen. She is an amazingly good actress for my taste. I am startled at times by the honesty of her performance. Now that I know the lady from whence it comes I know that she has an enormous vista yet to trod."

Through *Thoroughly Modern Millie* and *Star!* the friendship ripened into a full-fledged and semipublic romance. And on November 14, 1967, Julie, through her lawyer, Allen E. Susman, filed for a California divorce from Tony Walton, on the usual show-business grounds of mental cruelty. The thirty-two-year-old actress, who had been living apart from her husband for three years, said in a typically terse statement issued the same day she filed the divorce action in the Santa Monica Superior Court: "The varying demands of our careers have kept Tony and me apart for long periods of time, thus placing obvious strains upon our marriage. It has therefore become clear that a divorce will be in the best interests of all concerned."

Julie had taken the final step to end her marriage only after the most careful thought and in California, where it takes a divorce on any grounds one year from the date of filing to become final. And she did not appear to be any more eager to commit herself to a second marriage than she had been to finish the first. She and "Blackie" were spending more and more time together, at his new house in Malibu, with her daughter, with his children, in California and in Switzerland, where they spent part of the months of December, 1967, and January, 1968, and December, 1968, and January, 1969. But marriage was not yet on her mind.

One day in the late summer of 1967 I had lunch with Julie at Twentieth Century-Fox when *Star!* was in full swing, coincidentally the day after I had had a lunch interview with Ingrid Bergman at the Los Angeles Music Center, where she was about to star in the last-surviving Eugene O'Neill play, *More Stately Mansions.* Julie had met Miss Bergman only that once in her dressing room during *My Fair Lady,* but she had always had enormous admiration for the Swedish star, who twenty years before had held Julie's throne only to be driven off it and from the country—and for an adulterous affair with a director! Miss Bergman had returned to the city that had exiled her in 1952 for the first time (excepting the briefest trip in 1957 to accept her second Academy Award, for *Anastasia*—the first had been for *Gaslight*—the same American trip on which she had seen *My Fair Lady*) since the birth of her illegitimate child by Roberto Rossellini, whom she had since divorced. Miss Bergman had come back not out of love or forgiveness ("God, it's an ugly city," she had said to me before lunch, looking out from the music center patio), but simply because she considered O'Neill "your greatest playwright," and because the play would be taken on to Broadway, and "it is not so easy to get the parts now."

"It's a brave thing for her to do," said Julie, "especially in this town." But Julie was positively livid at the thought there were those in the Hollywood community who still disapproved of the way Miss Bergman had conducted her life and at the thought of her having to leave in the first place. "How dare 'they' judge another human being?" Julie asked. "Who knows what goes on in anyone else's life?" Julie opined that the form of hypocrisy was "the last dregs of the big star era, when the public and the press decided how a star should behave."

Julie, of course, at that time was feeling more than ever the weight of *her* public adultery. And she felt strongly that it was nobody's business but her own and Blake's (and possibly Emma's and Tony's). "I mostly do what I want to do and don't care what anyone thinks," she said. "I do try not to hurt anyone. People will talk and gossip, and there is nothing you can do, so you might just as well go your own sweet way. There is nothing I wish to announce or tell the world. When there is, I will. Until then I'd rather as well leave it alone. I don't think anybody goes out of her way to be a scarlet woman, but then there is very little I can do about it if that's what they want to make of it."

Blake agreed with Julie's sentiments about their affair. "You know that you're going to live your lives the way you want to anyway," he said, "but I'm in a better position than she because I'm not a celebrity. The fans and the fan magazines want to know every move she makes, but she is a very bright girl about that. We both feel that they're gonna say what they're gonna say anyway. You can't avoid that unless you get out of the business."

Certainly Blake and Julie had no intention of getting out of show business; in fact, they were just getting ready to go further into it together, despite their own instincts and pronouncements about working on the same projects with one's husband, wife, lover, friend. *Darling Lili, or Where Were You on the Night You Said You Shot Down Baron von Richthofen?* (the title was shortened in Europe when, but not necessarily because, the budget was lengthened) was, in Blake's words, "a play with music," using, as *Star!* had, existing songs of the period—in this case circa 1915, during World War I. Henry Mancini and Johnny Mercer, who had written the Academy Award-winning songs "Moon River" for Edwards' *Breakfast At Tiffany's* and "Days of Wine and Roses," for the director's film of the same name, were signed to write seven new songs for the picture, six of them for Julie. These included "Whistle Away the Dark" (Julie's favorite of the new numbers), "I'll Give you Three Guesses," "Smile Away Each Rainy Day," "Skal," "A Girl in No Man's Land" and "Chantons Comm' P'tits Oiseaux." The seventh Mancini-Mercer song, "Your Good Will Ambassador" was to be sung by an anonymous Parisienne nightclub entertainer, in much the same way Ann Dee had done "Rose of Washington Square" in *Thoroughly Modern Millie.*

Julie would also sing "Keep the Home Fires Burning," "It's a Long Way to Tipperary," "There's a Long, Long Trail A-Winding," "Red-Wing," "Beautiful Dreamer," "Mother Machree," and the French national anthem, "La Marseillaise," in her role as a British singing idol and secret German spy. The chief target of her espionage is a handsome American Dawn Patrol air squadron commander who knows all the crucial Allied aerial and troop maneuvers, played by Rock Hudson. She tries to extract the secrets from him by seducing him but ends up falling in love with him. A bit of image changing was provided by Julie's doing a comic striptease in a theater in which she is supposed to sing only, done in a jealous fit to make the commander mad; a little wrestling with Hudson in bed; and a shower scene in which she is bare to the cleavage and he is fully clothed, splashing her with cold water as punishment.

"I'm trying to be very still in this one," said Julie, describing Lili. "This isn't a lady who is bouncy. She's somebody who's cool and in perfect control and then gets all gibberish." And Blake blanched at any insinuation that *Darling Lili* was camp, like *Thoroughly Modern Millie*. "We're playing this for realism—the sets, the action, the people are all as honest as we can make them," he said. "Julie plays an English lady who is loved by England and turns out to be a German spy. The humor in it arises out of characters; Lance Percival is a cowardly Englishman who can only fly if he drinks, and he likes to drink, so he flies. He has destroyed six planes, the ones he has crashed in. There's absolutely nothing inconceivable about his character."

Darling Lili started filming on the Paramount lot in March, 1968. It was a congenial set, partly because Blake had his handpicked associates around him. His father was serving as studio production manager, and his uncle was executive producer; Ken Wales was associate producer, and Jack Bear was on wardrobe (although Donald Brooks had designed Julie's clothes). Also, Julie was new to Paramount, and there was great excitement at having her on the lot. The project was the object of a great deal of curiosity, and the interior scenes at the beginning of shooting were posing no particular problems. I visited the set one day to find things in a particularly happy frame of mind. They were doing the shower scene, and the director, the star, and her co-star were finding it all great fun, and therefore so was the crew.

The scene had been shot three times, and Blake was satisfied with the third take. Julie, ever the perfectionist, even when soaking wet, said: "Darling, would you like to do another take?"

"Would you?"

"Not if you're happy."

"You know what you need is to find a fellow, settle down, and marry him."

" 'ood 'ave me?" (Lapsing into Eliza-like Cockney.)

"Some damn fool director."

They kissed, and she reached to put her arms around him. "Oh, no, you don't," he said. "You're all wet, and I don't have a change of clothes with me."

While the set in general waited for her to change into a dry costume and wig (she was a vivid redhead much of the time in *Darling Lili*), Blake recounted yet another outrageous additon to the mythology surrounding his star and best girl. "You know, as long as I've been in this business, I'm still surprised by some of the things people in it say about each other. We were at David Niven's house in Gstaad on Boxing Day [December 26, on their first ski vacation in Switzerland]—he had an open house—and the next thing I heard was that he was telling people that Julie had sat in a corner the whole time, turning on. Can you see Julie Andrews sitting in a corner anywhere, blowing grass?"

When the *Darling Lili* company went to Dublin, the general hilarity continued, but the problems began. Julie and Blake lived at Carton, a castle outside Dublin that doubled as a movie set in several sequences. It was elegant, private, woodsy, and peaceful, all the things she liked, and Julie had never been happier anyplace. Carton had four gatehouses, several outcottages, and unlimited livestock. When Rock Hudson hurt his foot, she played Lady Bountiful and came down from the big house with a basket of goodies and a solicitous concern for his health. She went for a long walk in the summer rain along a secluded garden path. The whole atmosphere was so right that she and Blake rented the castle again in the summer of 1969, just to rest in. But they changed plans at the last minute, canceled Ireland, and settled for a shorter vacation in Hawaii, another of her favorite movie locations.

But on the picture the weather was uncooperative: When a gray day was called for, there was endless brilliant sunshine. There were several night scenes, and night began in the summer at 11 P.M. and lasted only until about 3:30 A.M. The Irish crews were not especially used to big Hollywood musicals, and their uncertain work slowed things down considerably. But when they left Ireland, the Irish extras serenaded Julie with "For She's a Jolly Good Fellow," and "Come Back to Erin." Julie couldn't wait to do just that.

The company went on to Brussels, where there were more weather problems, more night shooting, and the added obstacle of bureaucratic inefficiency when it came to granting official permission for the use of buildings—a problem that was to be even worse in Paris. "Everything that could have gone wrong went wrong," said Julie. Filming was costing $70,000 a day, and because of the variable weather, scenes weren't matching properly and had to be reshot. One cloudy day outside Paris, when sunshine was needed, Blake was trying to match outdoor close-ups of Julie and Hudson with footage that had been shot in Ireland.

When I visited the set at Eure-et-Loir, Diane de Poitiers' sixteenth-century Château d'Anet, I sensed a mixture of concern, a bit too-determined good-timing, and, of course, continued professionalism. They were already five weeks behind schedule and a projected $2,000,000 beyond budget. Blake was using, as he usually did, an expensive closed-circuit television tape system that showed him in black and white the scene that had just been shot by the camera. And Julie, who had never worked with it before, found it fascinating and helpful. "I was nervous at first, but this is all kind of fun," she said. "Blake very kindly defers to me when it comes to the singing, and if I want to redo something, he lets me redo it. Best of all is that we're together."

Blake, between shots and bouts of bad weather, played Frisbee, and took home movies of Julie and his children—Jennifer, a beautiful, blond twelve-year-old who had proved such a superb Heidi in the NBC television special directed by Delbert Mann (and also starring Maximilian Schell and Michael Redgrave and released in Europe as a feature film), and his nine-year-old son, also blond, Jeffrey, who was shyer than his sister but more closely resembled his father. Jeffrey was learning gymnastics, and Jennifer was riding horses, and both of them lived with their father and Julie and Ken Wales in a suite at the Bristol Hotel in Paris. (At that point Julie and Blake had been living together so long without the hypocritical pretense of separate hotel rooms that her secretary, Joan Mansfield, had to refer to "the Rising Glen house" [his] and "the Hidden Valley house" [hers] when talking about deliveries or merely where something was. He eventually sold his house in West Hollywood, bought a weekend one in Malibu, and moved in with Julie in Beverly Hills.)

I asked Julie and Blake about marriage. He said "I'd marry her tomorrow, but she can't right now [the divorce would not be final until November]. We're together, that's the important thing. Of course, if I do marry the leading lady, I'll get ten percent of the profits of the picture," he said jokingly. She said of the Hollywood rumormongers who couldn't count a year from the date she filed for divorce and were predicting an imminent merger: "Well, let 'em rumor for a while."

Julie, during this phase of *Darling Lili,* went shopping in Parisian shops and improved her French, a lifelong ambition, by speaking it to shopgirls and waitresses in restaurants. She mothered Jeffrey and Jennifer in a mock Mary Poppins voice (Emma was then visiting her father at *The Seagull* location in Stockholm), and, as usual, looked forward to returning to California, which had long since become home.

She and Edwards did go back to Hollywood and further delays and spending more money. Blake wanted to return to Europe to reshoot some scenes that he felt had not turned out well. But the studio said no.

Edwards' self-indulgence or perfectionism, depending on your viewpoint, left Paramount with, in the words of one top studio production executive, "fifteen million dollars of unusable film and no picture." There were individual scenes that were interesting, conceded some of the few Paramount officers who had seen rushes, but they didn't add up to a salable film of any sort, much less a big Julie Andrews road show, which is what it had been planned as and which it would have to be if there was any chance of recouping. The opening was postponed to March, 1970, in the hope that something could be done to salvage it, but in the meantime, not only was *Darling Lili* bringing in no return, but it also was costing money in taxes on unreleased film and interest on the capital, a total of $24,000,000. Edwards spent the extra time completely reassembling and recutting and rescoring *Darling Lili*. "Everything Blake does is going into *Lili* right now," Julie told me in October, 1969, when she was busy taping the TV special with Harry Belafonte and when Paramount was releasing *Paint Your Wagon*, another expensive ($20,000,000) musical that made the studio all the more nervous about its upcoming investment.

XIII

S *AY IT WITH MUSIC,* based on Irving Berlin's song
of the same name and employing perhaps some others
of his songs but otherwise not necessarily related to
the composer, was first seriously proposed in 1954, when
Don Hartman got Berlin to agree to let him use the song
title for a musical he would develop for Paramount. It was
not heard of again until April, 1963, nine years later, when
MGM picked up the project and discussed with Berlin the
possibility of using the title song and any of his fifty years'
worth of standards and six or seven new songs he would
compose for a large-scale musical to be produced by Arthur
Freed, a veteran who had produced many MGM musicals,
including Berlin's *Easter Parade,* and *Annie Get Your Gun.*
Arthur Laurents was reportedly signed to write the screenplay (although he said the announcement was premature),
and Vincente Minnelli was signed to direct. In November,
Julie, Sophia Loren, Robert Goulet, and Ann-Margret were
announced as cast for the musical that was budgeted at more
than $4,000,000, then close to a record for an MGM musical.
It was to be Miss Loren's musical debut. Jerome Robbins was
named one of two choreographers, and he and Mr. Freed
were to select the other one jointly. One dance number
was to be a ragtime ballet including "Alexander's Ragtime
Band," Berlin's first hit.

Shooting was scheduled to begin in the spring of 1964
after a long rehearsal period. The plot was a secret, but a

189

fourth woman star was being sought and Freed would only say, "I think this will be something new in the field of movie musicals." It was certainly supposed to be something new for Miss Loren, who was reportedly signed after Freed heard some private recordings she had sent him from Italy. But the elements began to fall apart, and a succession of scriptwriters couldn't make them come together again. One by one, the principals withdrew, Julie among them, although perhaps more reluctantly. "It just wasn't good enough," she said. "And we agreed to disagree."

Typical of the vagueness surrounding the project was Sophia Loren's reaction when I asked what had happened to her and *Say It with Music,* in the summer of 1969 in Moscow, where she was making *I Girasoli* for her producer-husband, Carlo Ponti, and director Vittorio De Sica. She swore that my mentioning it was the first she had heard of the film ("What would I do in a Julie Andrews musical?") and speculated that Carlo had indeed said yes to MGM "and didn't tell me about it because he knew that it was never going to happen and didn't want to worry me."

Suddenly in January, 1968, *Say It with Music* was very much alive again, and Julie was signed to star, and Blake Edwards was signed to direct, replacing Minnelli. Freed was still a producer, but Edwards was named co-producer. MGM planned to release it as a 70-mm reserved-seat road show. The seven new Berlin songs were still in, and the musical was conceived as a record of the composer's contributions to popular music and a tribute. It would be Blake Edwards' first full-fledged musical (*Darling Lili* being counted as, in his words, "a play with music") . Shooting was set to begin in the spring of 1969 for double the original budget, although no other stars were signed.

The film went through several more scripts and scriptwriters, ending up a year later with George Axelrod (as the sole writer) who described it thus: "It will not be like the image one would have of an Irving Berlin-Julie Andrews musical. It is very dramatic with a strong love story, and a movie director is the romantic interest." Axelrod was then conferring with Blake, Julie's own romantic interest and director, who had finally more or less finished *Darling Lili* since Paramount was reluctant to send him and cast and crew back to Europe, as he had asked. Julie had signed for $1,000,000 against 10 percent of the gross plus 35 cents from each cast album sold. Reportedly, she would play a manufactured star totally dependent on her husband, who dies, causing her to go into a suicidal collapse. It was all rendered highly academic two months later, when MGM, in the throes of management reshuffling and financial losses, dropped twenty of its pending projects, *Say It with Music* among them. Instead, the studio set Julie and Blake to do the screen version of *She Loves Me*, the 1963 Broadway musical based on *The Shop Around the Corner*, with Julie in the Barbara Cook role (Daniel Massey had been the male lead) and with Blake writing, producing, and directing. But in October, 1969, MGM again changed hands, and Jim Aubrey, who had been fired by CBS in early 1965, became the new president, replacing Louis F. Polk. It looked as if MGM would be mounting no musicals, major or minor, for some time. "I think *She Loves Me* will go under," said Julie.

XIV

THE ROLE JULIE really liked—and played—best was that of Mum. "She is a goddamned good mother," said the person in the likeliest position to know, Elsie Giorgi, Emma Kate's doctor (Julie, except for a bilateral bunionectomy in November, 1966, and frequent exhaustion from overwork, was never sick). "She feels safer with her baby," said actress Tammy Grimes, an acquaintance of long standing. "She becomes all warm and kind of mummy." "She is a very good mum," echoed Svetlana Beriosova. Julie guarded Emma Kate's privacy obsessively, never telling the names of the schools she attended for fear of kidnapping, and from the time her daughter was eighteen months old, Julie absolutely forbade pictures to be taken of herself with Emma or of Emma alone—except once, in early 1968, by her friend Zoë Dominic, a London photographer.

She was always jealous of her own time with her daughter, and even when dutifully delivering Emma to Tony in New York for a few days' visit, she would try to preserve the important days—like Emma's birthday and Christmas—for herself. Weekends, whether she was working on a movie or not, were devoted to Emma, as were late afternoons, when possible. Julie cited as one of the major reasons for her latter-day strong preference for films over the stage "the more normal hours free to be with Emma." When Emma was in nursery school, five mornings a week Julie drove her there and picked her up in a black 1965 Falcon with simulated wood sides and the "Mary Poppins Is a Junkie" sticker that Mike Nichols provided on its bumper. (Emma's governess, Kay, whom Julie termed "an absolute angel, a real friend, Emma's kind of rock," drove the red 1966 Mustang that Universal had provided during *Torn Curtain* and *Thoroughly Modern Millie*.) "Julie drove up just like all the other mothers," said her business manager, Guy Gadbois, "slightly apologetic about being there."

Emma—sometimes pronounced *Emmer*—was clearly the central focus of Julie's life before and even during Blake Edwards. Julie did go all warm and "mummy" whenever the blue-eyed blonde, tanned by the California sun (who actually looked more like her father), bounced into a room or paid an unexpected visit to the movie set of the moment. The two girls shared the same hairdo, some mannerisms, and many interests. "Emma is going to be Julie's biggest competition," said Dr. Giorgi. Emma and Julie walked around their house whistling and singing songs like "Daisy, Daisy" in a British accent. When Julie took up oil painting in the summer of 1966, Emma emulated her, and whenever Julie retreated to her pool house to paint, Emma was likely to be right alongside with her little box of water colors. Once when Julie had an interview at home, six-year-old Emma sat quietly in the living room with a sheaf of paper. Julie asked her what she was doing. "I'm having an interview, too, Mummy," was the answer.

Emma loved to watch her mother on-screen—and sometimes would greet her in real life with "Hi, Julie Andrews!" She saw *Mary Poppins, The Sound of Music, Thoroughly Modern Millie,* and *Star!* and skipped *The Americanization of Emily* and *Torn Curtain*. "I think I'll let her see *Hawaii* half at a time—not that I think she couldn't take it all, but she might fall asleep, and then I'd be terribly embarrassed," said Julie.

Emma Kate also loved to be sung to sleep by that true,

Julie singing and dancing an English music hall number in her first
NBC-TV special. 1965. NATIONAL BROADCASTING COMPANY.

Mike Nichols and Julie frug it up at a party at the Daisy for George Segal. UNITED PRESS INTERNATIONAL PHOTO.

Julie as would-be flapper Millie Dilmount, in *Thoroughly Modern Millie.* 1967. UNIVERSAL PICTURES.

Julie as Millie in *Thoroughly Modern Millie,* dancing "The Tapioca" with James Fox as Jimmy. UNIVERSAL PICTURES.

Julie and Paul Newman in *Torn Curtain*.

Julie vamps an inattentive John Gavin, her boss in *Thoroughly Modern Millie*. UNIVERSAL PICTURES.

Julie leaves her shoes in the wet cement as she becomes the hundred and fifty-first film star to place her footprints in the sidewalk at Grauman's Chinese Theater in Hollywood. March 26, 1966. UNITED PRESS INTERNATIONAL PHOTO.

Julie with Bruce Forsythe and Beryl Reid (playing her father and stepmother) as a sixteen-year-old Gertrude Lawrence in the "Piccadilly" number in *Star!* (later retitled *Those Were The Happy Times*). TWENTIETH CENTURY-FOX.

Julie as Gertrude Lawrence singing "Burlington Bertie" in *Star!*

Julie as Gertrude Lawrence dancing (with Don Crichton) "Lime-house Blues" in *Star!*

Julie as Gertrude Lawrence and Daniel Massey as Noel Coward in *Star!*, 1967.

Gertrude Lawrence and Raymond Massey in *Pygmalion*, 1945. TWENTIETH CENTURY-FOX.

Julie and Rock Hudson in Hollywood during *Darling Lili*. 1968.

Blake Edwards directs Julie in a bedroom scene with Rock Hudson in *Darling Lili* at Paramount Studios in Hollywood. PARAMOUNT PICTURES.

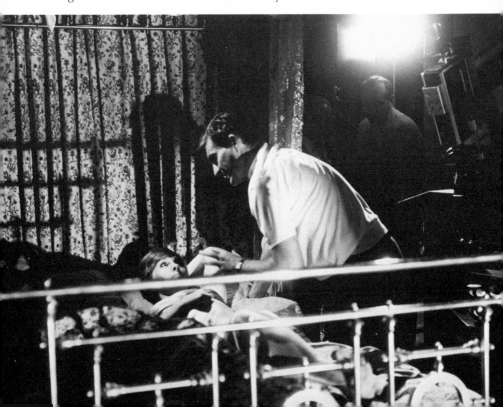

Julie with latest *Lili* script revision and Jennifer Edwards, Blake's daughter, Jennifer, who played Heidi on the NBC special. Dublin, 1968.

Julie with Blake and Rock Hudson, *Darling Lili*. Ireland, 1968. PARA-MOUNT PICTURES.

At home in the sunny living room in Beverly Hills. CURT GUNTHER.

Two stars and director Gower Champion combine their talents in
An Evening with Julie Andrews and Harry Belafonte, the AT&T
special staged by Gower Champion on NBC in November, 1969.

Blake Edwards and Julie laughing over a story in *Time* magazine.

Julie and Blake mugging during *Darling Lili* in Ireland. 1968. PARA-MOUNT PICTURES.

clear soprano voice the world had come to love, too. "But she hates for me to *practice* singing," her mother said during the particularly musical period of *Thoroughly Modern Millie* and *Star!* "She bursts into tears, real tears, whenever I do practice. She shouts, 'Stop it; I don't want you to do it.' She keeps trying bravely to conquer it. One day Andre and I were here at home practicing, and Emma came in. She said, 'Mummy, if I sit very quietly, may I watch?' which she never would have thought of asking before. She sat for a few minutes, looking very uncomfortable, and then asked to leave the room. She had heard all she could stand."

In those days, when she was not yet five, Emma took a nap in the early afternoon, well within range of the pool house where Julie practiced, making it sometimes difficult for Julie to rehearse her songs for the films. "The only time I could do it was driving to the studio early in the morning. There I was, driving down Coldwater Canyon, clinging to the wheel for dear life, completely oblivious to everything around me, singing at the top of my lungs. I'm sure when I pulled up to a light the person in the next car thought to himself, 'Now, who's that crazy woman?'"

If Emma missed her father, she filled in by "clinging to my brother," Chris Andrews, who lived with them for a few years, and later to Blake Edwards. She was always a genuinely interesting child, who painted well, made up clever word images, and increasingly showed creative tendencies. "She's a worse romantic than I am," her mother said. Julie "wouldn't mind her being an actress if she wants to; I don't think I could stop her if I tried." Julie was determined that if Emma wanted a career in entertainment, she would have all the dancing and drama lessons her mother never had. One of Emma's favorite stuffed toys epitomized her, in Julie's opinion. It was a white and purple fabric hippopotamus about a foot long, around whose neck she had placed a dog's collar and leash. "That's my daughter—one day she'll put a leash on a hippopotamus," said Julie.

Julie had the same sort of maternal instincts toward Blake's children, Jennifer and Jeffrey, whom she saw often in Europe and in Malibu. They were five and three years older than Emma, respectively and they called her Julie. Jennifer particularly responded to her as she might to an older sister or a youngish aunt. On the *Darling Lili* locations Jenny and Julie sang a song about their expanded "family" that they had made up, to the tune of "My Favorite Things": "Blackie and Julie, and Jenny and Jeffrey/Emma and . . ." I lost track of all the half brothers and just who from which family was included and who was not, but the punch line had something to do with all of its adding up to a very full living room.

In 1965 Julie bought the spacious, lovely, but not elegant eight-room house once owned by physical fitness expert Vic Tanny in a hidden corner off Coldwater Canyon, above Beverly Hills, that she and Emma and later Blake called home. Near neighbors were Charlton Heston, Lana Turner, and Rock Hudson, and television producer Aaron Spelling, whom Julie at first didn't know, lived next door and sent her flowers to welcome her to the neighborhood. Julie's youngest half brother, Chris, who had stayed with her and Emma in Hawaii came to live with them in Beverly Hills at the end of the summer of 1966, when he was twenty. He was studying photography at the Art Center school in Los Angeles.

Other members of the household included two dogs and a cat. The dogs, an almost white toy poodle named Q-Tip ("because he looks like a used one," Julie explained) and a black standard poodle named Cobie, lived in harmony with the cat, a black, white, and gray mixture named Bimbo ("he used to be called Contrapuntal, but Emma thought that was a bit much") . Emma romped regularly with the three animals, but Julie gave them scant attention.

The house was until late 1969 in the firm charge of a Negro butler, Covington, called Cov by his mistress and her more

familiar friends. He had been found by Guy Gadbois, as had
Mrs. Mansfield. He answered the door and the phone and did
most of the cooking. "The Army got him for a month, and
three cooks tried to take over in the kitchen." Julie recalled.
"He was as distraught as I was. I pleaded with the Army to
let me have him, but they won." Covington at one time slept
in, but Chris Andrews took over his room. A laundress
came in most days and doubled as a baby-sitter when the
nanny was away. Julie had a secretary—first an Englishwoman, Bea Hopkinson, who had worked for Joan Fontaine, Zsa Zsa Gabor, and Nobel Prizewinning physicist Willard Libby in similar capacities, and then an American, Joan
Mansfield, who had worked for Edie Adams. The job usually
entailed three days a week at Julie's house or on the set.

Once when Emma was between live-in English governesses
(Kay left to get married and have a child of her own), a
happy mother, briefly between pictures, provided the transition herself. Their kitchen was being completely remodeled,
and Julie wasn't much of a cook anyway, so Julie and Emma
took to having their suppers together at a local "Hamburger
Hamlet." (The replacement governess turned out to be a
German woman of whom Emma was very fond, but Julie replaced her quickly with another Englishwoman who was less
competition, and then there were others for short terms.)

Even after her divorce, Julie wanted more children, "and
she should have them," pronounced Elsie Giorgi. "I do want
more babies," said Julie, who was envious every time Carol
Burnett got pregnant. In her lapsed marital state, even in an
era of new Hollywood freedom, it would have been difficult,
so Julie turned her energies to her house. It was ideally lo-
cated about fifteen or twenty minutes from all Hollywood
studios and about twelve minutes from downtown Beverly
Hills. Despite its centrality, it was in semiwild canyon country, with the appearance of being totally isolated—and it was
off the routes of most "visit-the-homes-of-the-stars" sight-
seeing buses. Julie, of course, preferred it that way. "I like

being out of doors, and I like the country better than the city. My real Dad taught me to love the country. The only salvation for an apartment in London or New York is if you can see trees, a park, or a river."

Given her nomadic early existence, brought on first by the war and divorce, then by show business, it wasn't surprising that Julie had long sought a place to call home. What was surprising was that she found it in Southern California. She had first"fallen in love with it" when she went there on her honeymoon with Tony in 1959. When she returned to work in *Mary Poppins,* she said she'd never been happier anyplace," Carol Burnett recalled. "And she fell in love with the movies. If you like the work and place you're living in, you're doing beautifully." Five years later, she still loved the area and the work, if not Tony. "Having bought this house has made me feel truly at home here," she said one day in Hollywood. "When I first came here, I put it down like everyone else and said that there was nothing going on here. I didn't know a soul when I arrived. I hated the fact that I had to drive everywhere—and I very nearly got a ticket once for driving too slowly. But now I think that Hollywood is as real as New York or as real as London or as real as Venice. But to really appreciate it, you must go away and come back again. Sometimes when I feel lonely or depressed, it helps me to think that Venice *is* at that moment—that Rome is teeming. It keeps one from being too isolated."

While California was her favorite home ("There is no place I'd rather be. When I'm away for very long, I can't wait to get back"), she retained a bit of nostalgia for the old house in Walton-on-Thames, with its bay windows and fireplaces. And she was crazy about her cottage on Alderney, in the Channel Islands. She seldom got there, and her father looked after it, supervising its use by any members of her family who cared to use it. "Personally, I never intend to lose it," she said. "It's sweet and small. Alderney is small enough and wild enough and free enough to be totally removed. For the first two days you damn near die and say, 'Oh, I'll never stand for all this wind through me,' but it's so totally fresh a climate that you never want to leave, and when you do, you're completely exhilarated."

The house remodeling in Hollywood was a sure sign of a frugal woman's intended permanence on the Hollywood scene. In addition to the kitchen's being completely redone to her specifications, an adjacent sun porch was converted to a family-breakfast room opening onto the kitchen. Central air conditioning was installed, and all the oak parquet floors were stained dark. And bougainvillaea bushes were added to the garden she inherited. "What's been fun is finding out what blooms and what doesn't," she said.

The modern white brick, wood, and glass house was plunked onto a private hillside. A pool and a pool house were across the driveway, and beyond them was an extra lot containing Emma's playground (swings, seesaw, and slide) and still with room for a tennis court should Julie pursue another lifelong ambition. "Tennis is something I really would like to learn one day. I've never had the time to learn, much less to practice." The lot was ringed by pear, apple, and avocado trees and wild canyon plants. In front of the house was a flagstone courtyard, with a fountain which was lighted at night. In back of the house was an extension of the driveway that was converted, in the best California tradition, to an eating patio.

Julie had fireplaces in both her living room and her dining room, and she installed one in her huge bedroom (the whole upstairs of the house), which also housed a king-size bed and bookcases containing books that had been read, including *Hawaii* and Moss Hart's *Act One*. She had several chairs and a sofa in shades of white in the living room. Julie eschewed smooth fabrics and surfaces, and the living-room sofa was rough white satin; it sat on a shaggy white rug that had a sunburst in five shades ranging from off-white to yellow to orange to brown and was backed by a white brick wall.

Opposite was a white brick fireplace and more bookshelves, containing mostly reference and picture books about art and music. A Grotian Steinmeg grand piano was at one end of the room, under a straight open staircase leading down from the bedroom; behind the staircase was a virtual glass wall, facing south, allowing the room to be filled with sunlight for most of the day.

The furnishings ran to elegant things like white Wedgwood bone china. She had the nucleus of an art collection, one of her ardent ambitions. There were two bronzes by Anna Mahler, daughter of the composer Gustav, and a friend of Julie's: a highly unsuccessful head of Julie and a delicate, graceful three-foot-high statue of an anonymous girl. There were five oil paintings by the Oakland, California, artist Henrietta Berk. Blake Edwards, who had several large Berks of his own, had introduced Julie to the artist's works—semi-abstracts of flowers, children, trees, oceans, and fields in bright warm reds, oranges, and blues and greens that Julie favored. Guy Gadbois, who had a large blue Berk in his office, thanks to Julie's influence, and who had to approve the expenditures of several hundred or a thousand dollars for each new one, would comment only on the fortyish married artist's prolixity: "She grinds them out like popcorn," he said.

Among Julie's other art treasures were a Gyneth Johnstone Italian landscape, an African fertility doll and two dozen art books, leaning heavily to the romantics, as she did in music. She would have liked to buy $30,000 pantings, but it was business manager Gadbois who wouldn't let her have them. "We feel it's just a little too early for that," Gadbois said. "In Hollywood terms, she has not been a great earner until very recently, and she is young in her business career."

Julie and Blake and Andre and Dory Previn used to play a five-favorite-paintings game. "If you could buy any five paintings in the world for yourself, which five would they be?" explained Previn. I played it with Julie one afternoon, not limiting her to five, and she chose "anything by Turner,

but that really is daydreaming—that's just for the game,"
and more possibly "any of the strange wonderful birds and
winged creatures by Braque, and anything by Manet, Monet,
Pissarro, Sisley—especially 'The Canal,' 'The Woodcutter,'
and 'The Orchard'—Daumier ('The Refugees'), and any
still life of Redon, like 'Bouquet of Wild Flowers,' and any
of Nolde's watercolors.

"The trouble is one wants so much," she said, and she
seemed reluctant to buy just one or two paintings and build
a collection slowly, perhaps one painting for each of her
moving pictures. Dory Previn insisted Julie could afford at
least almost any one of her innermost heart's desires. "Why
doesn't she just go out and buy it?" asked the lyricist. Although Julie listened closely to Gadbois' advice anent the art
collection (the Berks were in place on the walls, but there
was room for some better known names as well), she weak-
ened where Blake was concerned. For the Christmas of 1967
she gave him Emil Nolde's "The Singer" ("Somewhat appropriate, I thought"), and for his birthday in 1968 she gifted
him with a Persian water jug from 1000 B.C. that she had ac-
quired in Brussels during *Darling Lili*.

Julie frequented no particular gallery. Since she was not a
big buyer, no dealer put things aside for her or did her col-
lecting for her. She loved to browse on gallery row on La
Cienega Boulevard in West Hollywood, and sometimes
"did" La Cienega with Blake, like any other art lover.

Tony Walton recalled that Julie had "little interest in the
business side of her career and always found it difficult to discuss money." But Gadbois, who also handled the personal
finances of Jimmy Stewart, Edie Adams, and Rock Hudson,
found Julie with "a good awareness of her business affairs.
She is a very conservative person. She wants to know what's
going on all the time, and she's very inquisitive about where
her money's going."

Gadbois, a baldish man of middle years, like all Hollywood business managers—as opposed to personal managers

—handled merely his clients' money after it was made and had nothing to do with directing their careers. In Julie's case, Arthur Park negotiated all contracts, and very well, thank you. "Uncle Charlie" Tucker, who had been Julie's personal manager since that first show at the Palladium, "and I decided to part company" (that was in 1965) was the crisp way Julie put it. "There were too many people around. We still ask his advice from time to time." Park said that there was an advisory arrangement, but that no money and no contract were involved.

Tony Walton remembered that the arrangement with Tucker had been a "bizarre" one, and other friends said that Julie had long wanted to get rid of him, but because he had been with her since the beginning of her career, she couldn't bring herself to it—even if he had taken money from her—until Gadbois and Park in effect ordered her to sever the connection.

"It's their own money, and if they want something badly enough, they'll get it," said Gadbois. "If they have a business manager who won't let them buy something, they'll fire him and get one who will. But Julie's sensible enough to know that we're right about the art collection." Gadbois' investments on Julie's behalf, he said, "are of a conservative nature and conservatively diversified." They included the interest in the orchard in Hawaii. Julie and Gadbois discussed every major expenditure, and when she was in town and not working, they met once a week to discuss business, sometimes at her house, but often at his office on Wilshire Boulevard, making her a highly unusual superstar. Their major disagreement was over a white Mercedes 280 SL she wanted and eventually got. But he urged her to make do with the 1965 Falcon for a while longer, and she did.

Gadbois took care of all household expenses, based on a budget that Julie had approved. She had a small allowance for very, very personal expenses. "It isn't a question of sitting down and saying, 'Julie, you can do this, and you can't do

Julie Andrews

that.' We always discuss it, and she almost always agrees with the policies we set." ("I suppose my money isn't invested in any big way, but I love anything to do with land and houses and the feeling of security they give you," she said.)

Julie was a woman with a great need for simplicity in everything: her house; her clothes; her grooming; her work. During *My Fair Lady,* when she was still wearing her hair parted in the middle with stupid English curls on each side, she greeted an interviewer with her hair pulled back with a rubber band. "I can't bear all that ironmongery one goes through for a perm," she said. "I can't stand the thought of spending two days a week in a beauty parlor having my hair teased," she told me fourteen years later. "With my hair [a short-cut style evolved with help from several stage and screen stylists], I literally wash it and set it." She had it cut once a month by a California stylist named Hal Saunders, whom she termed "a genius," which meant "he agrees with me that this is right for me—far different from what most hairstylists would think."

In place of a two- or three-piece suit, Julie would rather wear a one-piece dress; "instead of stockings and a garter belt, I would rather wear something that is both. The less one wears the better. I don't like jewelry. I have about four pieces that I wear off and on." For the Hollywood premiere of *Hawaii,* she borrowed a diamond brooch, and around the house she wore a plain watch with a plain black strap and, of course, no engagement or wedding ring. After *Star!* her taste ran to more jewelry on the few glamorous occasions, but at home and in her dressing room during the day she wore none. Rehearsing her 1969 TV special, she wore a brass ankh, a peace symbol, on a chain around her neck.

Her taste in clothes ran from what Dory Previn described as "old-fashioned" to what less charitable observers sometimes called "frumpish." In the mid-1960's she belied the whole English mod thing. At one Hollywood party, she arrived "looking like the chaperone," according to Andre Previn. "She didn't act it, but she looked it. She was younger than most of the other guests there, but she looked older." Tammy Grimes, who also attended the same party, a sit-down dinner with live rock-band dancing afterward, said: "She wore white gloves. I thought the press was gonna come and give her an award."

"I don't deny that I adore clothes," said Julie. "My greatest pleasure is picking out a new gown. I used to be influenced a lot by Tony. I used to wear a lot of black for some somber reason. He informed me rather tartly one day that black made my skin look all blotchy."

As her career soared, and as women in stores recognized her and came up for a close look and asked for autographs, Julie found she had less and less time and inclination for shopping, even for Emma Kate. She had stores send merchandise in on approval, or she went out and bought a lot at once, "in spurts, three or four pairs of shoes, six dresses, ten half-slips. I do love to shop; to go shopping is like having a treat." She had designer clothes from time to time but until Donald Brooks had no particular favorite. She looked forward to the day when she would have a French or Italian designer, to whom she would take material. "I do love to choose fabrics for myself; that's a great pleasure for me."

At home, Julie "always" wore slacks, often of an old-fashioned cut and sometimes with the little white anklets that everybody's mother wore in the 1940's and stopped wearing in the 1950's ("God knows where she gets them," remarked a woman friend). She finished off her casual outfits with round-collared blouses and brightly colored pullover sweaters or velour cardigans. She often wore slacks to the studio and a variety of housecoats in her dressing room at work when she wasn't in costume. And she once flew across country in a fashionable purple pant suit.

Growing up, and particularly thanks to the influence of her father, Julie loved to read, particularly poetry (hers and

Ted Wells' favorite books were *The Oxford Book of English Verse* and *The Golden Treasury*) , and in later years in rare leisure and Emma-less moments, she read as much as possible. "I'm a great lover of poetry. When I'm very busy, it's hard to get into a deep novel. But you can pick up a book of poems and read as much as your heart desires. I go off into a whole other world." Her favorite poet was Robert Frost, for his simplicity and outdoorsiness. The other books on her shelves included show-business biographies like *Chaplin* and novels that have been made into movies, her own and others.

Recorded classical music was another important part of home life. "Whenever I call her or go over there, the record player is going, and it is not for my benefit," said Andre Previn. "She really knows it and loves it." Svetlana Beriosova said Julie had "great love and understanding for music and dance. I visited her in California when she was in the midst of *Mary Poppins,* and one night we just sat listening to Benjamin Britten's *War Requiem* and ended up hearing it twice."

By her own admission, Julie cooks very rarely and only adequately. Dilys Lay did the cooking during *The Boy Friend,* but by the time Julie married Tony, she was able to manage to get him breakfast every morning. In her movie years, "Mom"—Lorraine Roberson, who had been with her even on foreign locations since *The Sound of Music* ostensibly as a hairdresser—was responsible for breakfast and lunch and always saw that she ate well. Julie did have three culinary specialties which provided her with at least minimal fame in Hollywood. She made boiled potato sandwiches, "all squashy and gorgeous," although Bea Hopkinson couldn't ever remember seeing one. They consisted, according to Julie, of brown bread, butter, salt and pepper and boiled potatoes, although "chips"—both the American and English varieties—could be substituted. Then there was a secret bullshot recipe over which Carol Burnett went into raptures.

"And every Christmas, to everyone's annoyance and chagrin, I make mulled wine, all icky and sticky. I'm the only one who likes it."

Julie never dieted as such. "My Mum was a great one for balanced meals—fruits and salads, seldom fried things and all that. Because she was so strict, I now have a passion for things like rice pudding and potatoes." She picked up "the Moss Hart diet" during *My Fair Lady*: Eat everything you like, but in half quantity. "I still do that when I need to think about food. For *Hawaii,* I went on a fairly strict diet because I didn't want it to have to be just a makeup job."

XV

I N 1964, DURING *The Sound of Music* filming, Julie
underwent psychoanalysis. "I needed some answers. I
had been going toward it for some time, asking about
it," she said. "I thought it would be pleasant to try one day,
for a lot of reasons—all of them obvious. One day I just
did it. I rang up everybody I knew who had a psychiatrist
and asked who would be good." Julie had been partly in-
duced by a London friend, Masud "Sudie" Khan, Svetlana
Beriosova's husband, himself a psychiatrist. John Calley also
influenced her strongly toward it, and Blake Edwards, himself a subject, urged her to continue in it and work hard at
it after he came on the scene.

At first she kept it a secret, not from her friends or even
her fans. But she told co-workers on *The Sound of Music* and
Hawaii not to say anything about it, for fear her mother
would find out. Eventually, of course, Mrs. Andrews did, and
she pronounced the whole psychiatric profession and Julie's
alleged need for its services as "bloody nonsense. Of course,
you understand we still look on them as quacks in England."

Blake felt it had helped her greatly. Elsie Giorgi, a dissat-
isfied subject of analysis, wasn't so sure. "In analysis she has
become a student of it, rather than a patient," Dr. Giorgi
said. "I sometimes wonder who's treating whom. She has
great intuition, as well as a great intellectual curiosity about
everything, and I think this is just one more thing she's
learning about." Julie, who visited her analyst once a week

when she was in town, said, "It's hard to be objective about it. I felt I needed it, and I went, and it helped. I think I'd have been a rotten mother without analysis. I'm only beginning to crystallize the bits and pieces of my life, and it takes some sorting out."

Julie never got or attempted to get "important help and answers" from a somewhat more conventional source: religion. "I'm not an atheist or anything like that, but I've never had any religious upbringing. My family were not religious at all, and neither were Tony's. We never went to church. It's hard to know what to do about Emma. She has to be taught some basic things, I know, prayers and things. But she'll get enough at a good school, I think." Julie, for her part, only prayed when she was in the theater, just before she went on stage, and it was always something like "Oh, God, don't let me fall on my face."

She refused to be very specific about the things that led her into analysis, but the breaking up of her marriage was one reason. Her other psychological failings, she felt, were a too tightly controlled temperament, near total ambivalence about most decisions, and a fear of scenes and good-byes. "I have enormous phobias about singing, stemming from the Broadway days when I was trotted out every night and was pretty much mixed up. I do have phobias, and there's no doubt about it. Some of the neurotic idiosyncrasies of worry about my throat during the Broadway run of *My Fair Lady* really hung me up. I was in an absolute tizzy. I got phobias and complexes and everything else. It really made my life miserable for no good reason. The same was almost true of *Star!*. I was on-camera constantly for months, and the pressures were enormous, and I worried more than I should have."

Her earliest memories were of World War II. "I was lucky because we weren't hit, but it was sort of scary at times. Sometimes I think I've almost forgotten those childhood memories, and then I go to an utterly beautiful land like Hawaii, and the banging came back to me all at once," she said. On the set of *Darling Lili* an actor fired a gun containing blanks, and Julie turned terrified white. She hated violent noise coming suddenly, another irrational fear that in analysis had been traced to a specific blitz during the war.

Another of her concerns was her tendency to anger, but to express it very differently from most people. "I do have a temper, an absolutely fearful one," she said. "But I think I am too controlled a human being to let it be said that I have a temper most people would recognize. What usually happens, funnily enough, is that when I'm really blue, I get wacky. It seems to me I get to be the funniest when things are really down. But at times I am an angry young lady—and maybe not so young anymore. I do hate scenes of any kind. They upset me desperately, and I go out of my way to avoid them. I used to hate good-byes to an extent that was ridiculous. I still hate them both, but now I know why."

Both Richard Burton and Max von Sydow saw her temper, which surprised her because "I thought I was kidding them the whole time." Others, like Tammy Grimes, wished she would show it more. "She's sad and boring," said Miss Grimes. "She's lost Eliza. Her accent is too high. She does just what's right; it would be groovier if she'd do just what's Julie once in a while."

"I suppose another of my failings is that I am a totally ambivalent person," said Julie. "Ambivalence can either be a vice or a virtue. But I am able to see both sides of anything to such an extent that it is terribly hard for me to make a decision or do anything involving a drastic change.

"My kind of temper, when it does come out, is the stewing kind. I grit my teeth at the things that really do get me upset, and I simmer for a while. It's the little things that get me mad. I'm terribly good about coping with big problems. One of my ambitions used to be to throw a great screaming temper tantrum. I can't see myself actually doing it, but I have fantasized it. To do it, you have to be pretty damn sure

you're right or you look damn foolish. And because I'm ambivalent, I'm never that sure."

One of the things that made Julie angry was "mothers who
force their children to recognize Mary Poppins. The children are barely two or three, and their mothers make them
wave at me, actually make them look closely, to mark the
date, so to speak. It puts me very uptight." And "I always
get very upset when people don't get on with the job at hand.
I always say—or feel like saying—to people, 'Let's get on
with it; it's the piece that matters, not our own personal
thing.'"

Because she was so totally committed to her career (she
once spent an entire evening exacting advice from George
Burns at a party, riveted by his explanation of how he and
Jack Benny had made their stardom last a lifetime—he told
her to embrace all entertainment media), her social and professional lives were hard to separate. And her friends attributed Julie's stardom to the very qualities they found in her
as a person.

Julie's friendship with the later estranged Previns, whom
she had met through Mike Nichols when she first went to California to do *Mary Poppins,* was partly based on a mutual
loathing of large crowds of any sort ("Going out with her was
a little like blockade-running," said Andre) and a distinct
preference for small groups with lots of conversation. Julie
found these evenings "truly memorable." She hated big parties, never gave them, and seldom went to them. When she
did, it was out of a sense of obligation. Another reason for
their closeness was that the Previns, like Nichols, knew her
before movie stardom and refused to treat her as a superstar.
"She gets vehement razzing from all of us whenever she does
something 'big star,'" said Previn, "like when we say, 'Let's
go to a movie,' and she says, 'No, I'll have it screened at
home.'"

The home screenings at Julie's "to catch up on movies or
to preview them" had a practical impetus: Julie was likely to

be mobbed in a movie theater. "I screen the movies on the smooth wall of the playroom if it's a good movie, on the brick wall of the living room if it's a bad movie." She declined to give examples of each category but said her own favorite movie stars were Audrey Hepburn, "the other Hepburn, particularly in her movies with Spencer Tracy, and I also like old Fred Astaire-Ginger Rogers movies. Whenever I see Sophia Loren, I am staggered by the amount of work she puts into a role—she never does it by half. She may be in the world's worst movie, but one knows that at the time she did it she was committed to her role. Audrey Hepburn is the same: totally committed."

When she and Blake went out, it was often to small dinner parties ("Ten is the perfect number"), but most often they didn't go out at all. "I seem to be a little quieter in my old age. I don't go out as much as I used to," Julie said. She was an investor in New York's Arthur, "like everyone else," but never went there. The owner of The Daisy in Beverly Hills gave her a free membership, which she used just once. "If one were in one's twenties even, it would be fun to go more often," she said. "I must say I admire and envy all the kids who do all those dances." Sometimes there was the offbeat entertainment, like the night Andre conducted at the Hollywood Bowl and Julie showed up with fried chicken on which they picnicked before the Mahler.

In small groups Julie was both at her wittiest and most enigmatic. "She has a far-out sense of humor," said Previn. "She loves to be the clown, and she is very amusing, much more broadly amusing than you would suspect. She is not above saying things you could not say on a movie screen. I don't know why she is such a reserved lady or seems so, but while she's saying all these things and while she's at her funniest, you're never quite sure what she's thinking."

Carol Burnett knew Julie well as a performer before she knew her well as a person. But when it comes to humor, Carol said, it made no difference: "Julie's funny onstage or off—a little bawdier, perhaps, off." There was one elaborate gag in particular that Carol recalled.

In January, 1965, Mike Nichols, Julie, and Carol had been summoned to Washington to perform at President Johnson's inauguration. It was in the middle of a snowstorm, so Julie arrived by train, skipped a party at Perle Mesta's, had an early dinner, and returned to her hotel, the International Inn, to wait for Nichols. When he did arrive, Carol invited him to their room on a different floor. Julie, in her inevitable slacks, and Carol, in Joe Hamilton's bathrobe, went out to the elevator to wait. "We sat on a settee across from the elevator and tried to think of something to make Michael laugh," Carol said. "We tried a lot of pigeon-toed stuff, then with our feet out, but nothing was funny enough. Julie said, 'I know wot—let's be kissing.' I said, 'I like you a whole lot, Julie, but I don't know.' She talked me into it, and we went into a mad embrace the minute the elevator doors started to open. A woman got out. She didn't recognize us, but the look she gave us— Next time the doors opened we went into another mad embrace, and this time it was about ten male heads—none of them Mike's—who had stopped at the wrong floor. By now I'm on the floor in hysterics. Back comes the lady. She keeps looking and very solemnly says, 'You're Carol Burnett, aren't you?' I said, 'Yes, and that's Mary Poppins.' I wasn't gonna be the only one recognized. She goes, and the elevator opens again, and we go into our mad embrace. And damn Mike Nichols! He walks right out and by and says, 'Hi, girls,' like we did it all the time."

Julie has her "earthy moments," according to Carol. "I remember when she was pregnant with Emma in England. She and Tony sent me little limericks they made up—they were a little off-color, but funny." When Julie thought she might be pregnant, Carol asked her, "How are you going to know for sure?" Julie replied, "Oh, they take a little mouse and shoot him full of something, and if he dies, you're pregnant." Later Julie called Carol up and said simply, "The mouse is dead." "When I got pregnant a year later, I just wired Julie, 'The mouse is dead.' "

Carrie Hamilton, Carol's oldest daughter, who was a year younger than Emma Walton, played with Julie's daughter whenever possible. And Carol did the same with Julie. "Whenever we get together it's slop time," said Carol. "One time I went to her house for dinner, and we had it on the living-room floor. She made bullshots, of course. I always insist on it, and I'll never drink any bullshots but hers, the best bullshots in the world. Neither of us drinks much at all ["I'm too cautious, too careful a person," said Julie in explanation of why she turned down drinks in public as if they were poison, "I'd be terrified of what I'd reveal if I ever really let go"], but I always think—soup and liquor, so good for you. Cov made a steak and kidney pie, and we sat on the floor in slacks and bobby socks and made a real hen party out of it."

Naturally, Carol had nothing but admiration for Julie as a co-star: "She always calmed me down. I always drew strength from her. Not that she never needed calming down. Before the special we were so nervous we were like zombies, and perhaps sometimes she felt I was the strength. But she was never fidgety or running around. Unfortunately there are few women who work well with other women. Julie is one; so is Gwen Verdon, and so is Lucy Ball, and so, oddly enough, is Eileen Farrell. They throw themselves into whatever they are doing, and there is no feminine thing about working with them. That's security in your talent. You don't have to prove your talent—you know you've got it. That's Julie."

Both Previns—and Mike Nichols for that matter (although he was not completely sure she would survive superstardom with herself intact)—were absolutely admiring when it came to Julie's abilities, although they had strong objections to some of the properties she involved herself in. On screen or in the recording studio, the Previns felt, she was nothing short of superb. *"Mary Poppins* is like drowning in peppermint, but *The Sound of Music* makes it look like *The Deputy,* and yet she came through both so dryly, so absolutely *sec,"* said Previn. "She showed no sentimentality in those grossly sentimental pictures," added Mrs. Previn.

"There is musically nothing she cannot do," said the permanent conductor of the London Symphony and alumnus of Debbie Reynolds movies. "She is not Leontyne Price, nor should she be that kind of singer. When she was twelve, she was on her way to being Gloria Jean, but what was that? She is naturally very musical, with a great love for music. She's an inveterate concertgoer. And the best present anyone can give Julie is a classical record. Her tastes are varied but she likes the nineteenth century by far the best." (Julie's favorite composition was Rachmaninoff's Second Symphony.)

Dory Previn felt that "whatever it is in Julie that people love so, she is comparable to one old-time star: Irene Dunne. She was a very sexy woman who was a lady. She sang and was in innocently sexy comedies, looking like she was straight out of the PTA. She was rowdy, and yet her skirt was always below the knees. Men fantasize that if they ever got to know her, they could find out the real Julie, but different men view her differently. Billy Wilder says she's not only sexy, but erotic. I would adore seeing Julie in a Billy Wilder movie; it would bring out the rollicking English music hall thing complete with funny faces. Hitchcock used her for the obvious Hitchcock thing, and that was a waste."

Elsie Giorgi, the other friend who knew Julie before she exploded on the big screen, was also not impressed with her stardom, although she loved and admired the girl within. "She hasn't changed one iota, except that she is a little older and learning to be alone." Julie first met Elsie at a dinner party, through Anna Mahler, a mutual friend, but got to know her in a crisis. When Emma was still an infant, she had the croup late one night. Julie, not knowing any other doctor, called Elsie, who was also a near neighbor. "On the phone she was worried sick, but restrained as always. When I got to her house the first thing she said was 'Babies always get better, don't they?' " Emma Kate, who had been "dreadfully sick," did recover quickly, and Julie and Elsie became intimate friends.

One Christmas Julie returned the favor in kind, when Elsie was expected at her house for dinner but canceled because of the flu. Julie visited Elsie in her sickbed, bearing Guinness stout and port wine. She urged Elsie to drink, Elsie the whole time protesting that she couldn't face it. "It cured my uncle's consumption," said Julie, as if that settled the matter. "That sounded like a line from *My Fair Lady*," said Elsie.

"The first impression of Julie stays with you forever," said Dr. Giorgi, a woman who didn't usually mix with the show-business set. "My notion of movie people is that they have a part to play. She doesn't. She's everybody's daughter. You can't say she's the girl next door because she doesn't look like the kid next door. The opening scene of *The Sound of Music* is Julie: fresh, with absolutely no pretense." Success, Elsie felt, had not changed Julie much except that she was "more aware of things." And "she does miss being able to make a move without being recognized. I'm sure she misses the old days when she could go to the supermarket herself.

"She has great vitality. She is not going to be typed readily. Her friends are all different kinds of people, all interesting for different reasons. She gives a great deal—more than she should, enough for ten Julies. And she wears success lightly. She acts as if the next day it's all going to disappear. She's her own severest critic. There are no three faces of Julie. There is just Julie, intelligent, curious, a student of everything. She knows and does what is instinctively right and decent. Yet while intelligent and mature, she is sometimes like a small girl. She is childlike about the way she loves her home. She has great dignity, but she is the Sarah Bernhardt of slapstick (something Julie would like to do professionally), as well as being everybody's darling. She is reserved and dignified, but there is no subterfuge about her. She has great integrity. She's exceptional, with a hell of a lot to give. She has good instincts, and whatever happens, she lands on her feet. She is wholesome and sophisticated, and that is a rare combination. She wouldn't want to be anything different from what she is. She always belonged to somebody since she was twelve, someone who ran her life or owned her. Now she's entitled to be by herself and run her own life."

If Julie has a major fault, Elsie thinks, it is that "she hates to disappoint anyone. As a result, she does things that are overtaxing and not even worthy of her. She has a great sense of duty and great conscience. Who else would take two years to say, 'We are separated'?"

Previn knew her as a friend before he knew her as a performer, and making a record and then a movie with her was a revelation. In 1966 he conducted and Julie sang an album of Christmas carols for RCA Victor (the first year of its release it was distributed in the United States by Firestone Rubber as a premium item, but RCA retained the rights abroad and for subsequent American sales). The same year he conducted the musical numbers for *Thoroughly Modern Millie*.

"Working with her," he said, "you find out why she makes it so big. Singers are generally a dangerous, unpredictable lot. But Julie comes to any session completely prepared and knowing exactly what to do. She is totally willing to take suggestions, but I don't mean everybody can walk all over her. She is a very good singer who acts rather than a movie star who sings, and it is an unadulterated pleasure to work with her."

Recordings were a medium she tried to embrace, heeding George Burns' advice, but unsuccessfully except for the cast albums and sound-track recordings on which she starred. *The Sound of Music* was the best-selling long-playing record album of all time (8,500,000 copies), and the original-cast

My Fair Lady was second with 7,000,000. Even *Star!* was a best-selling album that was better than the picture. Her collections of songs in the late 1950's and early 1960's, like *The Lass with the Delicate Air, Julie Andrews Sings,* and *Don't Go in the Lion's Cage Tonight,* did not do well and prevented her from making more albums later on. It bothered her that this was the one medium in which she had not succeeded on her own, despite her fantastic success with all the others, and she envied Barbra Streisand's making it with records as well as movies, stage, and television.

Julie didn't even like to hear the cast album of *My Fair Lady,* and she "never" played it. "It hurts too much. Sometimes I might hear an orchestra playing 'I Could Have Danced All Night,' and then it is marvelous. But not my own voice. Maybe in a few years I'll want to." She abhorred recording sessions until the one with Previn. "I admire his quiet affirmation that all is right," she said. "In one of the orchestrations for the Christmas album there was a top G at the end, and I hadn't sung a top G since 'I Could Have Danced All Night.' He said I could do it, and I did it."

For the album, the last that she had recorded apart from the *Millie, Star!* and *Darling Lili* sound tracks, Previn found some obscure Welsh and English carols to go with the more traditional "Joy to the World" and "O Come, All Ye Faithful" and a piece written by a Firestone executive and forced into the album. Some of the old carols were on odd clefs, but Previn said, "I really think after one hearing she had two-thirds of it down cold. She evidently has instant retention for music." Julie herself was "quite secretly pleased with the Christmas album," which made use of most of the Los Angeles Symphony as a studio orchestra.

Dory Previn noticed that whenever Julie began to sing a brand-new song, she would ask the lyricist, "What does the song mean?" "We would discuss lyrics, and sometimes she will even lead you into making a change," said Mrs. Previn.

In two of her most musical movies, *The Sound of Music*

and *Star!*, Julie worried as much about the sound track as she did her own performance, according to the director of both. "She would always want to do one more take, to make sure the track was exactly right," Robert Wise recalled. "And we would discuss everything that went into it."

Virtually all superstars are true professionals and at least technically competent. Some are superperfectionist and unpleasant, something Julie was often accused of on her later pictures. But until *Star!* at least, she was perfectionist *and* fun, which made her something to marvel at.

She was sublimely aware of her perfectionist tendencies, and she said they started back in the London company of *My Fair Lady.* "I suddenly began to see that it could be a very honorable thing to do one's job well. Fancy spending all that time flopping around on a stage and not feeling that before. I began to see that discipline was the key thing. I began to practice instead of being forced to practice. And now I think I can do well anything that I really set out to do. Now I love discipline; I suppose it's a form of Mary Poppinsism, but it's the only thing I can function with, and I get panicky without it—it's fun to put to use, and I enjoy the challenge."

Julie's perfectionism was part, but not the whole story of her superstardom. Marty Ransohoff attempted to explain the complete phenomenon: "In an industry bloated with sex symbols and manufactured stars, every now and then as a wholesome or refreshing change a Grace Kelly, an Audrey Hepburn, a Julie Andrews comes along. A stream of girls are pushed into stardom, amidst great cheesecake, frolic and horn blowing. Then a reaction sets in, an audience backlash, and every seven or eight years a girl comes along—A. Hepburn in 1950, Grace Kelly in 1956, and Julie in 1964— who does not make it on overt sex, but on personality, talent, honesty, plus *joie de vivre.* Julie's a rare talent, and she came along at a time when the audience backlash was overdue. That is what makes her unique—a flower on a hill of bushes."

Her other co-workers attempted to assess the phenomenon and most often pointed to her qualities as a person that helped to make her a star. Ross Hunter, the producer of *Thoroughly Modern Millie,* gave her high marks for unconventional cooperativeness. "Most women stars," he said, "take about a day and a half of shooting time to get their hair done. She always said, 'Don't worry, love, I'll do it on Saturday.' "

And Robert Wise, who was not always gallant where Twentieth Century-Fox's stars were concerned (he once said of Raquel Welch, "She's ten years too late, thank God," to which Miss Welch replied indirectly with a certain understandable petulance, "You're not allowed to be pretty anymore"), paid Julie the supreme compliment, aside from the obvious ones for an actress, like looks: "She is always prepared. She is pliable and open to suggestions, but with a mind of her own; she is not a piece of putty that can be molded any way. She is aware of the talent she has and of the ways she is able to use it. She is quite willing to experiment, to play something out to see how it works. But she is a perfectionist, always waiting and trying to do something the best way."

Cy Feuer believed she was unique in being a combination of "great actress, performer, and star. These are not the same. Some great performers and actresses are not stars, and some stars can't act or perform. In addition to being of star quality, she has great professional qualifications as an actress, and furthermore, she is a wonderful soprano." Julie's "star quality" to Feuer was "her freshness, her vitality, her energy. It comes off the stage at you. She just has that Julie Andrews exuberance that you feel."

"With Julie," offered Carol Channing, "it's not 'who loves me? How sweet am I? Do you think I'm dear?' and all that sort of stuff. Instead it's work, work, work. She's completely career, completely dedicated. There's everything businesswoman about her. I can't say she's sweet; what she is is businesslike. She's all for the goal, and it doesn't matter if she's subtle about it—and to me that's the most feminine thing there is: she's dead-on honest. What she wants is ability around her; it makes her better. If you have that ability, or can develop it, she's all with you. It's sort of, well, if the ship is going down, we'll go down together; if it's going to be well, you are going to be well with me." Miss Channing also found Julie, as a person, "wise and intelligent, a little bit giggly at times."

Herman Levin, the producer of *My Fair Lady* called Julie "one of the calmest, most cool, most collected people I have ever run across in the theater. She's like a block of ice."

"She is one of the very few people in this profession with script sense," said sometime scriptwriter Blake Edwards (there were at least three new versions of *Darling Lili* and a first draft by Edwards of *She Loves Me* for Julie to test that script sense on). "Her story sense is amazing. I have seen her confidence grow daily. It will be more and more her decision what she will do. She'll listen to other people and then she'll decide."

And Julie's adoring agent, Arthur Park, exulted: "I can praise Julie to the skies all day and still feel I haven't said enough nice things about her. She is unusual among actresses and actors I've known. In spite of all her years as a performer she approaches every job as if it were her first. That's spectacular, but it is rough on Julie. She has to be satisfied artistically with everything she does. To her nothing is as important as the whole. She is absolutely peerless in this respect. She broadens her view to take in everybody's problem. Most actors are so busy thinking about themselves that they haven't got time for that. She's not necessarily everyone's keeper, but she likes to know what's going on, and she has great respect for her fellow workers in all areas. She has perfect warmth [a description at which Julie blanched when I relayed it to her] and there is nothing phony about it. She doesn't put it on; it's just there."

After praise like that, Julie should be allowed the last,

self-deprecating word. Tim White was always saying about Julie that "you have to pay her a compliment every five minutes or she'll pay herself one." That meant, Julie recalled, that "he was always patting me on the head and saying 'pretty Julie,' 'nice girl,' 'well done' for no reason at all." But despite a propensity for saying things like "I think I did that rather well" when indeed she had done it superbly, Julie was her own toughest critic and was always asking to do things over long after her director or musical director was satisfied she had done her best. And she knew she sacrificed some human qualities at the expense of her mania for professional perfection. Even she had to laugh at the appropriate parallel she found between her own attitude and image (sometimes self-created) and that attributed to Gertrude Lawrence at the very end of *Star!* as she was riding off on her honeymoon with Richard Aldrich: "What's important is understanding and love and being absolutely genuine all the bloody time."

XVI

J ULIE, AS AN INNATELY SHY (and innately honest)
person, has always found herself uncomfortable with
the press, and she would rather avoid encounters with
newsmen—and particularly newswomen—altogether. A superstar, of course, cannot do that completely, but she has the
right to close the set of her pictures to any particular person
or to journalists in general. And Julie did, particularly and
appropriately on *Star!* when she insisted that an especially
acid New York free-lancer and an LA-based woman telecaster
not be admitted to the set, even when she wasn't there, which
wasn't often. On *Darling Lili,* Blake Edwards and his assistant, Ken Wales, acted as buffers and more often than not,
elected to refuse reporters audiences with Julie, in spite of
the pleadings of the Paramount-assigned publicists, Harry
Mines and Mac Hamilton. "Do we really need this?" Blake
would ask. "No; then let's don't waste time doing it," he
would say to the publicist, sometimes with the reporter in
earshot.

Among the Hollywood press corps she was known as a
tough interview, too discreet, too controlled. She found private revelations "unnecessary—who wants to know all that
about you? I used to feel I had to tell everything. I don't anymore. Really I think it is a way of purging oneself of guilt,
for having suddenly been given so much."

In her early days, on the vaudeville stage in England,
Julie's mother took care of the reporters and told her daugh-

ter to keep her mouth shut. The most persistent question in those days was: "How much money does little Julie make?" Barbara Andrews was determined not to tell anyone—even Julie herself—until she was sixteen years old and firmly in the $450-a-week bracket.

Her first brush with American newsmen was when photographers met the plane bringing her from London to New York for *The Boy Friend*. "As we got off the plane, these men aimed their cameras and shouted, 'All right, girls, let's have some cheesecake.' We didn't know what the word meant then. Now I know, and I don't like cheesecake." Her biggest fear about the writing press in those days was that they might "think I'm too ugly because of the baggy costumes I have to wear," but American reporters in the early days found her nothing but captivating, and if they invented romances, it was to enhance her charms. "Your columnists are so maddening," she allowed during *The Boy Friend*. "They have linked me with a couple of men I know only very slightly—no love or anything. Why do they do that?"

With this minor annoyance of occasional romance-mongering, Julie's honeymoon with the American press continued almost unbroken for the next thirteen years. We all said she was so beautiful, talented, and nice that even she got a bit sick of it. For most of this time she was unfailingly available to all, although her former secretary, Bea Hopkinson, remembered her playing favorites, giving expensive Christmas presents to some journalists, the cold shoulder to many more. I can't vouch for either.

She got tired of interviews, but callous about them as well. And she refined a technique for saying exactly the same thing in a slightly different way to several different journalists. But by the time of *Star!* her attitude was "these damn interviews . . . well, if it will help get back ten million dollars, what's twenty minutes?"

Ordinarily movie stars never bother to sue or otherwise take public notice of the usually outrageous stories of the movie fan magazines, with their imaginary interviews, or of the newspaper gossip columnists, with their somewhat imaginary "sources" (more often than not a disgruntled producer or studio executive, a frustrated competitor, or a co-star who is getting upstaged). Julie herself told me in the summer of 1968 that she and Blake were not going to do anything about a particularly scurrilous attack by Joyce Haber in the Los Angeles *Times* in April anent *Darling Lili*. Haber, then struggling to build circulation for her newly syndicated gossip column, had taken to blasting Barbara Streisand—then the big new star on the Hollywood scene—whenever possible, but that had begun to pall, and her new method of attracting attention was a series of "blind" items about celebrities, usually involving bizarre sexual exploits. The personalities were noted only by descriptions or vague nicknamey initials, and the game was to figure out just who was being hatcheted.

In the case of Julie and Blake, Haber had used the not very subtle initials Miss P and P (Prim and Proper) for her; Mr. X, for the director of a major musical now being filmed who is conducting an affair with his leading lady, Miss P and P; and Mr. VV (Visually Virile) for co-star Rock Hudson. Haber contended that Julie and Blake had been making fun of Hudson for his supposedly less than manly behavior on the set. (This was the least of it but this much was true, at least in Blake's case. Hudson, a genuinely nice man who is nonetheless plodding when it comes to work and not in the same snappy-dialogue set as Julie and Blake, would ask a lot of questions about scenes that would annoy Blake, who thought the answers were obvious. Once I heard Blake say, in total and on-the-set public exasperation at one of Hudson's questions: "What a leading man!") Haber had it that Blake said, "I don't understand people like that" and that Julie had said to Hudson, "Remember, *I'm* the leading lady."

Julie and Blake both said that to try any legal action against Haber or the Los Angeles *Times* would have been wasteful and unsatisfying and would probably call much too much attention to the columnist, which, of course, was what she wanted. "Suing her would dignify her," said Julie, who had been the victim of previous attacks by Haber and would be the subject of many more. "There is simply nothing we can do."

The experience turned both Blake and Julie, who had never exactly been enamored of the press, even further against the journalistic profession, and suddenly interviewers were even less welcome on the set of *Darling Lili*. Both star and director wanted to be told which newsmen were coming on which day, and for how long, and exactly what they wanted. Julie cited the impartial example of a recent book review in *Time* magazine that had torn the novel and the author (whom she did not know) to shreds. "They gave him no credit for the two years of his life he probably spent writing the book," she said. "There has to be some recognition of what people are *trying* to do, whether or not they succeed. You can't dismiss a creative person's work in a few well-chosen words of put-down."

Miss Haber always, in her attacks and even in private conversation, affected an intimate knowledge of Miss Andrews and her every thought that she simply did not possess. Pressed on the point in mid-1969, Haber would confess to having met Julie only once, "several years ago" and to finding her "rather nice." In point of fact there were two meetings and perhaps two faulty memories at work. Julie recalled only once, too, but it was a different once. As a "Show Business" section researcher for *Time* magazine in New York, "she came up to Boston during the *Camelot* tryout to do a story, and we rather liked her, thought she was a bright lady and one of us. We spent a lot of time with her and told her everything she wanted to know. Then she went back and wrote the most vicious thing imaginable about all the trouble we were in, and we were really hurt." (John McPhee actually wrote the *Time* cover story on Lerner and Loewe, which

some observers said led to their breakup, but Haber had
supplied the raw material.)

Haber was my predecessor as *Time*'s Hollywood correspondent, and it was during her tenure there that she
met Julie, according to the magazine's files. It was just
after Julie had been nominated for the Oscar for *Mary
Poppins* and seemed the favorite to get it, and the editors
in New York had assigned Haber to do a takeout on the
young star, which Haber was loath to do and did everything
she could to avoid doing. Finally, she was ordered to do
it and so set up an interview, which she reported on in the
most childish I-don't-know-why-I'm-seeing-this-silly-woman-
when-everybody-knows-Ava-Gardner-should-win tone, but
concluding, "All we can say is that if Julie Andrews does win
the Oscar, it couldn't happen to a nicer girl." Had Julie and
Joyce really changed that much in four short years?

The blind item in Haber's column was the first of the
major anti-Julie attacks in the press, but it really was just the
beginning, as it was followed closely by the *Star!* premieres
in London and New York and Julie's nonattendance. Also at
this time, *Life* magazine turned down an expensive takeout
done by their Hollywood correspondent reportedly "because
it wasn't bitchy enough." The reporter, who resigned shortly
after the incident and partly because of it, had spent two
months on nothing else, with considerable access to Julie and
Blake and everyone involved with *Star!* and come up with an
essentially positive but far from glowing portrait. Not a line
of it ever appeared.

The British popular press, excepting the critics, who had
sometimes said negative things about a particular performance, had always been respectful of Julie Andrews and
seemed even to work with her in protecting the reserve she
had built up. They did not dredge deep for scandal in her
private life, and even the divorce from Tony had been handled delicately. But now, it seemed, all knives were bared. By
not appearing for her own most important premiere she had

offended (besides two major film studios, an adoring public, royalty, and her friends) all Fleet Street, England, and what was left of the Empire. The American papers, in the summer doldrums anyway, took up the anti-Julie cry as they never had before, and suddenly this superstar was no longer a sacred cow.

The fan magazines, which, because Blake Edwards was such public knowledge, had been relatively bland on the subject of Julie Andrews, also began to hit harder, once they saw it was possible to get away with the most outrageous things. Two of them in particular went out on limbs for sensational stories about Julie. *Modern Movies,* a minor entry in the pulpy sweepstakes for popularity at American beauty parlors, had a story in its January, 1969, issue headlined JULIE ANDREWS: THE SENTENCE THAT ALMOST STOPPED HER MARRIAGE! "I DON'T WANT THAT MAN FOR A DADDY!" The story contended that Julie was indifferent and unconcerned about the welfare of her daughter, Emma Kate, and that she and Emma had had emotional scenes about Blake, culminating in Emma's illness as a result of the liaison. The January, 1969, issue of *Screenland* screamed JULIE ANDREWS DEFENDS HER INTIMATE DATES WITH SIDNEY POITIER, and the story that followed was the purported account of her flaming romance with the black actor, complete with supposed quotes from her.

Still, it was a surprise when, in the midst of her second winter vacation with Blake and Emma in Switzerland, Julie's lawyer, Allen E. Susman, filed libel suits in her name totaling $6,000,000 against the two publications. The suits, filed on January 7, in the Santa Monica Superior Court, where she had divorced Tony, were against the publishers and West Coast editors of the magazines and against the writers of the stories, and in each case for $1,000,000 compensatory damages for the impairment of her reputation and $2,000,000 punitive damages, on the basis that the defendants knew the stories to be false and libelous. Julie said, in her complaint, that she respected Poitier's professional competence but that she had never gone out with him. She accused the writer, who used the name Dick Fogarty, of having fabricated the statements attributed to her in his piece. Of the other story, written under the name of Madeline White, the complaint said that "in truth and in fact, a very close and enduring relationship exists" between Emma and Edwards. The two suits were still in an out-of-court limbo a year later, "but at least, if nothing else, they have kept the fan magazines quiet about me," Julie said.

No one, among her fans or foes, suspected that there was anything to the charge that Supernanny was neglecting her child; Mary Poppins simply wouldn't do such a thing. And anyone who knew her at all well knew that Emma always came first, even ahead of Blake, so this suit seemed unnecessary but also open-and-shut in Julie's favor. But some segments of the public and even some entertainment industry types who should have known better were more than prepared to believe the Poitier fable, although it simply was not true. Julie and Poitier had appeared together in public, of course: twice at the Academy Awards, once when she received her Oscar in 1965 from him as the previous year's male winner and once in 1968 when she presented the best picture award to *In the Heat of the Night,* in which he was starred. In both cases they posed together for publicity pictures, croppings of which, with him in white tie and tails, were used to illustrate the *Screenland* and other "stories" of their intimate dating life.

She had been Blake Edwards' constant companion during the period of this supposed romance, as everyone knew. But those who were ready to accept the story did so because it was assumed by them that all movie stars, whatever their image, had sordid sex lives, and the sweeter the image, the more sordid the sex. Hollywood gossip had also linked Julie with Ike Jones, the black musician who had been married to the Swedish-born star Inger Stevens, although secretly since she was starring in a television series, *The Farmer's Daughter,* based on the old Loretta Young movie, at the time and it was thought her fans wouldn't accept the interracial marriage.

Haber used the Poitier story suit as an example of her assertion that Julie's "behavior lacks dignity," although in an earlier day she had been only too happy to include Julie in the select list of people who by their mere presence could make any party an A party (as opposed to a tacky B party, where the food was merely catered and the guests were common and Joyce Haber never appeared, sending instead an underpaid assistant but later writing how awful it had been; Haber, who reported *ad nauseam* about A and B lists even said there were A and B members of the press but had the good sense not to differentiate between them in print).

But the anti-Andrews blasts reached their nadir in the January, 1969, issue of *Esquire,* a magazine which had been trying to get a job done on Julie for two years. And a free-lance writer named Helen Lawrenson did the job. Had she not appeared in the magazine, she would surely have been a prime candidate for one of *Esquire*'s "Dubious Achievement" awards for her totally tasteless article, whose prime thrust seemed to be Miss Lawrenson's pique at not having the star delivered to her at a prescribed hour each morning, spouting juicy tidbits entirely unprompted by the journalist, who, of course, would not have to walk four feet herself to attempt to strike up a conversation with her subject. Her noninterviewing was done on the locations for *Star!* and *Darling Lili,* and she behaved and wrote as if they were her first visits to a movie set. When I arrived on *Darling Lili* outside Paris, Miss Lawrenson had left the day before, but the set was abuzz with stories of her rudeness to all on the picture, her constant guzzling of studio-provided liquor, and her ill-tempered demands for all kinds of time alone with Julie. An on-budget, on-schedule movie being shot on the backlot in Hollywood is not the most ideal situation for an interview, and *Darling Lili* in its late days of production was that much worse.

Once the Blake Edwards picture had returned to Paramount in Hollywood, things got worse still, and yet another incident occurred which worsened Julie's press. The studio, which, despite the problems with *Darling Lili*, then was enjoying uncommon corporate success as a division of the conglomerate Gulf and Western, with the success of *Romeo and Juliet, The Odd Couple,* and *Rosemary's Baby* suddenly found itself with more stars making movies on its lot than at almost any other time in its history. Barbra Streisand and Yves Montand were shooting *On a Clear Day You Can See Forever,* John Wayne was making *True Grit,* Lee Marvin and Clint Eastwood were finishing *Paint Your Wagon,* and Julie and Rock Hudson were there for *Darling Lili.* The studio decided to get them all together one afternoon on the steps of the administration building for the kind of star group picture that hadn't been taken officially since the heyday of movies at MGM and Columbia. The actors, uncommonly, were all close to on time, except for Julie, who didn't show at all. The six other stars, including Hudson, waited, and Wayne said to Robert Evans, vice-president in charge of production, "Are you going to furnish chairs while we wait for the queen?" Evans himself went to the *Darling Lili* set to see where she was and found her in a difficult crying scene that she had to do over and over because it was not going well. Edwards told Evans he would not interrupt shooting for a publicity photograph, which Evans was forced to tell the other stars, who posed without her. The next morning Julie went to the dressing rooms of Barbra Streisand and some of the other stars, to apologize for holding them up in vain. Bob Evans, after rushes the next afternoon, sent Blake a note: "It was well worth missing the picture yesterday. You got a hell of a scene out of Julie."

However the incident was or was not resolved at Paramount, off the lot it was more grist for the relentless mill of anti-Andrews feeling, which by then was incorporating wholly unsubstantiated reports of Julie's pregnancy, abortion, and impending marriage to Edwards, possibly while they were in Switzerland. Sheilah Graham had noted in December, 1968, that Julie had been free for two weeks to marry Blake but that they were concentrating on finishing the picture. While they were in Switzerland in late December and January, 1969, Rona Barrett took to the ABC-TV airwaves with the pregnancy story, and others picked it up. Hank Grant in the *Hollywood Reporter* and others printed the story about the wedding, which had a certain minimal logic because Blake's children lived in London with their mother and Emma was with them in Switzerland, in case all the kids wanted to attend the nuptials. Then on February 6, columnist Grant wrote:

> All those rumors about Julie Andrews and Blake Edwards having had a secret wedding in Switzerland are just that— rumors. They're not yet wed and have yet to even take out a license. . . . All this bum-rapping of Julie kinda makes me ill. We've never seen her less than gracious to press and fans alike, gracious being what I'm not to callers who phone in "juicy" items on her but refuse to identify themselves.

Another columnist in the *Hollywood Reporter,* Radie Harris, that same week took note of all the down-with-Julie sentiment and the new popularity of a star who, with Academy Award time coming close and *Funny Girl* a hot contender, had chosen to modify her troublesome reputation:

> Julie Andrews is dead! Long live Barbra Streisand! This seems to be the new slogan in Hollywood these days. Without detracting from Barbra's superstar appeal, this hostility towards Julie seems highly unjustified, at least to this reporter. . . . The last two times I saw Julie was when she

was filming "Star!" (both at 20th-Fox and in NY) and "Darling Lili" at Paramount. On both occasions she couldn't have been more cordial in her welcome or more accessible. There were no delusions of big star grandeur but the same unaffected friend I've known for many years. She even willingly posed for publicity stills with me. . . . Like most Britishers, she doesn't enjoy sharing her private life with strangers. If she wants to marry Blake Edwards in secret in Switzerland, rather than over here, she feels that's her own business.

But the last straw, even for the most ardent pro-Julie elements in the American press, came the next Sunday night, February 9, 1969. The occasion was Alan Jay Lerner's twenty-fifth anniversary as a librettist and lyricist, and all the stars who had sung his songs and many who had not, his good friends in and out of the theater, and the most important members of the show business press corps were invited to a formal testimonial dinner with entertainment, for the benefit, at the suggestion of Lerner, of the American Academy of Dramatic Arts. Julie, of *My Fair Lady* and *Camelot*, was one of four co-chairmen, along with Barbra Streisand, of the movie version of *On a Clear Day You Can See Forever*, then just starting filming in Hollywood, Richard Burton (*Camelot*), and Rex Harrison (*My Fair Lady*). Burton was busy on a film in Europe and not expected to be able to attend, but the other three were. Then Miss Streisand was excused with Lerner's permission and urging because she was needed in Hollywood for *On a Clear Day*. Julie agreed to appear in the entertainment portion of the program, singing "I Could Have Danced All Night" and, with Harrison and George Rose, one of the replacement Alfred Doolittles in *My Fair Lady*, "The Rain in Spain." Although she had some understandable reluctance about appearing onstage singing after a seven-year absence, she agreed out of respect to Lerner, the launcher of two of her most successful vehicles, and to the other performers, who included Harve Presnell, Van Johnson, Constance Towers, Karen Morrow,

Diahann Carroll, Harrison and John-Michael King, live; and Gene Kelly, Louis Jourdan, Hermione Gingold, Maurice Chevalier, Jane Powell, Fred Astaire, and Miss Streisand, on film.

The show was written by Sidney Michaels, staged by Stone Widney, and produced by Jean Dalrymple, and in some respects resembled a Broadway production except that there were only two days for rehearsal, Saturday and Sunday. The out-ot-town guests were flying in Friday (Rex Harrison and his wife, Rachel Roberts, from their home in Portofino, Italy) and staying at the Waldorf-Astoria, where the party was to be in the Grand Ballroom. Blake was not coming with Julie, and she had agreed to sit with me. Rex Harrison, not noted as one of show business' spendthrifts, almost hadn't come because the academy had not agreed to pay for his and his wife's plane tickets, but thanks to some adroit behind-the-scenes maneuvering by Mrs. Lerner, the academy had sprung and that crisis had passed. But only in time for a new one to erupt, Friday evening, February 7. Julie called Alan Lerner from California at about the time she had been due in New York, to say that she was terribly sorry but she had a spot on her throat and the doctor had told her she shouldn't go to New York, and besides, Blake was sick with bronchial pneumonia and she had to stay home and take care of him. She, of course, had called the one person who couldn't plead with her to relent or tell her to come off it, and so Alan Lerner said he understood and good-bye.

Karen Lerner, Alan's wife, didn't understand, however, and she tried desperately to get Julie to honor her commitment, even calling Andre Previn, Lerner's collaborator on *Coco* and the additional songs for *Paint Your Wagon* and Julie's friend in London, where he was conducting the London Philharmonic, to get him to call Julie and plead with her to reconsider. Karen was deeply disappointed and knew Alan was, too, and she knew it would mean further problems with Harrison, who had a big-star complex about singing with understudies—even assuming an understudy could be found. Sally Ann Howes, who had planned to participate until she found out that Julie was definitely back from Switzerland and had reiterated her plans to be at the Waldorf, had committed herself elsewhere and was unavailable. The lifesaver turned out to be Margot Moser, another fair lady of very good voice who had played Eliza on Broadway. "They called me at home this morning and said, 'You're going on tonight, come down to the Waldorf for rehearsal,' and I said, 'But I'm having people in for drinks tonight,' and so there are people at my house drinking and here I am," said Miss Moser at an after-banquet party.

The whole benefit affair, which raised more than $60,000 for the academy, was complicated by the worst snowstorm of the season, which had begun falling at about midnight Saturday. By Sunday evening all New York was snowed in, and all late arrivals, even including Alan Lerner's eldest daughter and her husband on Long Island, were snowed out. Still, an estimated two-thirds of the 2,500 ticket buyers somehow appeared, many in high boots, having walked down a deserted Park Avenue through deep drifts of snow. The show, from "It's Almost Like Being in Love," from *Brigadoon,* to a new number, "Let's Go Home," from *Coco,* went as planned except that Miss Moser sang "I Could Have Danced All Night" and "The Rain in Spain" was quietly dropped. Harrison talked "I've Grown Accustomed to Her Face," but the familiar face wasn't there—except as a cartoon of Eliza as the flower girl along with Harrison as Higgins and Burton as King Arthur. Film clips were shown from *Royal Wedding, Brigadoon, Gigi, My Fair Lady,* and *Camelot* and the only reference to Julie was made by the master of ceremonies, cartoonist Al Capp, who read a congratulatory wire from President Nixon, and then said, "There are many other wires. I think the one we love the most was the one from the universally beloved Julie Andrews, which says 'I can't make it.' It is signed by her doctor, Sam Sheppard, and I believe him and I believe her." There was embarrassed laughter from those who knew what had happened.

Everybody knew what had happened a few days later when Joyce Haber devoted a full syndicated column to it (the part of her column that detailed the latest acquisitions for her wardrobe and which industry bigwig buttered her up at which A party which night ran only in the Los Angeles *Times*) . "Poor Julie will soon run out of excuses," wrote the columnist, "and what will her fans, her public defenders say then? (I assure you, she has few important defenders in the industry.) " But Radie Harris had the last word on February 21. After mentioning a "sweet note" from Julie thanking Miss Harris for her defense of her "in this pillar" Radie Harris said: "Blake Edwards called to assure me that the ONLY reason that he and Julie didn't attend the Tribute Dinner to Alan Lerner was because they were both ill and their doctor had absolutely forbidden them to leave their sick beds." Unfortunately, there were indeed few people in the film industry who believed that at that point.

XVII

AT THE START OF 1970, despite the set back of *Star!*
and the siege of bad press, Julie Andrews was still
a reigning superstar. Whatever she had to prove to
Blake, or herself, or her critics, she had little to prove to the
public or to the producers who cater to that public. She was
Miss Movie Musical, and almost any singing part she wanted
was hers for the asking. When *She Loves Me* didn't work out,
there was the chance that she might work at Warner Brothers
after all, in *Mame,* even though Elizabeth Taylor, who had
done well by that studio with *Who's Afraid of Virginia
Woolf?* was making noises about having her musical debut
in the film version of the Jerry Herman-Jerome Lawrence-
Robert E. Lee hit (something she had wanted to do with
Hello, Dolly!). It mattered little that Julie was ten years too
young for *Mame* or that Angela Lansbury, who had created
the part on Broadway, could not be surpassed. She still had
a large loyal audience, and there was a strong feeling among
her advisers and others that she should get back to a proven
property as soon as possible, after two experimental musical
flings. John Wayne even had some words on the subject:
"Julie Andrews, a refreshing, openhearted girl, a wonderful
performer. Her stint was *Mary Poppins* and *The Sound of
Music.* But she wanted to be a Theda Bara. And they went
along with her, and the picture [*Star!*] fell on its face. A
Goldwyn would have told her, 'Look, dear, you can't change
your sweet and lovely image.' "

Looking back, she considered herself "sublimely lucky. When I look at my life, one should be fairly happy." For the most part, she had been in hit after hit, in vehicles that were fun, sprinkled with a fair share of challenges. "It's only later that you gather it together and see what it all means," she said. "I was one of those people who was able to learn by doing on the job and get away with it. Half the time I was running to keep up with myself trying to learn what everybody thought I knew."

She had had an extraordinary run of male co-stars, all of whom she termed "dishy." She once rated them, as *Variety*, the show-business trade paper, might have: "Burton—socko; Garner—winger-dinger; Van Dyke—perks show biz; Rex Harrison—daddy of them all, socko, boffo, whammo; Von Sydow—a classy package."

They, with Christopher Plummer and Richard Harris perhaps the exceptions, returned the compliment with continual raves for her, sometimes for the oddest reasons. James Garner claimed, "She has one of the greatest figures in the business, and I fancy myself something of an expert."

Her life-style guaranteed that she would be isolated from her enemies, most of whom were, in George Roy Hill's words, "very quiet ones." Her success meant that she could stay in Hollywood and make movies of her own choosing. "If the part is good enough, I am interested in anything," she insisted. "I am worried about my image only to the extent that I would hate to be totally bracketed, but I'm not wildly concerned about it. I think there is probably nothing I *couldn't* play, but it is hard enough to find out the ones I can do well. I have an enormous inferiority complex when I work with very good actors. I often feel so shallow in my work, and I would love to have a technique to fall back on. I'd be devastated if I had to do Shakespeare. It's very difficult to make an experimental film, and in a way one shouldn't lay oneself open to failure without looking into all the possibilities. Anything I do would have to stack up on my side."

That her image concerned Julie at all concerned Carol Burnett. "Image shmimage, she's an actress. That's what she's trying to prove, and that's what she proved in *The Americanization of Emily*. She shouldn't try to live it down. Julie's not out to be an evangelist. She's not Mary Poppins. She's Julie Andrews, an actress who can play Mary Poppins but who can also play Emily Barham."

But for all her acclaim, she had gone only a short way toward reaching her potential or at least aspirations. "Julie has artistic ambitions and is quite adventurous," said Andre Previn. "But she winds up giving in to her agents and the people around her." And Dory added: "She'd love to do a Truffaut movie. And every once in a while she'll hear of a play or read a book that's a little offbeat that she'd like to do, but she can't because of these people."

"These people" included especially her agent, Arthur Park, and his associates at Chasin, Park, Citron. Julie was criticized by her friends—Calley, the Previns, Blake—for leaning too much on their judgment. It was they who insisted that she do *The Sound of Music* and *Torn Curtain*. Julie said, "God, look at the results—who's to knock that?"

Her own choices were *The Americanization of Emily* and *Thoroughly Modern Millie,* choices to which Arthur Park was unalterably opposed. "The great public would like to see Julie Andrews play Julie Andrews, Paul Newman play Paul Newman, and Gary Cooper play Gary Cooper," said Park. "If she made nothing but pictures like *The Americanization of Emily*, she would not be a star." He defended his agency's choice of *Torn Curtain* somewhat lamely: "We banked on Hitchcock being a good director."

Park, in addition to being a shrewd businessman, was a political conservative who refused to let Julie participate in political gatherings of any sort (such participation was against her instincts anyway, as a British citizen living and working in America and as an ambivalent person) and once wouldn't even let her appear at a benefit on behalf of the United Nations. Against the protests of her friends, Julie defended him as a nice man who had done very well by her (he was and he had).

"Ultimately, the final decision is mine," said Julie. "It has to be. I know I have fairly good instincts for something good. The times when something excites one are really rare, and failing that, you have to pick something that is interesting for some reason, or a work that is solid. But somehow you always find something about every part that is stimulating."

Blake Edwards, on whom she became increasingly dependent for advice on work and almost every other aspect of her life, agreed with her assessment: "She has become more independent. She has taken a lot of steps away from other people's making decisions for her. She is learning what it is to be independent and free and not forever tied to someone else." And even Arthur Park conceded, "She decides these things for herself now."

The freedom to decide, which came with superstardom, was a freedom Julie cherished. She had finally learned to say no, even to some of the musicals she preferred. As Marty Ransohoff put it: "Family musicals—forget it—she owns that game." Andre Previn, with four Academy Awards for film musicals lined up in his study, put it a slightly different way: "You find that whenever a film musical is going to be made these days, someone says, 'Get Julie Andrews.' And the thing is, it's usually right for her."

Since she made the permanent switch to California, Broadway, of course, had been beckoning her back. She turned down *The Apple Tree* although she wanted to work with Nichols again. "A show would have to be planned well ahead because of Emma being in school and all, and I would want to sign for the least possible amount of time I could, nine months at the most. I certainly hope to do something again someday, but films are much more my level really. On Broadway I never felt quite *enough*. I had to pick myself up by the scruff and give more than I thought I had." She liked the five-day week movies offered and the precision in movies made possible by editing.

Singing was something Julie worked at constantly. She practiced frequently and sang, hummed, or whistled most of the time walking about the house. "Strangely enough, singing has never been particularly easy for me," she said, "particularly singing the way I want to. I have not found the totally easy enjoyable way of singing. I think I have a fear of finding it, probably from having a little too much of it when I was young. In the back of my mind and in the bottom of my heart, I want to lick that. God willing, one day I will have the strength to."

Julie objected to the use of the word "wholesome" to describe her, on-screen or off. "I don't want to be thought of as wholesome. It does rather lack any suggestion of mystery. What I suppose I'd like to be, one day, is someone who is fascinating—a person you want to look at or see no matter what they're doing. I'd like to be an original, to be myself and not a pale copy of someone else. The really marvelous actors and actresses we admire have qualities that can't be pinned down. I suppose I'd like to be that type of performer if I were to leave a mark.

"I don't pretend to be great, but I seriously could be good, and I would like to do light opera someday. That's probably more potentiality than reality, but I like to think I could do it if I wanted to. It's a sort of dream I have to lick it myself and so do something I haven't done in the singing department. I practice and work extremely hard when I have to. To get down to work is my problem."

Like almost everything else about her, Julie's summation of her goals was thoroughly professional and typically tentative: "In the long run, over a period of time, it is a person's body of work that matters. If the body of work is honest, with an integrity about it, and people sense a love of work in it, those are the things that last and that one is remembered for, possibly."

An Epilogue

THREE YEARS AND 80,000 words later, Julie Andrews is still something of an enigma to me. Hers is an unmapped psyche. What really deep down motivates her as a person and a performer is something known only to her and her psychiatrist, and I'm not even sure about him. Her defenses are as solid as her talent; she's worked hard at both for at least twenty-five of her thirty-four years. And her responses are as measured as her music, as automatic as her singing on pitch. She knows the truth but never stops acting long enough to share it.

But what is as crystal clear as her voice is the fact that given her determination and some of her less controversial qualities—like her talent—Julie Andrews was bound to "happen," as they say in the world of pop culture. If she hadn't happened in *My Fair Lady, Mary Poppins* and *The Sound of Music,* she would have emerged—nay, exploded—in other vehicles. For she has always given as much or more to her plays and movies as they have given to her. Her special magic—and that is a word I have carefully avoided in the text of this book, but it is the only one that will do here— was what was wanted in the 1960's and quite likely will be wanted in the 1970's, 1980's, and 1990's. She is an original; she replaced no one on the entertainment scene, and no one will replace her.

Her talent and sunny distinctiveness are nontransferable: She couldn't give them to Gertrude Lawrence (and couldn't take the late Miss Lawrence's qualities for herself; both their publics stayed away from *Star!* by any name). But like Miss Lawrence and all other superstars, she is durable. She has suffered some setbacks and will suffer more, but each time she will pull up her tacky anklets and take on something safe, like the movie version of a hit Broadway musical, and she will be back on top, singing, dancing, delighting. We have made her a star, and she is going to be the best bloody one that ever was or know why not. Thirty years hence, if she reverts to her original first name and returns to Great Britain—both, I think, strong possibilities—I fully expect we will see Dame Julia in the ninth revival of *My Fair Lady* on stage and *The Judy Garland Story* on-screen.

Image, which infected so much in the sixties, from politics to instant mashed potatoes, plays a more significant part in the Julie Andrews story than it does in the story of any other star. One reason is that she cultivated her own image long before anybody cared or responded to it. Whoever Julia Wells really was (and the objective facts of broken home, wartime, and second-string show business are almost too pat) was obscured early on by the layers of lacquer self-imposed by an embryo Emily Barham who wanted the world to think she was Mary Poppins. And the world did, during five years of psychoanalysis and three years of living openly with a man (two of those years before she was divorced from her husband), and does and will despite all that, even though the image now haunts even her. Her public believes what it wants to and discounts the rest.

The last time I saw Julie Andrews before this book went to press was in Hollywood in November, 1969, during the taping of her second NBC-TV special. Despite the obvious pressure she was under with the immediate project at hand, the recent disaster of *Star!*, the junking of *She Loves Me* with the Kirk Kerkorian-Jim Aubrey take-over at MGM, and the imminent release of her and Blake's problem-plagued *Darling Lili*, she was more relaxed and herself than I had ever seen her. In a light-blue denim work dress and a white blouse, her hair after two years of wigs back to its *Sound of Music* cut and color, she was like a college girl discussing her next semester's courses. With the failure of *Star!* which she had "slowly and sadly come to accept" and with her having survived the venomous press attack that seemed to have abated, it was as if all the pressure were off, as if she never had to be totally "on" again. Secure in her talent and knowing she would always be in demand and pretty much on her terms, she no longer had to worry about being what Carol Burnett had called "the great big star of the world." She had rested for a full year between *Darling Lili* and the special, long enough to know that unemployment wouldn't drive her crazy, but that it was nice to work in something good once in a while.

Blake Edwards, at last Julie's husband (thanks to a quiet, anticlimactic wedding on November 13, 1969), will serve to illustrate the essential paradox of Julie Andrews: While the times she is not working and is spending time with "family" are what make her most happy, career is what gives meaning to her life. She cannot force a total commitment to either, and so with "Blackie" she is clinging, sometimes badly, to both.

Index

Index